Daily Fundamentals

GRADE 2

The following illustrations were created by the artists listed (provided through Shutterstock.com) and are protected by copyright: Iosw (page 19); Reinekke (page 26); BlueRingMedia, Dave Barnard, GraphicsRF (page 28); Giraphics (page 31); ekler (page 33); lenoleum (page 37); AlexeyZet, Teguh Mujiono (page 38); Aaron Amat (page 39); TeddyandMia (page 40); Andrey Pavlov, livestock99, suns07butterfly (page 51); Mike Truchon, Shams Ashraf (page 61); Eric Isselee (pages 61, 98); Visun Khankasem (pages 69, 138); Mjosedesign (page 90); Kimazo (page 91); Ana Gram, VectorPot (page 94); nikiteev_konstantin (page 95); Macrovector (page 96); Alena Root (page 99); Rob Hainer (page 100); alexjuve10, freesoulproduction (page 106); Memo Angeles (page 110); Crisan Rosu (page 112); Luis Molinero (page 113); Constantine Pankin, Julia-art (page 114); Matt Benoit (page 121); graphixmania (page 126); ively, Spreadthesign, Viktar Malyshchyts (page 136); Ann Precious (page 139); d-e-n-i-s, Natalia Zelenina, Natykach Nataliia, ojal, Svetlana Guteneva (page 146); Aleksangel (page 156); Vectomart (page 157)

Writing: Guadalupe Lopez
Content Editing: Lisa Vitarisi Mathews
Kathleen Jorgensen
Copy Editing: Cathy Harber
Art Direction: Yuki Meyer
Design/Production: Jessica Onken
Susan Lovell
Paula Acojido

EMC 3242

Helping Children Learn

Visit
teaching-standards.com
to view a correlation
of this book.
This is a free service.

Correlated to State and Common Core State Standards

Congratulations on your purchase of some of the finest teaching materials in the world.

Photocopying the pages in this book is permitted for <u>single-classroom use only</u>. Making photocopies for additional classes or schools is prohibited.

For information about other Evan-Moor products, call 1-800-777-4362, fax 1-800-777-4332, or visit our website, www.evan-moor.com.
Entire contents © 2017 EVAN-MOOR CORP.
18 Lower Ragsdale Drive, Monterey, CA 93940-5746. Printed in USA.

CONTENTS

Introduction

What's Inside? 4
How to Use This Book 5
Skills Scope and Sequence 6
Student Progress Chart 8
Student Record Sheet 9

Week

Week 1 11
Week 2 16
Week 3 21
Week 4 26
Week 5 31
Week 6 36
Week 7 41
Week 8 46
Week 9 51
Week 10 56
Week 11 61
Week 12 66
Week 13 71
Week 14 76
Week 15 81

Week 16 86
Week 17 91
Week 18 96
Week 19 101
Week 20 106
Week 21 111
Week 22 116
Week 23 121
Week 24 126
Week 25 131
Week 26 136
Week 27 141
Week 28 146
Week 29 151
Week 30 156

Answer Key 161

What's Inside?

Daily Fundamentals has 30 weeks of cross-curricular skills practice. Each week provides targeted practice with language, math, and reading skills. The focused daily tasks progress in difficulty as students move from Day 1 tasks to Day 5 tasks. Item types range from multiple choice and matching to constructed response and open-ended questions.

Language items practice grammar, mechanics, spelling, and vocabulary.

Math items practice number and operations, algebraic thinking, geometry, measurement and data, and problem solving.

Reading items practice core reading comprehension skills such as inference, prediction, author's purpose, main idea and details, fact and opinion, nonfiction text features, and literary analysis.

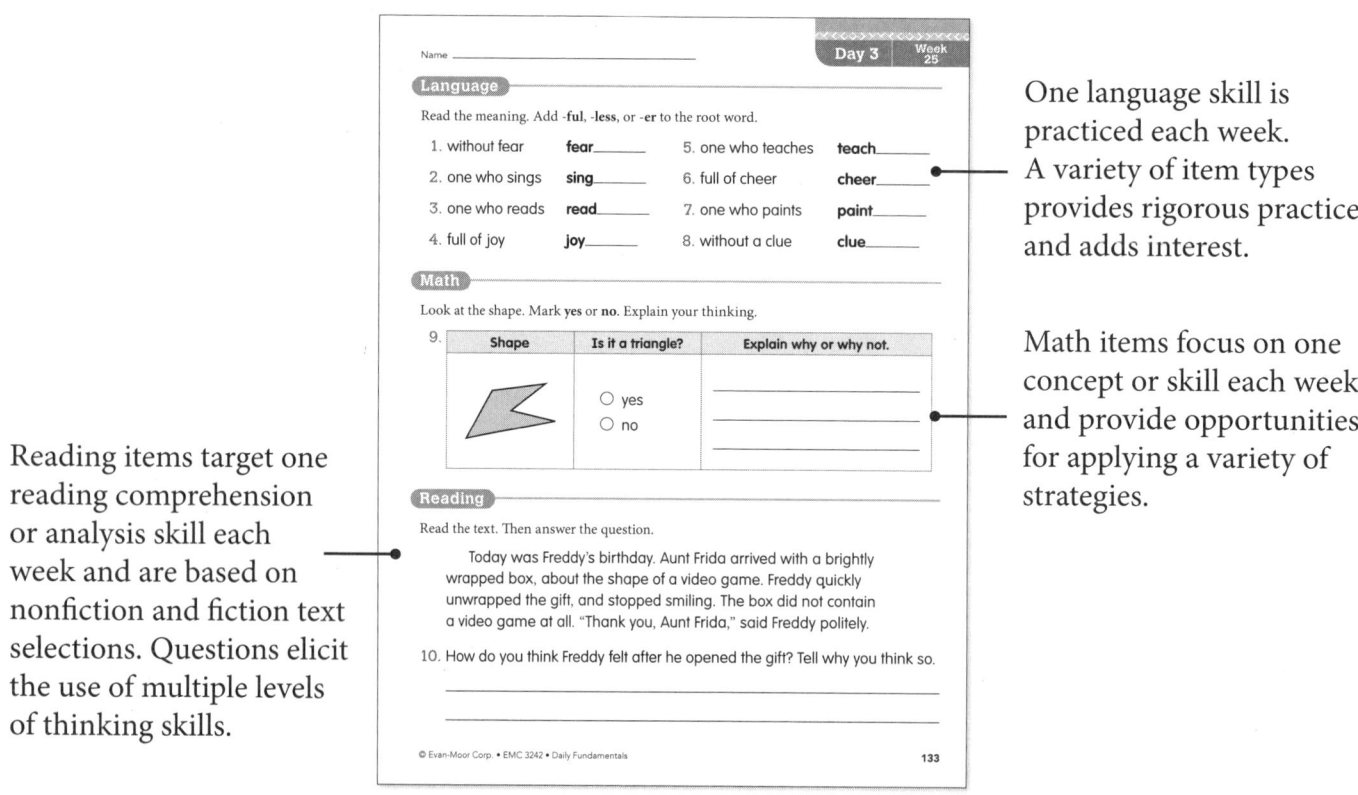

One language skill is practiced each week. A variety of item types provides rigorous practice and adds interest.

Math items focus on one concept or skill each week and provide opportunities for applying a variety of strategies.

Reading items target one reading comprehension or analysis skill each week and are based on nonfiction and fiction text selections. Questions elicit the use of multiple levels of thinking skills.

Answer Key

Correct or exemplar responses are shown on a reduced version of the actual page. An * is used to indicate an open-ended item or an item with many ways to word the answer. Accept any reasonable response.

How to Use This Book

Using *Daily Fundamentals* as morning work or bell ringers
Have the daily practice activity on students' desks when they arrive in the morning, after recess, or during a transitional period. Have students complete the assignment independently. Then have them share their answers and the strategy or approach they used. Encourage discussion about each item so students can share their thinking and provide support and insights to one another. These discussions may also provide you with teachable moments and information to guide your instruction.

Using *Daily Fundamentals* for homework
Assign one weekly unit at the beginning of each week. Students will have the autonomy to manage their time to complete the assignment, and they will benefit from the focused practice of language, math, and reading comprehension skills. At the end of the week, display the answer key and allow students to correct their own work. Facilitate a class discussion about the items and allow students to share their answers. Encourage students to model how to solve problems or answer items that their classmates may have struggled with.

Using *Daily Fundamentals* as an informal assessment
You may wish to use the weekly lessons as an informal assessment of students' competencies. Because each week's practice focuses on a particular skill or concept, the tasks provide you with a detailed view of each student's level of mastery.

Skills Scope and Sequence
Use the scope and sequence chart to identify the specific skills that students are practicing.

Student Progress Chart
Students can monitor their own progress by recording their daily scores and thinking about their success with different skills. Reproduce and distribute the progress chart to students at the beginning of each week. For older students, you may wish to have them write the number correct out of the total number of items.

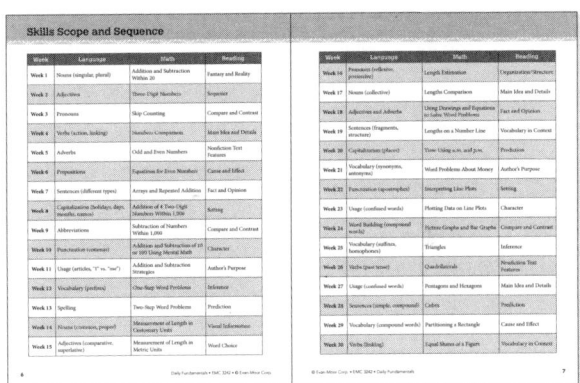

Student Record Sheet
Record students' scores on the record sheet. This form will provide you with a snapshot of each student's skills mastery in language, math, and reading and serve as a resource to track students' progress throughout the year.

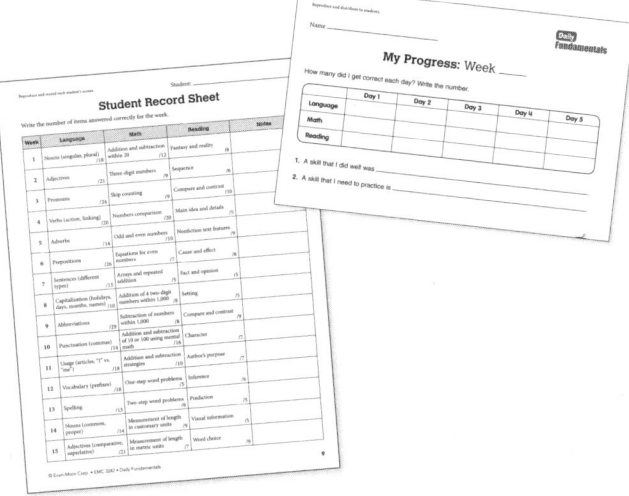

Skills Scope and Sequence

Week	Language	Math	Reading
Week 1	Nouns (singular, plural)	Addition and Subtraction Within 20	Fantasy and Reality
Week 2	Adjectives	Three-Digit Numbers	Sequence
Week 3	Pronouns	Skip Counting	Compare and Contrast
Week 4	Verbs (action, linking)	Numbers Comparison	Main Idea and Details
Week 5	Adverbs	Odd and Even Numbers	Nonfiction Text Features
Week 6	Prepositions	Equations for Even Numbers	Cause and Effect
Week 7	Sentences (different types)	Arrays and Repeated Addition	Fact and Opinion
Week 8	Capitalization (holidays, days, months, names)	Addition of 4 Two-Digit Numbers Within 1,000	Setting
Week 9	Abbreviations	Subtraction of Numbers Within 1,000	Compare and Contrast
Week 10	Punctuation (commas)	Addition and Subtraction of 10 or 100 Using Mental Math	Character
Week 11	Usage (articles, "I" vs. "me")	Addition and Subtraction Strategies	Author's Purpose
Week 12	Vocabulary (prefixes)	One-Step Word Problems	Inference
Week 13	Spelling	Two-Step Word Problems	Prediction
Week 14	Nouns (common, proper)	Measurement of Length in Customary Units	Visual Information
Week 15	Adjectives (comparative, superlative)	Measurement of Length in Metric Units	Word Choice

Week	Language	Math	Reading
Week 16	Pronouns (reflexive, possessive)	Length Estimation	Organization/Structure
Week 17	Nouns (collective)	Lengths Comparison	Main Idea and Details
Week 18	Adjectives and Adverbs	Using Drawings and Equations to Solve Word Problems	Fact and Opinion
Week 19	Sentences (fragments, structure)	Lengths on a Number Line	Vocabulary in Context
Week 20	Capitalization (places)	Time Using *a.m.* and *p.m.*	Prediction
Week 21	Vocabulary (synonyms, antonyms)	Word Problems About Money	Author's Purpose
Week 22	Punctuation (apostrophes)	Interpreting Line Plots	Setting
Week 23	Usage (confused words)	Plotting Data on Line Plots	Character
Week 24	Word Building (compound words)	Picture Graphs and Bar Graphs	Compare and Contrast
Week 25	Vocabulary (suffixes, homophones)	Triangles	Inference
Week 26	Verbs (past tense)	Quadrilaterals	Nonfiction Text Features
Week 27	Usage (confused words)	Pentagons and Hexagons	Main Idea and Details
Week 28	Sentences (simple, compound)	Cubes	Prediction
Week 29	Vocabulary (compound words)	Partitioning a Rectangle	Cause and Effect
Week 30	Verbs (linking)	Equal Shares of a Figure	Vocabulary in Context

Reproduce and distribute to students.

Daily Fundamentals

Name _____

My Progress: Week ____

How many did I get correct each day? Write the number.

	Day 1	Day 2	Day 3	Day 4	Day 5
Language					
Math					
Reading					

1. A skill that I did well was _____.

2. A skill that I need to practice is _____.

Daily Fundamentals

Name _____

My Progress: Week ____

How many did I get correct each day? Write the number.

	Day 1	Day 2	Day 3	Day 4	Day 5
Language					
Math					
Reading					

1. A skill that I did well was _____.

2. A skill that I need to practice is _____.

Reproduce and record each student's scores.

Student: _____

Student Record Sheet

Write the number of items answered correctly for the week.

Week	Language	Math	Reading	Notes
1	Nouns (singular, plural) /18	Addition and subtraction within 20 /12	Fantasy and reality /8	
2	Adjectives /21	Three-digit numbers /9	Sequence /6	
3	Pronouns /24	Skip counting /9	Compare and contrast /10	
4	Verbs (action, linking) /20	Numbers comparison /20	Main idea and details /5	
5	Adverbs /14	Odd and even numbers /10	Nonfiction text features /9	
6	Prepositions /26	Equations for even numbers /7	Cause and effect /6	
7	Sentences (different types) /15	Arrays and repeated addition /5	Fact and opinion /5	
8	Capitalization (holidays, days, months, names) /10	Addition of 4 two-digit numbers within 1,000 /8	Setting /5	
9	Abbreviations /29	Subtraction of numbers within 1,000 /8	Compare and contrast /9	
10	Punctuation (commas) /14	Addition and subtraction of 10 or 100 using mental math /16	Character /7	
11	Usage (articles, "I" vs. "me") /18	Addition and subtraction strategies /10	Author's purpose /7	
12	Vocabulary (prefixes) /18	One-step word problems /5	Inference /6	
13	Spelling /13	Two-step word problems /6	Prediction /5	
14	Nouns (common, proper) /14	Measurement of length in customary units /9	Visual information /5	
15	Adjectives (comparative, superlative) /21	Measurement of length in metric units /7	Word choice /9	

© Evan-Moor Corp. • EMC 3242 • Daily Fundamentals

Student Record Sheet, continued

Week	Language	Math	Reading	Notes
16	Pronouns (reflexive, possessive) /14	Length estimation /5	Organization/structure /6	
17	Nouns (collective) /13	Lengths comparison /5	Main idea and details /5	
18	Adjectives and adverbs /9	Using drawings and equations to solve word problems /5	Fact and opinion /7	
19	Sentences (fragments, structure) /16	Lengths on a number line /10	Vocabulary in context /8	
20	Capitalization (places) /9	Time using *a.m.* and *p.m.* /16	Prediction /5	
21	Vocabulary (synonyms, antonyms) /23	Word problems about money /5	Author's purpose /5	
22	Punctuation (apostrophes) /17	Interpreting line plots /5	Setting /5	
23	Usage (confused words) /15	Plotting data on line plots /5	Character /5	
24	Word building (compound words) /17	Picture graphs and bar graphs /5	Compare and contrast /8	
25	Vocabulary (suffixes, homophones) /23	Triangles /5	Inference /5	
26	Verbs (past tense) /17	Quadrilaterals /6	Nonfiction text features /9	
27	Usage (confused words) /15	Pentagons and hexagons /7	Main idea and details /8	
28	Sentences (simple, compound) /14	Cubes /5	Prediction /6	
29	Vocabulary (compound words) /20	Partitioning a rectangle /5	Cause and effect /5	
30	Verbs (linking) /30	Equal shares of a figure /5	Vocabulary in context /10	

Name _____

Day 1 | **Week 1**

Language

Circle the noun in each pair of words.

1. blue lake
2. tall man
3. big brother
4. small cat
5. pretty flower
6. good work

Math

Add.

7.
$$7 + 2 \qquad 8 + 2 \qquad 4 + 5 \qquad 0 + 9 \qquad 4 + 2 \qquad 9 + 5 \qquad 2 + 11$$

8.
$$8 + 5 \qquad 3 + 8 \qquad 16 + 0 \qquad 4 + 9 \qquad 18 + 1 \qquad 2 + 15 \qquad 8 + 8$$

Reading

Read the text. Then mark the item. Write how you know.

Mother Bear was crying because she couldn't find her two cubs. She called the animals of the forest together. She cried, "Help me, my friends! My babies are missing! We need to find them!"

9. ○ real   ○ make-believe

10. Tell how you know. _____

Name _____

Day 2 | **Week 1**

Language

Underline the noun in each sentence. Then circle **person**, **place**, or **thing** to tell what the noun names.

1. The park is not far away.   person   place   thing
2. The children want to go now.   person   place   thing
3. The big slide is new.   person   place   thing

Math

Subtract.

4. 6   6   9   9   9   7   15
   −4   −5   −8   −6   −4   −7   −5

5. 7   7   10   8   17   12   20
   −5   −4   −6   −6   −3   −3   −9

Reading

Read the text. Then mark the item. Write how you know.

　　Anna and her family were in the car for five hours. Dad had planned a family vacation at a cabin in the mountains. They finally arrived. Anna's big brother, Matt, took out his phone. "Great," he said. "There's no service. Now I can't use my phone!"

6. ○ real   ○ make-believe

7. Tell how you know. _____

_____

12   Daily Fundamentals • EMC 3242 • © Evan-Moor Corp.

Name _____

Day 3 | **Week 1**

Language

Write **S** if the underlined noun is **singular**.
Write **P** if the underlined noun is **plural**.

1. My <u>sisters</u> read every day.　　　　_____

2. One sister likes chapter <u>books</u>.　　　_____

3. The other <u>sister</u> likes fairy tales.　　_____

Math

Read the problem. Then answer the items.

> 20 children were playing soccer. 3 children had to leave early. How many children were still playing?

4. You will find out how many children _____.

    ○ left early　　○ were playing in all　　○ were still playing

5. There were _____ children still playing.

Reading

Read the text. Then answer the items.

> A family of rats lived under the chicken coop. All day long they scurried about, eating the chicken feed and hiding from the cat.

6. Mark the sentence that would make this story make-believe.

    ○ One day, Father rat said, "It's time to find a new home!"

    ○ The rats under the coop were a problem, so we got another cat.

7. How do you know? _____

_____

Name _____

Day 4 | **Week 1**

Language

Read the sentence. Write a plural noun from the word box.

> sandwiches   peaches   benches

1. Let's sit on these two _____.

2. We can eat our cheese _____.

3. I also have some sweet _____ you will like.

Math

Read each number sentence. Then write the missing number.

4. _____ + 10 = 16

5. 15 − _____ = 7

6. _____ + 16 = 20

7. 19 − 2 = _____

Reading

Read the text. Then answer the item.

    A poor fisherman lived alone in a tiny boat on the sea. He was tired of eating fish for lunch. He wanted a hot dog. He jumped off his boat and quickly flapped his wings. He flew more than twenty miles to land. He ate a hot dog, rested his wings, and flew home.

8. Write something from the story that is <u>not</u> real.

_____

_____

Name _____

Day 5 — Week 1

Language

Look at the bold noun. Write the plural form of the noun above it.

1. Many _____ are coming to the party.
   family

2. They are all from different _____.
   country

3. It will be fun to play with the _____.
   baby

Math

Find the sum or difference. Show a way to think about it.

4. 9 + 8 = _____

5. 9 − 5 = _____

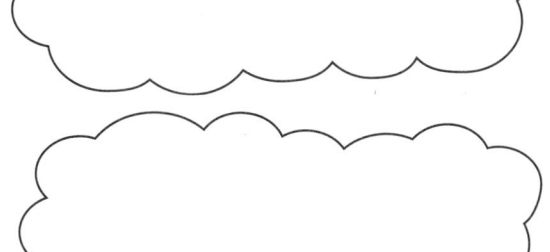

Reading

Read the text. Then answer the item.

One summer day, the wind and the sun were mad. The wind blew and said, "I am stronger than you!"
The sun got very hot. "That's not true! I'm stronger than you!" said the sun.

6. Write something from the story that is real.

_____

_____

© Evan-Moor Corp. • EMC 3242 • Daily Fundamentals

Name _____

Day 1 | **Week 2**

Language

Write an adjective to describe the noun.

1. _____ flowers
2. _____ men
3. _____ houses
4. _____ hats
5. _____ deer
6. _____ dress
7. _____ hand
8. _____ bed

Math

Match each digit to its set of cubes. Then write the value below the cubes. One is done for you.

9. 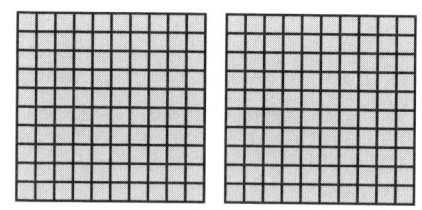 258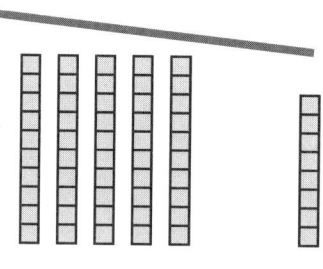

_____   _____   8

Reading

Read the text. Then answer the item.

   Ron put food in a bag and got into a raft. The raft slipped into the water. Right away, the river pulled them around a bend. The raft lifted and turned.

10. Write a number to show the order in which it happened.

_____ raft slipped into the water   _____ put food in a bag

_____ got into a raft   _____ raft lifted and turned

16   Daily Fundamentals • EMC 3242 • © Evan-Moor Corp.

Language

Read the sentence. Write an adjective from the word box.

> new   friendly   blue

1. My house has a _____ rug.

2. My pets are all very _____.

3. I have a _____ backpack this year.

Math

Mark the number that matches the set of cubes.

4.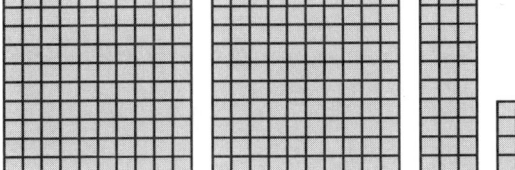
   - ○ 240
   - ○ 234
   - ○ 232

5.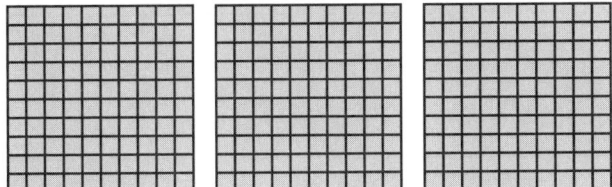
   - ○ 329
   - ○ 310
   - ○ 320

Reading

Read the text. Then answer the questions.

   Tom had a busy morning. Before he could run out the door to catch the bus, he had to eat breakfast. Then he had to find his book and brush his teeth.

6. What was the <u>first</u> thing Tom had to do before he caught the bus?

   _____

7. What was the <u>last</u> thing Tom had to do before he caught the bus?

   _____

Name _____

Day 3 | **Week 2**

Language

Write a noun on the first line. Then write an adjective to tell about it on the next line.

1. The _____ is _____.

2. The _____ is _____.

3. The _____ is _____.

4. The _____ is _____.

Math

Complete the table to show each number in three ways.

	Base Ten Numeral	Written Form	Expanded Form
5.	118	one hundred eighteen	
6.	436		400 + 30 + 6

Reading

Read the text. Then answer the item.

It is easy to make lemonade. First, fill a pitcher with water. Add the juice of four lemons. Add a cup of sugar and stir. Finally, add ice and enjoy.

7. Write a number to show the order in which it happened.

_____ fill a pitcher with water   _____ add a cup of sugar and stir

_____ add ice   _____ add the juice of four lemons

Name _____

Day 4 | **Week 2**

Language

Write three adjectives that tell about the color, shape, or size of the moon.

1. _____
2. _____
3. _____

Math

Mark the value of the underlined digit.

4. 83<u>4</u>
   - ○ 4
   - ○ 40
   - ○ 400

5. 6<u>0</u>7
   - ○ 60
   - ○ 1
   - ○ 0 tens

Reading

Read the text. Then answer the question.

   Once upon a time there was a poor shoemaker. He measured enough leather to make one pair of shoes. He cut out the leather. He laid it on the table. In the morning, he would sew the shoes.

6. Which one tells about the shoemaker's third step?
   - ○ He cut out the leather.
   - ○ He laid it on the table.

© Evan-Moor Corp. • EMC 3242 • Daily Fundamentals

Name _____

Day 5 | **Week 2**

Language

Circle the adjective that best completes the sentence. Then write it on the line.

1. The branches are _____ with apples. **fun**   **heavy**

2. Look at all those _____ apples! **beautiful**   **noisy**

3. Let's put the apples in _____ baskets. **itchy**   **strong**

Math

Read the problem. Then answer the items.

The tallest tree in the world is three hundred eighty feet high.

4. Write the height as a number. _____

5. Write the height using place value.

_____ hundreds, _____ tens, _____ ones

Reading

Read the text. Then answer the question.

On Saturday mornings, Aaron feeds his dog. First, he gets his dog Spot. Then he makes Spot sit next to his empty bowl. Next, he puts the dog food on the counter. He tells Spot to stay when Spot gets up. Then he pours the food into the bowl. Finally, he tells Spot he can eat.

6. Do you think the steps above are in the right order? Tell why or why not.

_____

_____

Name _____

Day 1 | **Week 3**

Language

Underline the pronoun in the sentence.

1. I have a cheese sandwich.
2. Do you want a bite?
3. I can share the sandwich.
4. She does not have a lunch either.
5. It is a big sandwich.

Math

Answer the item.

6. What number comes next?

   600, 610, 620, 630, _____

   Ⓐ 700
   Ⓑ 640
   Ⓒ 631
   Ⓓ 635

Reading

Read the text. Then answer the items.

   We put food in the yard for the birds. We put out different kinds of food. Most birds eats seeds. Pigeons and doves eat corn, too. But hummingbirds drink their food. They like the sugar water we put out. The birds come again and again to our yard.

7. Which bird is different from the others?
   ○ hummingbird
   ○ dove

8. Tell why the bird you chose is different from the others.

   _____

   _____

Name _____

Day 2 | **Week 3**

Language

Write a pronoun to replace the underlined noun or nouns.

1. <u>Dad</u> likes to bake. _____

2. <u>Dad and I</u> ate some pie. _____

3. <u>Mom and Jen</u> want some pie, too. _____

4. Does <u>Rita</u> like pie? _____

5. <u>The pie</u> is still warm. _____

Math

Skip count to find the number of cubes.

6.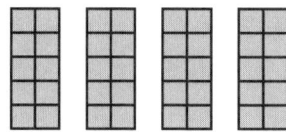

○ 40 cubes
○ 4 cubes
○ 400 cubes

Reading

Read the text. Then answer the items.

Lina and Tina are twins. They look alike and they talk alike. They live in the same house. They wear the same clothes. But Lina and Tina are also different. Lina loves math and science. Tina loves art and music. Both girls are hard workers and they will do great things.

7. How are the twins different?
   ○ Lina likes to talk and Tina is quiet.
   ○ Lina loves math and Tina loves art.

8. Write a sentence from the text that tells how the twins are the same.

_____

_____

22   Daily Fundamentals • EMC 3242 • © Evan-Moor Corp.

Name _____

Day 3 | **Week 3**

Language

Circle the plural pronoun in the sentence.

1. We are going to play soccer.
2. Jen and Kim, do you want to go?
3. We will see Sam and Jairo.
4. They will be there, too.
5. We can all meet by the swings.

Math

Answer the items.

6. What number comes next?

    55, 60, 65, 70, ____

    Ⓐ 80   Ⓒ 75
    Ⓑ 71   Ⓓ 72

7. Tell why.

    _____
    _____

Reading

Read the text. Then answer the items.

   The Miyata family wants to go on a vacation. They like the beach, but they also like the lake. Both places are pretty. Both places have water. At the beach, they can play in the sand. At the lake, they can row a boat and catch fish. It is hard to decide where to go because both places are fun!

8. Write how the beach and the lake are alike.

    _____
    _____

9. Write the different things the family can do at the beach and at the lake.

    _____
    _____

© Evan-Moor Corp. • EMC 3242 • Daily Fundamentals

Name _____

Day 4 | **Week 3**

Language

Rewrite the sentence. Write a pronoun to take the place of the underlined noun or nouns.

1. <u>Mom</u> baked a cake.

   _____

2. <u>Dad</u> grilled hot dogs.

   _____

3. <u>Mom</u>, <u>Dad</u>, and <u>I</u> celebrated.

   _____

Math

Skip count to complete the pattern.

4. 45, 50, _____, _____, _____

5. 100, 200, _____, _____, _____, _____

6. 20, 30, _____, _____, _____, _____

How did you skip count the last pattern?

I counted by _____.

Reading

Read the text. Then answer the items.

    Oranges and lemons are both fruits. They both grow on trees. They both have seeds on the inside. However, oranges are sweeter than lemons. Oranges and lemons are also different colors. Oranges are orange and lemons are yellow. Which fruit do you like better?

7. How are oranges and lemons different?

   _____

   _____

8. Write a sentence from the text that tells how the oranges and lemons are the same.

   _____

24   Daily Fundamentals • EMC 3242 • © Evan-Moor Corp.

Day 5 | **Week 3**

Language

Underline the pronoun in the sentence.

1. Ms. Mendes lent me a book.
2. I shared the book with Emily.
3. Emily will read it tomorrow.
4. We both liked the book.
5. Ms. Mendes always thinks of us.
6. Emily gave her some flowers.

Math

Answer the items.

7. What number is missing?

    600, 700, 800, ____, 1,000

    Ⓐ 850
    Ⓑ 999
    Ⓒ 900

8. How do you know?

    _____
    _____

Reading

Read the sentence next to the picture. Then answer the items.

Tyler is a Cub, but Jerome is a Blue Jay.

9. Write a sentence that tells how the boys are the same.

    _____

10. Write a sentence that tells how the boys are different.

    _____
    _____

© Evan-Moor Corp. • EMC 3242 • Daily Fundamentals

Name _____

Day 1 | Week 4

Language

Is it a verb or a noun? Circle the six verbs in the word box. Then write them on the lines.

> boy   write   sing   night   walk
> sit   jump   bed   run   story

1. _____   3. _____   5. _____
2. _____   4. _____   6. _____

Math

Write >, =, or < in the circle to compare the numbers.

7. 607 ◯ 607

8. 936 ◯ 671

9. 208 ◯ 421

10. 234 ◯ 240

Reading

Read the text. Then answer the question.

Acrobats can do amazing things! Their acts are fun to watch. A woman swings from a bar that hangs from the top of the tent. She lets go of the bar and flips three times in the air. A man rides a bike across a wire. He goes forward and backward. How do they do this?

11. What is the main idea?

○ Acrobats have many acts.

○ Acrobats do many amazing things.

26   Daily Fundamentals • EMC 3242 • © Evan-Moor Corp.

Name _____

Day 2 — **Week 4**

Language

Circle the verb in the sentence.

1. Sara sings a beautiful song.

2. I listen carefully.

3. She sits near my bed.

4. Soon, I sleep quietly.

Math

Write >, =, or < in the circle to compare the numbers.

5. 640 ◯ 529

6. 198 ◯ 190

7. 305 ◯ 305

8. 98 ◯ 212

Reading

Read the text. Then answer the question.

Long ago, before airplanes and trains, it was not easy for people to move across the country. People used wagons covered by tents. Some people rode in the wagons and others walked beside the wagons. Many wagons traveled together in a long line.

9. What is the main idea?

_____

Name _____

Day 3 | **Week 4**

Language

Read the sentence. Underline the verb.

1. I am so hot today!

2. My dog is thirsty on this hot day.

3. My two cats are in the tree.

4. Missy and Tina were in the pool earlier.

Math

Write >, =, or < in the circle to compare the numbers.

5. 2,000 ◯ 200

6. 876 ◯ 950

7. 50 ◯ 500

8. 29 ◯ 29

Reading

Read the text. Then answer the question.

The big island of Hawaii was made by five volcanoes. One volcano called Kilauea is an active volcano. Another volcano, Mauna Kea, is the tallest volcano on Earth.

9. What is the main idea?

○ The big island of Hawaii was made by five volcanoes.

○ Another volcano, Mauna Kea, is the tallest volcano on Earth.

28   Daily Fundamentals • EMC 3242 • © Evan-Moor Corp.

Name _____   Day 4   Week 4

Language

Read the sentence. Write the verb on the line.

1. This peach tastes so sweet.   _____

2. It smells good as well.   _____

3. Peaches from the farmers' market feel firm.   _____

4. Each one looks fuzzy and ripe.   _____

Math

Write **>**, **=**, or **<** in the circle to compare the numbers.

5. 1,000 ◯ 100

6. 435 ◯ 453

7. 776 ◯ 670

8. 321 ◯ 123

Reading

Read the text. Then answer the item.

   Ben Franklin invented many things to help people. For example, in 1742 he invented an iron stove. In those days, people made fires in a fireplace. But the fireplace did not do a good job of warming their homes. It also gave off a lot of smoke and used a lot of wood. Franklin's iron stove stood in the middle of the room. It gave off more heat, used less wood, and warmed people's homes for hours and hours. It was called the Franklin stove.

9. Underline the main idea. Then circle details that tell about the main idea.

Name _____

Day 5 Week 4

Language

Write two sentences about school. Use verbs that tell what is happening **now**.

1. _____

_____

2. _____

_____

Math

Write **>**, **=**, or **<** in the circle to compare the numbers.

3. 344 ◯ 444

4. 1,000 ◯ 999

5. 67 ◯ 67

6. 325 ◯ 355

Reading

Read the text. Then write the main idea.

The stem holds the apple to the tree. The leaf uses water, sunlight, and air to make food for the tree. The core holds the seeds. The skin protects the apple. The flesh is the part of the apple that tastes good.

7. _____

_____

Name _____

Day 1 | **Week 5**

Language

Read the sentence. Then read the question. Write the adverb that answers the question.

1. Jenna walks quickly to school.

   How does Jenna walk to school? _____

2. Jenna never arrives late to school.

   When does Jenna arrive late to school? _____

Math

Write the number of objects. Then mark **even** or **odd**.

3.  _____ ○ even ○ odd

4. _____ ○ even ○ odd

Reading

Read the glossary. Then answer the item.

Glossary

crust   Earth's hard outer layer

lava   the hot liquid rock that pours out of a volcano

mantle   the part of Earth between the crust and the core

5. The words in the glossary would most likely be in a book about ____.

   Ⓐ what is inside Earth
   Ⓑ the human body
   Ⓒ the planets

Name _____

Day 2 | **Week 5**

Language

Read the sentence. Then answer the question about the bold word.

1. My dog **excitedly** wags his tail when I get home.

   How does the dog wag his tail? _____

2. The word **excitedly** tells "how."

   Is **excitedly** an adjective or an adverb? _____

Math

Write the number of objects. Then mark **even** or **odd**.

3.

   _____ ○ even
   ○ odd

4.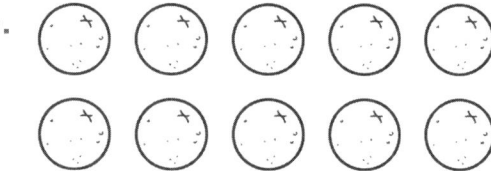

   _____ ○ even
   ○ odd

Reading

Read the table of contents. Then answer the questions.

Contents

Breakfast Foods 4
Lunch Foods 12
Snacks 19
Dinner Foods 23
Desserts 129

5. Which section begins on page 12?
   Ⓐ Desserts
   Ⓑ Lunch Foods
   Ⓒ Dinner Foods

6. Which section has the most pages?
   Ⓐ Lunch Foods
   Ⓑ Dinner Foods

Day 3 | **Week 5**

Language

Look at the bold verb. Circle the adverb that tells more about the verb.

1. Mom and I **walk** to school early in the morning.

2. We **shut** the door carefully.

3. We **laugh** quietly about the toys in the yard.

4. Mom and I **arrive** safely at school by 8:00 a.m.

Math

Write the number of objects. Then mark **even** or **odd**.

5.
   _____ ○ even ○ odd

6.
   _____ ○ even ○ odd

Reading

Read the ad. Then answer the questions.

7. What is for sale in the ad?
   Ⓐ party items
   Ⓑ grocery items
   Ⓒ school items

8. How many days is the sale?

   _____

   _____

Name _____

Day 4 | **Week 5**

Language

Read the sentence. Write the best adverb to tell **how**.

1. The kittens sleep _____ in the box.
   quietly   fairly

2. They meow _____ when they wake up.
   brightly   softly

3. I _____ put some food in their bowl.
   quickly   loudly

Math

Write the number of objects. Then mark **even** or **odd**.

4. ⚫⚫⚫⚫⚫⚫⚫⚫⚫⚫⚫⚫⚫ _____   ○ even   ○ odd

5. ▲▲▲▲▲▲▲▲▲▲▲▲▲▲ _____   ○ even   ○ odd

Reading

Read the flier. Then answer the items.

Fluffy
We cannot find our cat!
We miss him very much.
Please help us!
Call 555-5555 or bring him to 10 Cherry Lane

6. What is this flier about?
   Ⓐ a found cat
   Ⓑ a lost cat
   Ⓒ a cat for sale

7. Write one thing you can do if you find the cat.

   _____

34   Daily Fundamentals • EMC 3242 • © Evan-Moor Corp.

Name _____

Day 5 | **Week 5**

Language

Read the sentence. Underline the adverb. Does the adverb tell **when** or **where**? Circle the correct answer.

1. We visited the farm yesterday. **when** **where**

2. We ate lunch outside at a picnic table. **when** **where**

3. I want to visit this place again. **when** **where**

Math

Write the number of objects. Then mark **even** or **odd**.

4.

_____ ○ even
         ○ odd

5. Draw an odd number of hearts.

Reading

Read the sign. Then answer the questions.

POOL RULES
- WATCH YOUR CHILDREN
- DON'T SWIM ALONE
- NO DIVING
- NO RUNNING
- NO FOOD OR DRINK
- NO PETS IN POOL AREA
- NO TOYS IN POOL
- HAVE FUN!

6. Who is this sign posted for?

_____

_____

7. Why is this sign posted?

_____

_____

Name _____

Day 1 **Week 6**

Language

Underline the preposition in the sentence.

1. Today I walked to the park.
2. I rolled a ball through the dirt.
3. I sat on a bench.
4. A squirrel ate a nut near a tree.
5. A baby bird sat with its mom.
6. I ate a snack I brought from home.

Math

Read the number sentence. Draw objects to model the number sentence. Then write the sum.

7.

$2 + 2 =$ _____

8.

$3 + 3 =$ _____

Reading

Read the text. Then answer the question.

Last year, Anya saw that her lemon tree had tiny lemons on it, but the leaves did not look happy. They were droopy and dry. Anya looked in a book about taking care of trees. She read that lemon trees like a lot of sun. They need to be watered often. They need plant food. After Anya learned how to care for the lemon tree, it looked so much better!

9. After Anya learned how to care for the lemon tree, what was the effect?
   ○ The leaves did not look happy.
   ○ The tree looked much better.

36 Daily Fundamentals • EMC 3242 • © Evan-Moor Corp.

Name _____

Day 2 | **Week 6**

Language

Write **to**, **with**, **in**, or **on** to complete the sentence. Use each word only once.

1. Let's go _____ the beach.

2. We can sit _____ a big towel.

3. Let's dig a hole _____ the sand.

4. It's easy to dig _____ my toy shovel.

Math

Write a doubles number sentence that tells about the flowers.

5. _____ + _____ = _____

Reading

Read the text. Then answer the question.

   One day, Jack was playing video games with a friend. Jack had to be home by 6:00, and it was already 5:55. It always took him five minutes to get home, so Jack hopped on his skateboard and started rolling down the street. Suddenly... wobble, wobble, bump! Jack fell to the ground. His knee was hurt pretty badly, and so was his skateboard. The wheel had cracked! Jack had to limp all the way home. When he finally got home at 6:15, his mother was worried.

6. Why was Jack late coming home?

_____

_____

Language

Write **under**, **across**, **down**, or **up**. Use each word only once.

1. He climbed _____ the steps.
2. He walked _____ a bridge.
3. He slid _____ a rocky hill.
4. He rested _____ a big tree.

Math

Write a doubles number sentence that tells about the books.

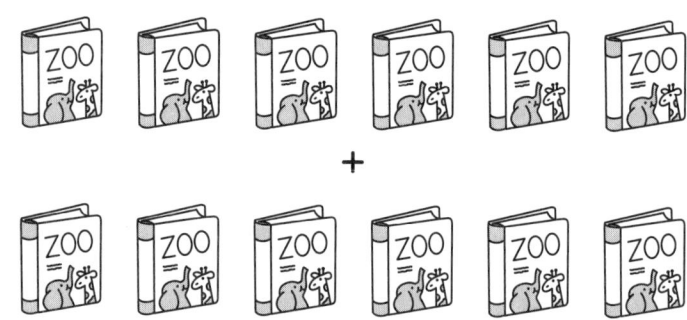

5. _____ + _____ = _____

Reading

Read the text. Then answer the question.

Mom and I were worried about our puppy, Pete. He did not want to play. He did not want to run after the ball. He was always tired. His belly looked bigger, too. But why? We fed him dog food twice a day just like we always did.

One day, I was picking up fruit that had fallen from our avocado tree. I saw that some of the dark green peels had been ripped open. Part of the inside of each fruit was gone. Now I knew how Pete had gotten so big!

6. Why was Pete's belly bigger?
   ○ He ate too many avocados.
   ○ He ate dog food twice a day.

Name _____

Day 4 | **Week 6**

Language

Underline the preposition in the sentence.

1. Come to my birthday party.
2. It will be at Albany Park.
3. We will be by the playground.
4. Walk across the parking lot.
5. Find the tree with balloons.
6. We will wait for you!

Math

Read the problem. Then answer the item.

Each box has 18 cookies. The cookies look like this:

7. The number of cookies in each row is _____.
   ○ different
   ○ equal
   ○ greater than 10

Reading

Read the text. Then answer the question.

    Sarah Josepha Hale felt that Thanksgiving should be a holiday that all Americans celebrate on the same day. Some states had Thanksgiving Day in October. Some had it in January. Many states didn't have a Thanksgiving Day at all. For seventeen years, Sarah wrote letters to presidents. She asked for Thanksgiving Day to be on the same day in all the states—a national holiday. In 1863, President Lincoln made Thanksgiving Day a national holiday. Every state would celebrate it on the last Thursday of November.

8. What happened because of Sarah's actions?

_____

_____

Name _____

Day 5 | **Week 6**

Language

Underline the preposition in the sentence.

1. Mom and I sit on a bench.
2. We like sitting near the pond.
3. Five little ducks are swimming in the pond.
4. We take a few pictures with Mom's phone.
5. We walk around the park.
6. Tomorrow we will come back to this same spot.

Math

Write a doubles number sentence that tells about the marbles.

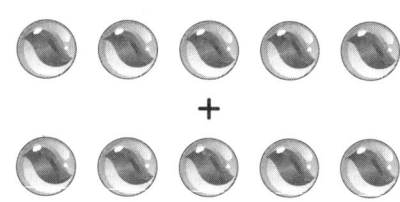

7. _____ + _____ = _____

8. Can you make a doubles number sentence with a sum of 5?
   ○ yes   ○ no

   Explain your answer.

   _____

Reading

Read the text. Then answer the questions.

    Kevin was playing soccer at the park. His team was doing great, and Kevin was kicking the ball toward the goal. Suddenly, he tripped and fell sideways. Kevin landed on his arm. It hurt so much!
    The next thing Kevin knew, he was in the hospital and the doctor was putting a cast on his arm. The doctor gave Kevin a black marker. Kevin's parents were the first to write "get well" on the cast.

9. What caused Kevin's arm to hurt?

   _____

10. What happened after Kevin hurt his arm?

    _____

Day 1 | **Week 7**

Language

What kind of sentence is it? Write **telling**, **asking**, or **exclamation** on the line.

1. It's time to pick the apples from our tree. _____

2. Look at all those big green apples! _____

3. Let's put the biggest ones in this basket. _____

4. Will you bake a pie for us? _____

Math

Write how many bugs are in each **column**.
Then complete the number sentence.

5. 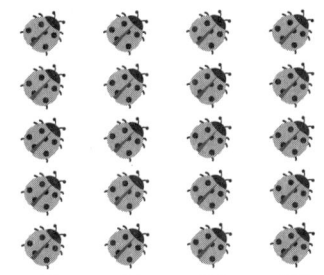   There are 4 columns of _____ bugs.

_____ + _____ + _____ + _____ = _____

Reading

Read the text. Then answer the question.

   Grandma's pies are yummy! We had some warm apple pie with vanilla ice cream. Grandpa told stories of when Mom was little, swinging on her apple tree.

6. Which one is an opinion?

   ○ We had some warm apple pie with vanilla ice cream.

   ○ Grandma's pies are yummy!

Name _____

Day 2 | **Week 7**

Language

Answer the question with a statement.

1. What is your favorite lunch? _____
   _____

2. What is your favorite color? _____
   _____

Math

Write how many hearts are in each **column**.
Then complete the number sentence.

3.

   There are 4 columns of _____ hearts.

   _____ + _____ + _____ + _____ = _____

Reading

Read the text. Then answer the question.

   Railroads in America were built long ago in the 1800s. Before trains, people traveled by boat or by horse. But rivers would freeze in the winter. Trains were the best because they never had problems.

4. Which one is a fact?
   ○ Railroads in America were built in the 1800s.
   ○ Trains were the best because they never had problems.

Name _____   **Day 3**   **Week 7**

Language

Write a period or a question mark to end each sentence.
Circle **S** if it is a statement or **Q** if it is a question.

1. I have a new puppy named Buddy____   S   Q

2. Would you like to meet him____   S   Q

3. When can you come over____   S   Q

Math

Write how many stars are in each **row**.
Then complete the number sentence.

4. ★ ★ ★ ★ ★   There are 3 rows of _____ stars.
   ★ ★ ★ ★ ★
   ★ ★ ★ ★ ★   _____ + _____ + _____ = _____

Reading

Read the text. Then answer the item.

   César Chavéz was born in Arizona in 1927. Arizona is the greatest state. His family had a farm and a grocery store. When César was ten years old, there was not enough water for the plants on the farm. Most of the plants died.

5. Write a sentence from the text that is an opinion.

   _____

   _____

© Evan-Moor Corp. • EMC 3242 • Daily Fundamentals

Name _____

Day 4 | Week 7

Language

Circle the question word. Then rewrite the sentence with an end mark.

1. When is the first day of school

2. _____

3. Who will be your teacher

4. _____

Math

Mark the number sentence that tells about the array.

5.

○ 2 + 2 + 2 + 2 + 2 = ?

○ 2 + 2 + 2 + 2 = ?

○ 5 + 5 + 5 = ?

Reading

Read the text. Then answer the item.

A magnet will attract some things made of steel. Many refrigerators are made of steel. So are things like paper clips, pins, nails, and cars. Magnets are fun.

6. Write a sentence from the text that is a fact.

_____

_____

Name _____

Day 5 | **Week 7**

Language

Read the sentence. Look at the picture.
Then write two sentences with **!** that go with the picture.

There's water all over the floor!

1. _____

2. _____

Math

Write a number sentence that tells about the array.

3. There are 5 rows of _____.

___ + ___ + ___ + ___ + ___ = ___

Reading

Read the text. Then answer the question.

A family of rats lived near a rice field. They visited the rice field every day to see if the rice had grown. There wasn't much rain, so the rice did not grow. Rice fields need to be flooded with water in order for the rice to grow. I think rats like to live near rice fields.

4. Does this text have both a fact and an opinion? Explain your answer.

_____

_____

Name _____

Day 1 | **Week 8**

Language

Read the sentence. Then rewrite it using capital letters for the holidays.

1. We will take Mom out to lunch on mother's day.
   _____

2. On valentine's day, we made cards for our friends.
   _____

Math

Solve the problem. Draw or write to show your thinking.

3. 62 + 24 = _____

4. 42 + 36 = _____

Reading

Read the text. Then answer the question.

After school, my friend and I ride our bikes to the park. We sit on the bench and watch the ducks in the pond. After a while, it's time to go home, but first we ride slowly on the bike path around the pond.

5. After reading the story, what do you know about the park? Write about it.
   _____
   _____

Name _____

Day 2 | **Week 8**

Language

Read the sentence. Then rewrite it using capital letters where they are needed.

1. On monday and wednesday I go to swimming class.

   _____

2. Paul's birthday party is this saturday.

   _____

Math

Solve the problem. Draw or write to show your thinking.

3. 33 + 44 = _____

4. 23 + 62 = _____

Reading

Read the text. Then answer the item.

One summer day, in a village in Mexico, Sergio and Lupe were married. They had no family and no money, so they had no party and no cake. Still, they were happy.

5. Tell when and where the story takes place.

   _____

   _____

Name _____

Day 3 | **Week 8**

Language

Read the sentence. Then rewrite it using capital letters where they are needed.

1. My sister's birthday is in june.

   _____

2. Thanksgiving is in november.

   _____

Math

Solve the problem. Draw or write to show your thinking.

3. 15 + 75 = _____

4. 12 + 76 = _____

Reading

Read the text. Then answer the questions.

One cool autumn day, a young hunter went out to find food for his family. He saw deer tracks and followed them. Before he knew it, the sky was dark and he was far from home. So he wrapped himself in his fur blanket and laid down to sleep under the tall trees.

5. Does the story take place in a city or in a forest? How do you know?

   _____

   _____

Name _____

Day 4 | **Week 8**

Language

Read the sentence. Then rewrite it using capital letters where they are needed.

1. sara lopez and mike anderson are my best friends.

   _____

2. sally ford has a cousin named richard.

   _____

Math

Read the problem. Then answer the item. Show your work.

Tyson has 26 students in his class.
Jordy has 30 students in his class.
Allen has 27 students in his class.
How many students are in all three classes?

3. _____ students in all three classes

Reading

Read the text. Then answer the questions.

   Hank looked out over the wide plains. He saw some folks coming on a wagon train, probably on their way out west. Hank rode out on his horse to meet them. He waved his hat and said, "Hello there! I reckon you are looking for a place to settle down?"

4. Does the story take place now or long ago? How do you know?

   _____

   _____

Name _____

Day 5 | **Week 8**

Language

Read the sentence. Then rewrite it using capital letters where they are needed.

1. bill, mary, and keith will visit us on thanksgiving.

   _____

2. They will stay until tuesday, december 5.

   _____

Math

Read the problem. Then answer the item. Show your work.

On Monday, Bree rode 12 miles.
On Tuesday, she rode 17 miles.
On Wednesday, she rode 8 miles.
On Thursday, she rode 13 miles.
How many miles did Bree ride altogether?

3. _____ miles altogether

Reading

Read the text. Then answer the questions.

The smell of candy drifted down the hall. The machines went cha-gug, cha-gug, cha-gug as they spat little yellow drops onto the long black belt. Workers with white caps and blue gloves checked every piece of candy to make sure it was soft and perfectly round.

4. Where does the story take place? How do you know?

   _____

   _____

Name _____

Day 1 | **Week 9**

Language

Write the abbreviation for the name of the month.

1. September _____
2. January _____
3. December _____
4. February _____
5. August _____
6. November _____

Math

Solve the problem. Draw or write to show your thinking.

7. $64 - 14 = $ _____

8. $98 - 92 = $ _____

Reading

Read the text. Then answer the questions.

Insects are everywhere. All insects have three body parts and six legs. However, insects differ in the way they move. For example, a butterfly moves by flying. A grasshopper hops and an ant crawls.

9. How are insects the same? How are they different?

_____

_____

10. Is the word **All** used to tell how insects are the same or different?

_____

Name _____

Day 2 | **Week 9**

Language

Write the abbreviation for the day of the week.

1. Monday _____
2. Tuesday _____
3. Wednesday _____
4. Thursday _____
5. Friday _____
6. Saturday _____
7. Sunday _____

Math

Solve the problem. Draw or write to show your thinking.

8. $48 - 23 =$ _____

9. $100 - 96 =$ _____

Reading

Read the text. Then answer the questions.

　　Lakes and oceans are alike and different in many ways. Both are bodies of water. Both are homes to plants and animals. Lakes are smaller than oceans. Lakes have land all around them, but oceans do not.

10. How are oceans and lakes the same?

_____

_____

11. How are oceans and lakes different?

_____

_____

52   Daily Fundamentals • EMC 3242 • © Evan-Moor Corp.

Name _____

Day 3 | **Week 9**

Language

Answer the question. Use an abbreviation for the person's name.

> Mr.   Mrs.   Ms.   Dr.

1. What is your teacher's name?

   _____

2. What is your doctor's name?

   _____

3. What is your friend's dad's name?

   _____

Math

Solve the problem. Draw or write to show your thinking.

4. $41 - 12 =$ _____

5. $302 - 292 =$ _____

Reading

Read the text. Then answer the items.

    My twin sister Martha and I both like the color blue. That is why our mom let us paint our room. We both like rainbows, too, so my dad ordered us a picture to put on the wall. My sister likes to sleep next to the window, but I do not. I like to sleep next to the door so I can see the hallway light. My sister wakes up early, but I try to sleep until our alarm goes off. Sharing a room isn't always easy.

6. Which word helps you know the sisters are alike? _____

7. Write a sentence from the story that tells how the sisters are different.

   _____

   _____

Name _____

Day 4 | **Week 9**

Language

Write the abbreviation for the underlined state.

> WI   IN   ME   NY   IL   TX

1. I live in Chicago, Illinois.   _____
2. We visit Wisconsin often.   _____
3. Indiana is a nice state.   _____
4. My aunt lives in Texas.   _____
5. I want to see New York.   _____
6. Mom wants to see Maine.   _____

Math

Read the problem. Then answer the item. Show your work.

> Mrs. Melon had 166 stamps. She used 22 stamps to mail letters. How many stamps does she have left?

7. _____ stamps left

Reading

Read the text. Then answer the items.

> On Wednesdays my mom buys my favorite bread from the farmer's market. She uses it to make sandwiches. Sometimes she makes grilled cheese sandwiches that are soft and gooey, and sometimes she makes turkey sandwiches that are meaty and tasty!

8. Underline the sentence that compares the sandwiches.

9. Is your favorite sandwich the same or different from the sandwiches in the text? Tell how.

_____

_____

_____

Name _____

Day 5 | **Week 9**

Language

Draw a line to match the name to the abbreviation.

1. Eagle Drive
2. Larkspur Avenue
3. Park Place
4. Hunter Street
5. Penny Lane
6. Davis Road
7. Sunset Highway

- Rd.
- Dr.
- Ave.
- Pl.
- Ln.
- St.
- Hwy.

Math

Read the problem. Then answer the item. Show your work.

Kareen has 27 cousins. Tami has 9 cousins. How many fewer cousins does Tami have?

8. _____ fewer cousins

Reading

Read the text. Then answer the question.

    My classroom library is in the corner of the room. It has all kinds of books. There are animal books, fairy tales, sports books, and even joke books. Most of them were given to us by parents, and a few came from our teacher. We are lucky to have so many books in our library.

9. Is the library the same or different from your classroom library? Tell how.

_____

_____

_____

Name _____

Day 1 | **Week 10**

Language

Write commas to separate the things in a list.

1. Maria plays baseball soccer and tennis.
2. Math science and music are my favorite subjects.
3. Mr. Edwards teaches English Spanish and French.
4. I need to buy milk eggs bread and cheese.

Math

Read the sentence. Mark the answer.

5. 10 more than 403 is _____.
   - ○ 413
   - ○ 503

6. 10 less than 179 is _____.
   - ○ 189
   - ○ 169

Reading

Read the text. Then answer the items.

Every summer, Ed helps Uncle Max on his farm. Ed wakes up early and gathers the eggs. Then he feeds the roosters. After that, he milks the cows and feeds the pigs. Next, he rides horses with Uncle Max and checks all the fences. By lunchtime, Ed is hungry!

7. Which word tells about Ed?   ○ lazy   ○ busy   ○ funny

8. Explain. _____

_____

Name _____

Day 2 | **Week 10**

Language

Rewrite the sentence. Write commas where they belong.

1. My favorite shirt is purple blue white and green.

   _____

2. My uniform includes blue pants skirts and shorts.

   _____

Math

Read the sentence. Mark the answer.

3. 100 more than 803 is _____.
   - ○ 813
   - ○ 903

4. 100 less than 172 is _____.
   - ○ 72
   - ○ 272

Reading

Read the text. Then answer the items.

    Miss Mae volunteers in the library. Every morning, she greets the students with a warm smile. She helps them with their homework. Before the students leave, she wishes them a great day and reminds them to walk, not run, to class.

5. Which word tells about Miss Mae?   ○ quiet   ○ angry   ○ helpful

6. Explain. _____

   _____

© Evan-Moor Corp. • EMC 3242 • Daily Fundamentals

Name _____

Day 3 | **Week 10**

Language

Write a comma where it is missing in the address.

1. Maricarmen Barrios
   8426 Coles Avenue
   Chicago Illinois 60617

2. Nelson Fields
   20105 River Road
   Denton Texas 76203

Math

Read the number sentence. Write the missing number.

3. _____ + 10 = 170

4. 895 − _____ = 795

5. _____ + 10 = 570

6. 695 − _____ = 595

Reading

Read the text. Then answer the questions.

Kayla saw Mia standing quietly in the kitchen doorway. Her eyes lit up and a big smile spread across her face. They hadn't seen each other in a year. Kayla jumped up and down with joy and ran to hug her little cousin Mia.

7. How does Kayla feel about Mia? How do you know?

_____

_____

Name _____

Day 4 | **Week 10**

Language

Write a comma where it belongs in the sentence.

1. Molly asked "May I borrow a pencil?"

2. Anthony answered "I have an extra pencil."

3. "Thank you. I will return it soon " said Molly.

4. "You can keep it " said Anthony.

Math

Read the number sentence. Write the missing number.

5. _____ + 10 = 480

6. 475 – _____ = 375

7. _____ + 10 = 870

8. 472 – _____ = 462

Reading

Read the text. Then answer the questions.

It was the first day at a new school. Henry waited, shifting from one foot to the other. What if the bus driver missed his stop? What if he couldn't find his classroom? What if no one liked him?

9. How does Henry feel on the first day of school? How do you know?

_____

_____

Language

Read the letter. Write commas where they belong.

1. Dear Grandpa

   When will you come to Texas? We miss you very much.

   Your grandson
   Marco

2. Dear Emmy

   Thank you for coming to my party. It was nice to see you.

   Love
   Belinda

Math

Read the number sentence. Write the missing number.

3. _____ + 100 = 532

4. 352 − _____ = 342

5. _____ + 10 = 765

6. 847 − _____ = 837

Reading

Read the text. Then answer the question.

Tomorrow was Grandma's birthday. Joey and Grandpa were shopping for a card. "How about this one?" asked Joey. "Or this one? It has pink roses, her favorite. No, wait. This one's better. It has pink and yellow roses. Come here, Grandpa! Here's another one!"

7. What does the story tell you about Joey?

_____

_____

Name _____

Day 1 | Week 11

Language

Write **a** or **an** to complete the sentence.

1. Do you have _____ banana in your lunchbox?

2. I usually eat _____ apple at lunchtime.

3. But this time I have _____ orange.

4. Would you like _____ piece of my orange?

Math

Read the problem. Then answer the item.

> 225 kids played at the park on Monday. 10 fewer kids played at the park on Tuesday. How many kids played at the park on Tuesday?

5. _____ kids played on Tuesday.

Mark the value in **225** that changes when you find **10** fewer.

6. ○ 5   ○ 20   ○ 200

Reading

Look at the chart. Read the text. Then answer the item.

Type of Beak	Spear beak	Scoop beak	Cracker beak
What it looks like			

Birds have different types of beaks that help them eat. A spear beak can stab fish. A scoop beak can scoop fish out of water. A cracker beak can crack seeds open.

7. The author wrote this text to _____.   ○ tell a story   ○ tell us facts

Name _____

Day 2 | **Week 11**

Language

Write **a** or **an** to complete the sentence.

1. Tomorrow my class will have _____ bake sale.

2. Aunt Cathy will bake _____ lemon cake.

3. Grandma will bake _____ angel food cake.

4. I will buy _____ oatmeal cookie from Miss Sanders.

Math

Read the problem. Then answer the item.

> Blake has 132 rocks in his collection. Kalia gave him 10 rocks from her collection. How many rocks does Blake have now?

5. _____ rocks

Mark the value in **132** that changes when you add **10** more.

6. ○ 2   ○ 30   ○ 100

Reading

Read the text. Then answer the items.

> Some things are not easy to recycle or reuse, but that doesn't mean you should throw them away. Think of how to use them in a different way. When we recycle, we make less garbage and that is good for Earth.

7. The author wrote this text to _____.
   ○ make us laugh   ○ get us to do something

8. Tell how you know. _____

_____

Name _____

Day 3 | **Week 11**

Language

Write **I** or **me** to complete the sentence.

1. _____ like to write stories about my life.

2. Grandma gave _____ a blue notebook.

3. _____ write in it almost every day.

4. Grandma always tells _____ to keep on writing!

Math

Read the problem. Then answer the item.

On Saturday, 468 planes flew out of the airport. On Sunday, 100 more planes flew out of the airport. How many planes flew out on Sunday?

5. _____ planes flew out on Sunday.

Mark the value in **468** that changes when you find **100** more.

6. ○ 8   ○ 60   ○ 400

Reading

Read the text. Then answer the items.

One day Mama Bear said, "It's time to have a party! Baby Bear, tell our friends that we are having a party today. Sister Bear, make the honey cakes and pick the berries. Oh, and Baby Bear…Baby Bear? Did he already leave?" Mama Bear went outside and saw all their friends. Baby Bear spread his arms and said, "I told them!"

7. The author wrote this story to _____.   ○ make us smile   ○ tell us facts

8. Tell how you know. _____

Name _____

Day 4 | **Week 11**

Language

Write **Gil and I** on the line in the naming part of the sentence.
Write **Gil and me** on the line in the telling part of the sentence.

1. _____ went to the park on Saturday.

2. Some kids asked _____ to play catch with them.

3. _____ played with them for a long time.

Math

Read the problem. Then answer the item.

Last month, my dad drove his truck 236 miles. This month, my dad drove his truck 100 miles. How many miles did he drive in both months?

4. _____ miles

Mark the value in **236** that changes when you find **100** more.

5. ○ 6   ○ 30   ○ 200

Reading

Read the text. Then answer the question.

The sun warms the land, air, and water. Sunlight warms the earth for people, animals, and plants to live. Sunlight makes plants grow. People and animals need plants for food. Without the sun, nothing could live on Earth.

6. What does the author want you to know?

_____

_____

Language

Write three sentences about your friend and you. Use **my friend and I** or **my friend and me**.

1. _____

2. _____

3. _____

Math

Read the problem. Then answer the item.

> Muds 'n' Suds washed 151 dogs last month. They want to wash 10 fewer dogs this month. How many dogs do they want to wash this month?

4. _____ dogs

Mark the value in **151** that changes when you find **10** fewer.

5. ○ 1   ○ 50   ○ 100

Reading

Read the text. Then answer the question.

> Chocolate-granola apple slices make a yummy snack. To make this snack, melt chocolate chips in the microwave. Dip slices of apple in the melted chocolate. Then dip the slices in the granola. Enjoy!

6. What does the author want you to know?

_____

_____

Name _____

Day 1 | **Week 12**

Language

Write the prefix **un-** to make a new word.

1. The family _____packed their bags in the hotel.

2. Dad _____folded his pants and hung them up.

3. Zack was _____able to lift a huge bag.

4. So Dad lifted the bag onto the bed and _____zipped the top.

Math

Read the problem. Then answer the item.

8 children arrived at Hector's party. 5 minutes later, 3 more arrived. How many children were at the party altogether?

5. ○ 8 + 3 = 11
   ○ 11 − 3 = 8
   ○ 8 − 3 = 5

Reading

Read the text. Then answer the question.

After loading his truck, Mr. Walker begins his work. He parks his truck and puts his bag over his shoulder. He walks up one side of the street, stopping at every house. Then he walks down the other side of the street. Many people say hello to Mr. Walker, and some even wait for him by the curb to give him their mail.

6. What is Mr. Walker's job? Tell why you think so.

_____

_____

_____

Name _____

Day 2 **Week 12**

Language

Write the prefix **re-** to make a new word. Then write the meaning of the prefix.

1. We _____ cycle paper.
2. We _____ fill the soap.
3. We _____ use brown bags.
4. We _____ sell things we don't need.
5. The prefix **re** means

   _____.

Math

Read the problem. Complete the model. Write a number sentence to solve the problem.

6. Soovin has 5 rabbits and 7 chickens. How many pets does Soovin have in all?

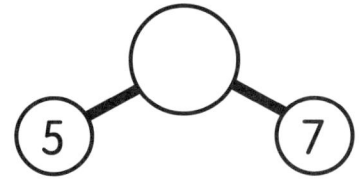

_____ + _____ = _____ pets

Reading

Read the text. Then answer the question.

Every Tuesday night I take my dog Kiwi to the dog park. Last Tuesday when I got to the park, there were at least fifty dogs running around. I let Kiwi off her leash to play. I saw a tall woman holding ten dog leashes. She called to her dogs and they came running. One by one, she clipped each dog's collar onto its leash. I watched her count the dogs and leashes two times. She kept looking around. She seemed worried.

7. What do you think the lady is worried about? Tell why you think so.

_____

_____

Name _____

Day 3 | **Week 12**

Language

Write the prefix **pre-** to make a new word. Then write the meaning of the prefix.

1. The cook _____ heats the oven.
2. I took a _____ test today.
3. My mom _____ plans my lunches.
4. Dad _____ paid the dog sitter.
5. The prefix **pre** means

   _____.

Math

Read the problem. Complete the model. Write a number sentence to solve the problem.

6. Meli has 4 red balls and 7 blue balls. How many balls does Meli have in all?

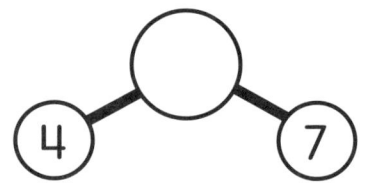

_____ balls

Reading

Read the text. Then answer the question.

David woke up early and rushed to the window. What a beautiful sight! Everything was covered in a blanket of white. He had been waiting for this day for months. David jumped up and down and shook his brother to wake him up. They rushed to put on warm jackets, mittens, hats, and boots. Then they ran outside to play.

7. What do you think David saw outside? Tell why you think so.

_____

_____

Name _____

Day 4 | **Week 12**

Language

Read the sentence and the bold word. Add a prefix to the word. Write the new word to complete the sentence.

> un-   re-   pre-

1. Dad has to _____ his shoes.   **tie**

Write the meaning of the new word.

2. The new word means _____.

Math

Read the problem. Then answer the item.

> Bret played a total of 4 hours today. If he played for 3 hours before dinner, how many hours did he play after dinner?

3. You will find out how many hours Bret played ____.
   ○ before dinner
   ○ in all
   ○ after dinner

Reading

Read the text. Then answer the question.

The people who live in a small town got together to create mosaic art. Mosaic art is pictures made with chips of colored glass. Each family made a mosaic to show what they liked about the neighborhood. Then all the tiles were put on a wall in the park.

4. Why do you think the people put the mosaic tiles in the park?

_____

_____

Name _____

Day 5 | **Week 12**

Language

Read the sentence and the bold word. Add a prefix to the word. Write the new word to complete the sentence.

(un-   re-   pre-)

1. Liam can't wait to _____ his gifts.
   wrap

Write the meaning of the new word.

2. The new word means _____.

Math

Draw a picture or a model for the problem. Then write a number sentence.

Nicki picked 8 peaches today. Mom used 5 to make a pie. How many peaches are left?

3. _____

Reading

Read the text. Then answer the questions.

There is a plum tree in Michael's backyard. It is April, and the tree has a lot of hard, unripe plums. Michael checks on the plums every day. The weather has been perfect. There have been many sunny days and a few rainy days. Michael wonders how much longer he will have to wait.

4. Do you think the weather has helped the plums grow? Tell why you think so.

_____

_____

5. Why does Michael keep coming back to the plum tree?

_____

_____

Name _____

Day 1 | **Week 13**

Language

Write the word. Then add the ending given. The first one is done for you.

1. happy **(er)**   happier
2. cry **(ed)**   _____
3. cherry **(es)**   _____
4. funny **(est)**   _____

Math

Read the problem. Mark the pair of number sentences that can help you solve it. Then write the answer.

Dori ate 12 red grapes and 7 green grapes. Grace ate 14 purple grapes. How many more grapes did Dori eat than Grace?

5. ○ 12 + 7 = ? and 19 − 14 = ?
    ○ 12 − 7 = ? and 14 − 7 = ?

6. _____ more grapes

Reading

Read the text. Then answer the question.

    It was a warm spring day, and Jaimee was outside drawing a yellow rose. Suddenly, dark clouds appeared and it began to rain. "Oh no!" said Jaimee. "My drawing is getting wet!"

7. What will Jaimee probably do next?
    ○ She will keep drawing and enjoy the rain.
    ○ She will run inside and start a new drawing.

Name _____

Day 2 | **Week 13**

Language

Read the sentence. Then write the correct word to complete the sentence.

1. I like _____ short stories about animals.
   writing   writeing   writting

2. My _____ story is about a funny rabbit.
   latist   latest   lattest

3. This story is much _____ than my other story.
   funnyer   funier   funnier

Math

Read the problem. Then answer the item. Show your work.

Roy has 64 crayons. Jerry has 6 fewer than Roy. How many crayons do they have altogether?

4.

Work Space

_____ crayons

Reading

Read the text. Then answer the question.

One summer day, Lori and Tim decided to sell cold lemonade. They set up a table in front of their house and put up a sign. Mom made a big pitcher of lemonade. In no time at all, the pitcher was empty. Thirsty customers were still coming. Lori and Tim had to act fast!

5. What will Lori and Tim probably do next?

   ○ They will take down the sign and go inside.

   ○ They will ask Mom to make another pitcher of lemonade.

Day 3 | **Week 13**

Language

Read the sentence. Underline the misspelled words. Then write the sentence correctly.

1. I thougt vanilla was your favorite flavor of ice crem.

_____

2. You allways get vanilla, but today you got a difrent flavor.

_____

Math

Read the problem. Then answer the item. Show your work.

52 dads went to back-to-school night. 12 more moms went than dads. How many parents went in all?

3.

Work Space

_____ parents

Reading

Read the text. Then answer the question.

The children have lots of fun during recess. They run, climb, and swing. After 20 minutes, the bell rings. The children quickly form a line.

4. What do you think the children will do next?

_____

_____

Name _____

Day 4 | **Week 13**

Language

Read the sentence. Underline the misspelled words. Then write the sentence correctly.

1. I like to play owtside with my best freind.

   _____

2. Woud you like to play with us, to?

   _____

Math

Read the problem. Then answer the item. Show your work.

13 children were playing. 8 more children joined them. Then 3 children left. How many children are still playing?

3.

Work Space

_____ children

Reading

Read the text. Then answer the questions.

   Kendra was sitting at the table eating breakfast. Toby, her dog, had just finished eating his food. Now he sat at the back door. Then he raised his paw and touched the door. "What's wrong, boy?" asked Kendra. "Do you need to go out?"

4. What do you predict will happen next? Why do you think so?

   _____

   _____

74   Daily Fundamentals • EMC 3242 • © Evan-Moor Corp.

Language

Read the sentence. Underline the misspelled words. Then write the sentence correctly.

1. I will stay home tomorow becus I am sick.

   _____

2. This is the furst time that Mom will miss wurk.

   _____

Math

Read the problem. Then answer the item. Show your work.

Joy had 58 stickers. She lost 15 stickers. Then her best friend gave her 24 more. How many stickers does Joy have now?

3.

Work Space

_____ stickers

Reading

Read the text. Then answer the questions.

It had been a beautiful day. Clara had opened her window to let the warm air in. In the evening, the air got cold. Clara felt very chilly near the open window.

4. What do you predict will happen next? Why do you think so?

   _____

   _____

Name _____

Day 1 | **Week 14**

Language

Circle **common** or **proper** to tell about the underlined word or words.

1. The students live in <u>Salinas, California</u>. **common**   **proper**
2. They are learning the history of their <u>town</u>. **common**   **proper**
3. There was an event at <u>Steinbeck Library</u>. **common**   **proper**
4. They saw old pictures of <u>people</u> of the town. **common**   **proper**

Math

Mark the length.

5.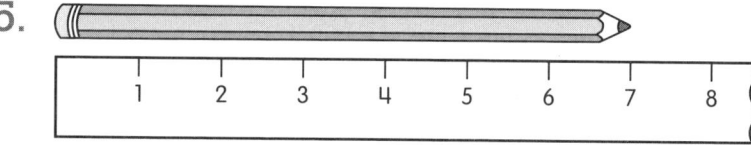
   - ○ 6 inches
   - ○ 7 inches
   - ○ 8 inches

6.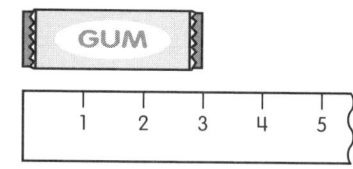
   - ○ 4 inches
   - ○ 3 inches
   - ○ 5 inches

Reading

Look at the map. Then answer the question.

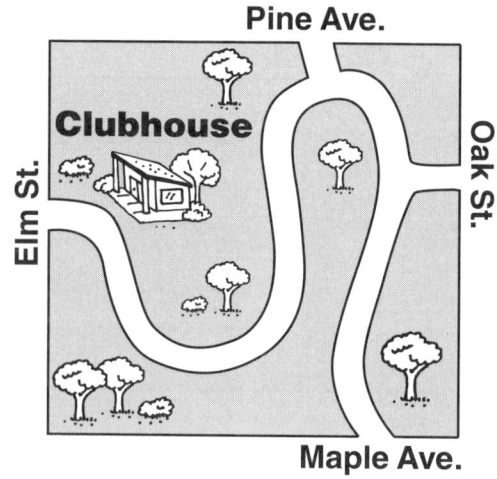

7. Which street is the closest to the clubhouse?
   - ○ Elm St.
   - ○ Maple Ave.
   - ○ Oak St.

Language

Underline the common nouns. Circle the proper nouns.

1. Tuesday is Valentine's Day.
2. I have a special card for Allison.
3. She and William are my best friends.
4. I also wrote a poem for Miss Lyons.

Math

Mark the length.

5.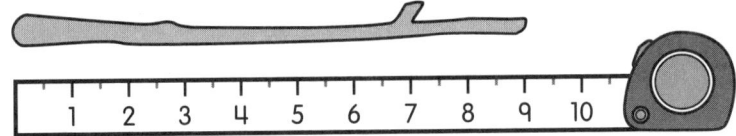
   - ○ 3 yards
   - ○ 2 yards
   - ○ 1 yard

6.
   - ○ 7 inches
   - ○ 8 inches
   - ○ 9 inches

Reading

Look at the poster. Then answer the question.

7. What is this poster about?
   - ○ a dog for sale
   - ○ a missing dog
   - ○ a new dog food

Language

Read the sentence. Rewrite it. Use a capital letter for each proper noun.

1. I walk to school with susie every morning.
_____

2. We go to crestview elementary school.
_____

Math

Read the problem. Then answer the items.

Gloria and Polly each measured the same feather. Here are their answers:

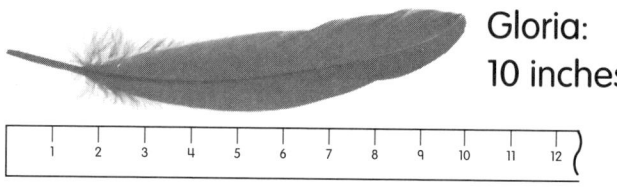 Gloria: 10 inches

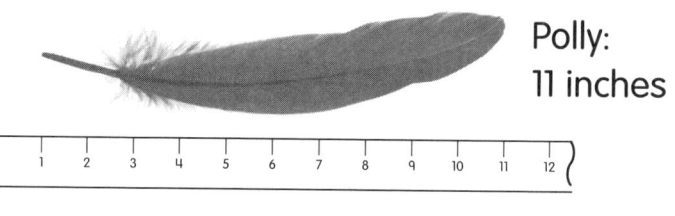 Polly: 11 inches

3. Which girl measured correctly?   ○ Gloria   ○ Polly

4. Explain why. _____

Reading

Look at the picture. Then answer the item.

5. This information is part of a _____.
   ○ menu
   ○ grocery list
   ○ recipe

Day 4 | **Week 14**

Name _____

Language

Read the sentence. Rewrite it. Use a capital letter for each proper noun.

1. Monday, wednesday, and friday I have swimming class.

   _____

2. My swimming teacher's name is mr. longman.

   _____

Math

Use your inch ruler to measure the scissors.

3. _____ inches

Reading

Look at the graph. Then answer the question.

Number of Books George Read

February
March
April
May

4. What does the graph show?

   _____
   _____
   _____
   _____

Name _____

Day 5 | **Week 14**

Language

Write two sentences about your school. Use proper nouns.

1. _____
   _____

2. _____
   _____

Math

Answer the items.

3. What can you measure with an inch ruler?
   _____

4. What can you measure with a yardstick?
   _____

Reading

Look at the graph. Then answer the question.

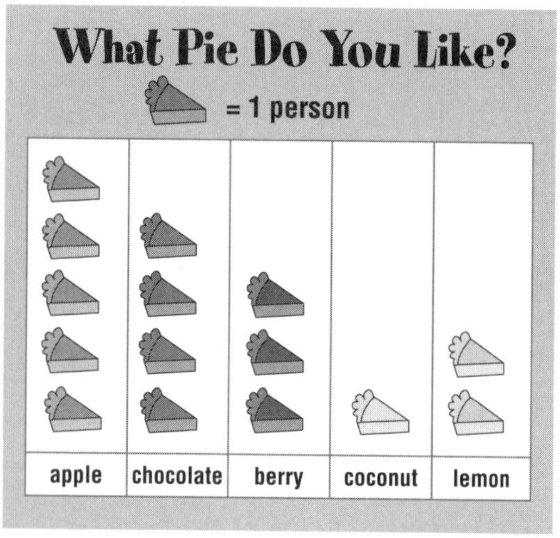

What Pie Do You Like?
🥧 = 1 person

apple	chocolate	berry	coconut	lemon
5	5	4	1	2

5. What does the graph show?
   _____
   _____
   _____
   _____

80   Daily Fundamentals • EMC 3242 • © Evan-Moor Corp.

Name _____

Day 1 | Week 15

Language

Circle the adjective that tells about the underlined noun.

1. Sunday is our last <u>day</u> at the lake.
2. It was a short <u>vacation</u>.
3. I want to stay another <u>week</u>.
4. Two <u>kids</u> from school are here.
5. Our tiny <u>cabin</u> is near the lake.
6. I hope we can visit next <u>month</u>.

Math

Mark the height.

7.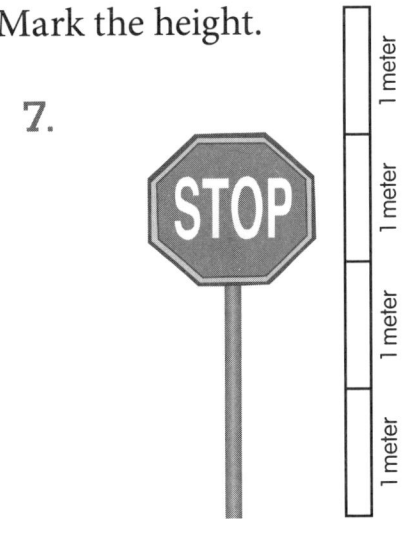

○ 1 meter
○ 3 meters
○ 4 meters

Reading

Read the text. Then answer the questions.

Mr. Wiggle liked to giggle. He giggled at flying pigs. He giggled at bugs dancing jigs. He giggled when it was sunny. He thought everything was funny. He giggled from morning till night. And when Mr. Wiggle giggled, he was quite a sight! His body shook up and down. His face looked like a clown. If only you could see Mr. Wiggle giggle!

8. What is special about the words in the story?
   ○ They rhyme.   ○ They are short.   ○ They are long.

9. Why do you think the author chose these words?

_____

_____

Language

Underline the adjective that is comparing two people, places, or things.

1. Annie is younger than me.
2. I am taller than Annie.
3. Her house is bigger than a castle.
4. The grass looks greener on that side.
5. This summer is hotter than last summer.
6. Maybe this winter will be colder than last winter.

Math

Mark the length.

7.

○ 3 centimeters
○ 7 centimeters
○ 9 centimeters

Reading

Read the text. Then answer the questions.

Suri wore a red silk robe as she brushed her long black hair. The golden handle of her brush sparkled in the sunlight. She blinked her large green eyes and held out her smooth, dark hand so the purple butterfly that flew in her window would have a place to land.

8. Did the words in the story help you imagine the girl?
   ○ yes   ○ no

9. What words told you about how the girl looked?

_____

_____

Language

Underline the adjective that compares.

1. I think robins are prettier than crows.//
2. Robins are bigger than hummingbirds.
3. Crows are louder than hummingbirds.
4. Hummingbirds are quicker than crows.

Math

Use your centimeter ruler to measure the paper clip.

5. _____ centimeters

Reading

Read the text. Then answer the questions.

    The green, slimy sludge came closer and closer. It almost looked like it was walking as it crept along the ground. Its terrible smell made me want to run. All of a sudden, I heard a loud rumbling sound and the ground started to shake. It was then that I decided to turn around and skip home.

6. How did you feel as you read the story?

_____

7. Did the ending of the story seem strange? Why or why not?

_____

_____

Name _____

Day 4 | **Week 15**

Language

Write the correct adjective to complete the sentence.

1. Ladybugs are the

   _____ insects.
   prettier, prettiest

2. I think they are

   _____ than bees.
   prettier, prettiest

3. However, bees are the

   _____ insects.
   busier, busiest

Math

Answer the items.

4. Which of these is the best tool to measure a bottle of glue?
   ○ centimeter ruler
   ○ meter stick

5. Which of these is the best tool to measure a driveway?
   ○ centimeter ruler
   ○ meter stick

Reading

Read the text. Then answer the questions.

   One beautiful morning, Mr. Takahashi whistled a happy tune as he went outside to feed his chickens. He tossed the feed onto the dirt and counted the chickens to make sure they were all there. Suddenly, his smile changed to a frown. He hurriedly walked inside the coop and looked around. He ran out of the coop shouting loudly, "Bessie! Bessie!"

6. How did Mr. Takahashi's feelings change in the story?

   _____

   _____

7. What words from the story helped you know how Mr. Takahashi was feeling?

   _____

Name _____

Day 5 | **Week 15**

Language

Use the word **smallest** in a sentence.

1. _____
   _____
   _____

Use the word **biggest** in a sentence.

2. _____
   _____
   _____

Math

Answer the items.

3. Centimeters are often used to measure _____ things.
   ○ big   ○ small

4. Meters are often used to measure _____ things.
   ○ big   ○ small

Reading

Look at the picture. Then use two words from the word box to write sentences about the picture.

happy   sad   crying   scared   worried

5. _____
   _____
   _____
   _____
   _____
   _____

© Evan-Moor Corp. • EMC 3242 • Daily Fundamentals

Name _____

Day 1 | **Week 16**

Language

Read the sentence. Then write the correct reflexive pronoun to complete the sentence.

1. The baby feeds _____ with a spoon.   **herself**   **myself**

2. I made a sandwich all by _____.   **myself**   **himself**

3. We helped _____ to some milk.   **ourselves**   **themselves**

Math

Answer the item.

4. The bead is 1 centimeter long. About how long is the pencil?

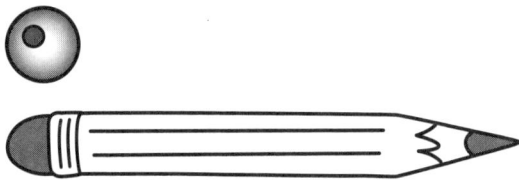

○ 7 cm   ○ 4 cm   ○ 3 cm

Reading

Read the text. Think about how it is written. Then answer the question.

Mr. Evans wakes up at 6:00 a.m every morning. First, he makes a cup of coffee. Second, he eats some toast and eggs. Next, he gets dressed and brushes his teeth. Finally, he gets into his car and drives to work.

5. How is the text written?
   ○ The text tells the order of events.
   ○ The text has a problem and a solution.

86 — Daily Fundamentals • EMC 3242 • © Evan-Moor Corp.

Name _____

Day 3 **Week 16**

Language

Look at the underlined word or words. Write the correct possessive pronoun to complete the sentence.

1. That red bike is <u>Billy's</u>. That red bike is _____.

2. The blue bikes are <u>the twins'</u>. The blue bikes are _____.

3. The yellow bike is <u>Mom's</u>. The yellow bike is _____.

Math

Answer the item.

4. The ruler is 1 foot long. About how long is the log?

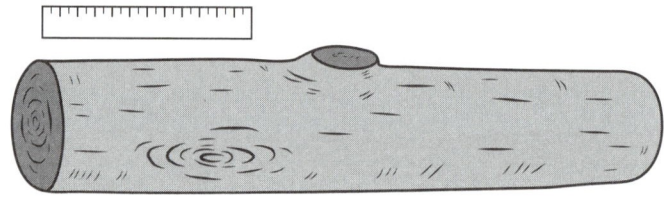

○ 3 yards   ○ 3 feet   ○ 2 feet

Reading

Read the text. Think about how it is written. Then answer the question.

   Simone had a problem. She kept losing her jackets! She left them on the bus, on the playground, and at her friends' houses! Her parents were not happy about this. Finally, Simone thought of a solution. She decided to tie her jacket around her waist when she took it off. So far, it's worked!

5. How is the text written?

   ○ The text tells the order of events.

   ○ The text has a problem and a solution.

88 — Daily Fundamentals • EMC 3242 • © Evan-Moor Corp.

Math

Answer the item.

4. The stick is 8 centimeters long. About how long is the bug?

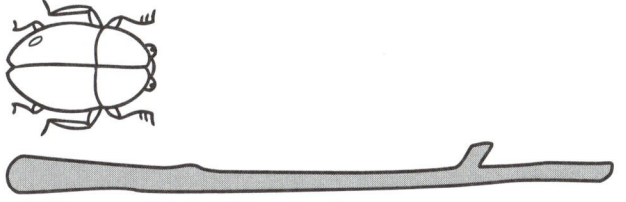

○ 1 centimeter   ○ 4 centimeters   ○ 2 centimeters

Reading

Look at the picture. Read the text. Then answer the questions.

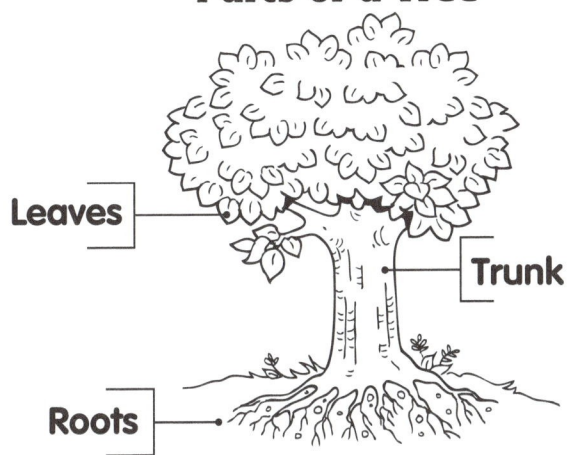

Parts of a Tree

5. Does the title help you know more about what the picture is showing?

   ○ yes   ○ no

6. What do the bold words and lines tell you?

   _____

   _____

Name _____

Day 5 | **Week 16**

Language

Write two sentences using a pronoun from the word box.

> theirs   his   yours   hers   ours   mine

1. _____

2. _____

Math

Answer the item.

3. The broom is 1 meter long. About how long is the ladder?

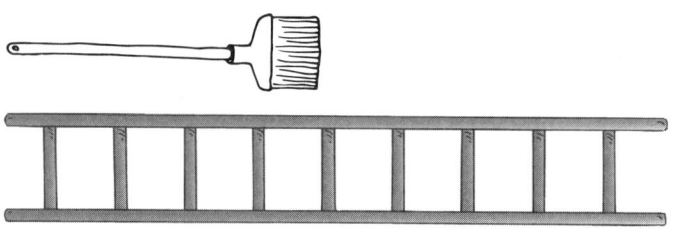

○ 2 meters   ○ 3 meters   ○ 1 meter

Reading

Look at the chart. Read the text. Then answer the question.

☀ Summer Months	Winter Months ❄
July	January
August	February

4. Why are the titles above the names of the months important?

_____

Name _____

Day 1 | **Week 17**

Language

Find and circle the collective noun in the sentence. Then write it on the line.

1. My team won the game on Saturday. _____

2. The crowd went wild when we scored. _____

3. Mom gave me a bunch of balloons. _____

4. Someone brought a stack of brownies. _____

Math

Compare the pair of objects. Then complete the number sentence.

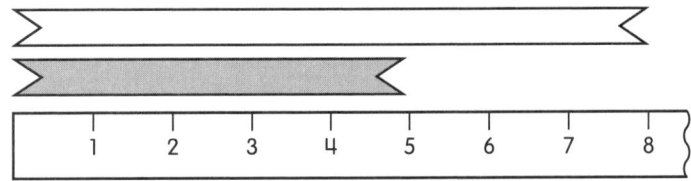

5. How much longer is the white ribbon?

   _____ ◯ _____ = _____ inches

Reading

Read the text. Then answer the question.

Ellen and Elisa are best friends. They play games, ride their bikes, and go to the park together. Elisa's dog can run very fast. Ellen and Elisa ride the bus to school together. They spend the night at each other's houses.

6. Which sentence does <u>not</u> belong in the story? Cross it out.

Name _____

Day 2 | **Week 17**

Language

Write a collective noun from the word box to complete the sentence.

> herd   colony   flock   pride   litter

1. We have a _____ of chickens in our yard.

2. My cat had a _____ of kittens.

3. A _____ of cows grazes in the field.

Math

Compare the pair of objects. Then complete the number sentence.

4. How much farther did the white rabbit jump?

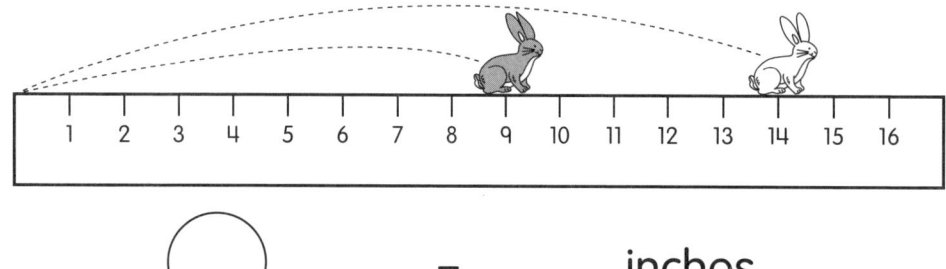

_____ ◯ _____ = _____ inches

Reading

Read the text. Then answer the question.

Some bears sleep all winter long. They cannot find a lot of food in the winter, so they sleep. Some bears use caves for winter homes. Deer eat leaves and twigs. Once spring arrives, bears awake very hungry.

5. Which sentence does <u>not</u> belong in the story? Cross it out.

Day 3 — **Week 17**

Language

Complete the definition. The first one is done for you.

1. A **colony** is a group of ants .
2. A **herd** is _____.
3. A **crowd** is _____.
4. A **class** is _____.

Math

Compare the pair of objects. Then complete the number sentence.

5. How much shorter is the sharpened pencil?

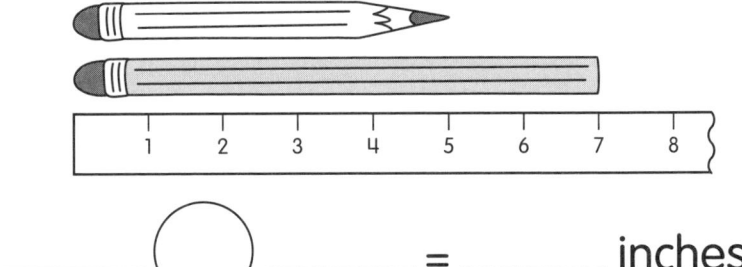

_____ ◯ _____ = _____ inches

Reading

Read the text. Then answer the question.

I just got a new T-shirt. It's soft and bright blue. It has a colorful peacock on the front. On the back, it has a little peacock.

6. What is the main idea?
   ○ It's soft and bright blue.
   ○ I just got a new T-shirt.

Name _____

Day 4 | **Week 17**

Language

Use the word **flock** to complete the sentence.

1. We looked up and saw

   _____

   _____ .

Math

Compare the pair of objects. Then write a number sentence.

2. How much shorter is Kai's skateboard?

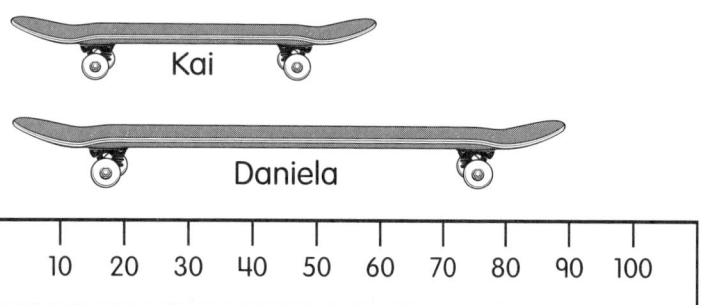

_____ centimeters

Reading

Read the thank-you note. Then answer the item.

Dear Aunt Susie,

   I am really enjoying your birthday gift! I've always wanted a purple raincoat. I'm happy that it has a hood. The raincoat is soft and fuzzy inside. It will keep me warm and dry.

Love,
Carla

3. Write the main idea.

_____

Name _____

Day 5 | **Week 17**

Language

Look at the picture. Then write a sentence about it using a collective noun.

1. _____
   _____
   _____

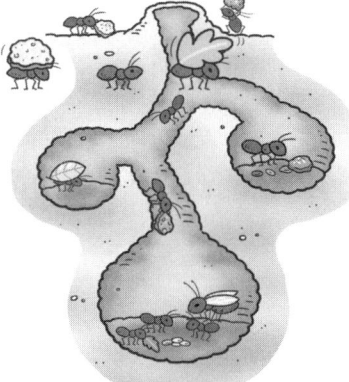

Math

Use your centimeter ruler to measure the flowers. Then answer the item.

2. How much longer is the rose than the tulip?

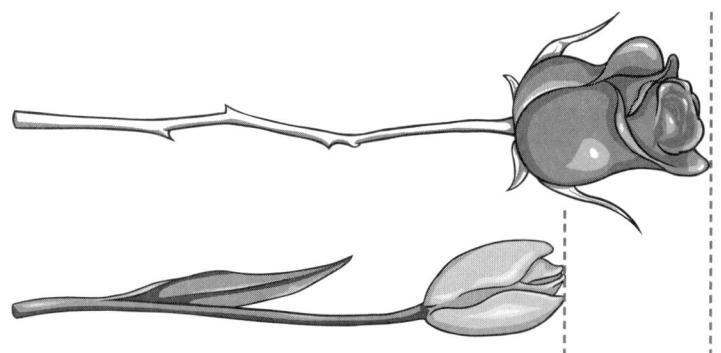

_____ centimeters

Reading

Read the text. Then answer the item.

My dog Bear can do all kinds of tricks. He can play dead. He can walk on his hind legs. He can jump through a hoop. Bear is such a great dog!

3. Write one detail that tells about the main idea.

_____
_____

© Evan-Moor Corp. • EMC 3242 • Daily Fundamentals

Name _____

Day 1 | **Week 18**

Language

Read the sentence. Then answer the question about the bold word.

1. I will **slowly** pour milk into each glass. How will I pour the milk?

   _____

2. The word **slowly** tells "how." Is **slowly** an adjective or an adverb?

   _____

Math

Read the problem. Then answer the item. Show your work.

Bo's shoe is 21 centimeters long. Rae's shoe is 30 centimeters long. How much longer is Rae's shoe?

3.
_____ centimeters

Reading

Read the text. Then answer the question.

There are all kinds of insects. They have 3 body parts. They have 6 legs. But they look very different. Insects are interesting. I can watch them for hours.

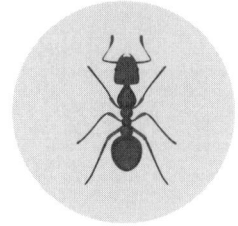  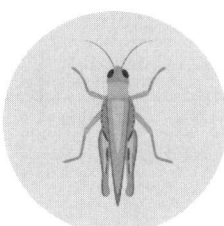

4. Which one is a fact?
   ○ They have 3 body parts.
   ○ Insects are interesting.
   ○ I can watch them for hours.

Name _____

Day 2 | **Week 18**

Language

Read the sentence. Then answer the question about the bold word.

1. The **slow** tortoise won the race. What noun does **slow** describe?

   _____

2. The word **slow** describes a noun. Is **slow** an adjective or an adverb?

   _____

Math

Read the problem. Then answer the item. Show your work.

Anh sweeps a 13-meter hall and a 28-meter hall each day. How many meters does Anh sweep in all?

3.
   _____ meters

Reading

Read the text. Then answer the question.

Spring, summer, fall, and winter are seasons. A season is a time of year. Each season lasts three months. My favorite season is summer. I can play all day!

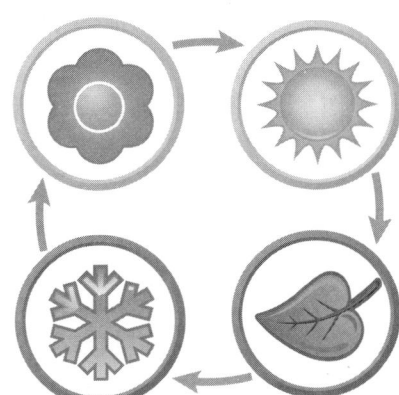

4. Which one is an opinion?
   ○ A season is a time of year.
   ○ Each season lasts three months.
   ○ My favorite season is summer.

Name _____

Day 3 — Week 18

Language

Write an adjective or an adverb to complete the sentence.

Adjectives	Adverbs
glad	gladly
sweet	sweetly

1. I will _____ accept a glass of lemonade.

2. This lemonade has a lot of sugar and tastes very _____.

Math

Read the problem. Then answer the item. Show your work.

Lin's kite flies 210 feet in the air. She adds another 164 feet of string to the kite. How high will her kite fly now?

3.

_____ feet

Reading

Read the text. Then answer the item.

Some animal babies look a lot like their mothers. They have the same body parts. They are the same shape. They are the same color. All animal babies are cute, but puppies are the cutest of all.

Write two facts from the text.

4. _____

5. _____

Day 4 — Week 18

Language

Write an adjective or an adverb to complete the sentence. Then answer the question.

1. We walked outside _____ during the fire drill.

   _____

   quick   quickly

2. Did you choose an adjective or an adverb?

   _____

Math

Read the problem. Then answer the item. Show your work.

A snail crawled 41 inches in the morning and 32 inches in the afternoon. How many inches did it crawl in all?

3.

_____ inches

Reading

Read the text. Then answer the item.

A sunny day is a wonderful day. Nothing feels better than warm sunshine on my face. The sun also warms the land, air, and water. Sunlight helps plants to grow. We need the sun to live. Without the sun, nothing could live on Earth. Hooray for sunshine!

Write two opinions from the text.

4. _____

5. _____

Day 5 | **Week 18**

Language

Write two sentences using the words **happy** and **happily**.

1. _____

Math

Read the problem. Then answer the item. Show your work.

The red bat is 34 inches long.
The blue bat is 36 inches long.
How much longer is the blue bat?

2. _____ inches

Reading

Read the text. Then answer the item.

Have you seen this symbol? It tells us to recycle. We can recycle many things, like glass, plastic, and paper. Some things are not easy to recycle. We can reuse them in another way. Whenever we recycle or reuse things, we make less garbage.

Write your opinion about recycling.

3. _____

Language

Read the group of words. Write **sentence** or **fragment** to tell what it is.

1. My birthday is tomorrow. _____
2. I will have a fun party. _____
3. My friends and family. _____

Math

Read the problem. Use the number line to solve it. Show your work on the number line.

Kim's book is 29 centimeters long. Ben's book is 21 centimeters long. How many centimeters shorter is Ben's book?

4.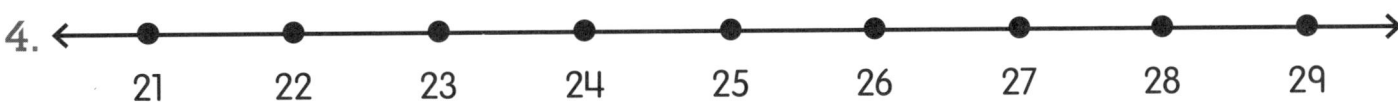

5. Ben's book is _____ centimeters shorter than Kim's book.

Reading

Read the text. Then answer the question.

Dad and I took a walk in the forest. I saw an old hollow tree, and there was a family of squirrels inside! Dad says a hollow tree is the perfect habitat for all kinds of animals.

6. What does **hollow** mean?
   ○ empty
   ○ heavy

Name _____

Day 2 | Week 19

Language

Read the group of words. Write **sentence** or **fragment** to tell what it is.

1. Opened the cage and flew away.   _____

2. I can't find my parrot Petey.   _____

3. Petey is small and white.   _____

Math

Read the problem. Use the number line to solve it. Show your work on the number line.

Beth used blocks to build a 31-inch tower. Rory came along and added 6 more inches. How tall is the tower now?

4.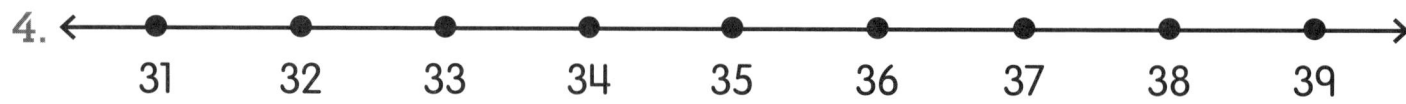

5. The tower is _____ inches tall.

Reading

Read the text. Then answer the question.

Today we went shoe shopping. I was excited to find shoes just like Janie's, but in a different color. I grabbed the box and said, "Okay, let's go!" But Mom insisted that I first try on the shoes to make sure they fit.

6. What does **try on** mean?
   ○ to look at
   ○ to test

Name _____

Day 3 | **Week 19**

Language

Join the two fragments to make a complete sentence. Remember to begin the sentence with a capital letter and end it with a period.

1. **Fragments:** My friend Greta. Goes to my school.

   Sentence: _____

2. **Fragments:** The yellow birdhouse. Is made of wood.

   Sentence: _____

Math

Read the problem. Use the number line to solve it. Show your work on the number line.

We need 15 feet of string lights to go across the window. We already hung 7 feet of lights. How many more feet of lights do we need?

3. ←—•——•——•——•——•——•——•——•——•——→
       7   ___ ___ ___ ___ ___ ___ ___ ___

4. We need _____ more feet of lights.

Reading

Read the text. Then answer the questions.

    We had been waiting a long time. We were so hungry. Finally, Elsa arrived with the mashed potatoes and set them on the table with the rest of the food. We all sat down to enjoy our feast.

5. What does **feast** mean?   ○ party   ○ big meal

6. What context clue helped you?
   ○ rest of the food
   ○ waiting a long time

Name _____

Day 4 | **Week 19**

Language

Underline the subject. Circle the predicate.

1. Three children were absent at school.

2. Many people at school have colds.

3. My friend Scott feels sick.

4. Miss Evans called Scott's mom.

Math

Read the problem. Use the number line to solve it. Show your work on the number line.

Mr. Rivas is making a fence. Yesterday he installed 5 meters, and today he installed 7 meters. How much fence has he installed so far?

5. ←—•——•——•——•——•——•——•——•—→
   ___ ___ ___ ___ ___ ___ ___ ___

6. He has installed _____ meters of fence.

Reading

Read the text. Then answer the questions.

Suli was the best speller in our class. We were proud when he became a finalist in the spelling bee. We felt happy for him. When they said his name, we all cheered with delight.

7. What does **cheered** mean?

   ○ screamed angrily   ○ yelled happily

8. What context clue helped you?

   ○ with delight   ○ best speller

104   Daily Fundamentals • EMC 3242 • © Evan-Moor Corp.

Language

Complete each sentence by adding a subject or a predicate.

1. A monkey _____.

2. _____ jumped over a rock.

3. _____ swims fast.

4. An elephant _____.

Math

Read the problem. Use the number line to solve it. Show your work on the number line.

A hummingbird flew 20 yards to a red flower. Then it flew 5 yards to a pink flower and 3 yards to a blue flower. How far did the hummingbird fly?

5. ←●——●——●——●——●——●——●——●——●→
   ___ ___ ___ ___ ___ ___ ___ ___ ___

6. The hummingbird flew _____ yards.

Reading

Read the text. Then answer the questions.

My sister Rae was just waking up in the next bed. She was talking, but since she was half asleep I couldn't understand her. "Rae, you're mumbling!" I said. "Speak up. I can hardly hear you."

7. What does **mumbling** mean?
   ○ talking softly   ○ talking loudly

8. What context clue helped you?
   ○ half asleep   ○ hardly hear you

Language

Answer the item.

1. Mark the sentence that has correct capitalization.
   ○ The city of Austin is in the state of Texas.
   ○ The City of austin is in the State of texas.
   ○ The City of Austin is in the State of Texas.

Math

Match the clocks that show the same time.

2.

3.

4.

9:35   2:30   4:10

Reading

Read the text. Then answer the question.

Santiago had finally found the book he was looking for. He walked up to the counter and greeted Ms. Seeley. He pulled out his card and handed it to her. "We'll see you back in three weeks!" said Ms. Seeley.

5. Which one will probably happen next?
   ○ Santiago will pay for the book.
   ○ Santiago will borrow the book.

Language

Rewrite the sentence. Use a capital letter where needed.

1. Our house in chicago was close to lake michigan.

   _____

2. Aunt mary lives in washington near the city of seattle.

   _____

Math

Write the time.

3.

   _____

4.

   _____

5.

   _____

Reading

Read the text. Then answer the question.

My name is Jerome. I have a dog named Hoover. If you drop any food—poof!—he eats it. I don't mind because it is my job to wipe the table and sweep the floor after dinner. I hardly have any work to do with Hoover around! I just wipe the food onto the floor. But Dad doesn't like it when Hoover eats food off the floor, so he started putting him outside.

6. How will Hoover being outside change Jerome's job?

   _____

   _____

Name _____

Day 3 | **Week 20**

Language

Read the sentence. Rewrite the sentence using capital letters where needed.

1. We rafted along the colorado river.

   _____

2. We drove six hours to the state of arizona.

   _____

Math

Mark the matching time.

3. 7 o'clock in the evening   ○ 7 a.m.   ○ 7 p.m.

4. 2 o'clock in the afternoon   ○ 2 a.m.   ○ 2 p.m.

5. 8 o'clock in the morning   ○ 8 a.m.   ○ 8 p.m.

6. 10 o'clock at night   ○ 10 a.m.   ○ 10 p.m.

Reading

Read the text. Then answer the question.

    This summer, Jada has a piano class that meets at 8:00 a.m. It's very early, but she really wants to learn to play. Jada has been late to class twice, and she doesn't want to be late again. Jada and her mom went to the store and bought an alarm clock.

7. What do you predict will happen next? Tell why you think so.

   _____

   _____

Name _____

Day 4 | **Week 20**

Language

Read the sentence. Rewrite the sentence using capital letters where needed.

1. Death valley national park is very hot.

   _____

2. The park is in the states of california and nevada.

   _____

Math

Write **a.m.** or **p.m.** to tell when each action likely happened.

3. Dad picked me up after school. _____

4. My brother and I got dressed for school. _____

5. We sat around the campfire after dinner. _____

6. After lunch, we went for a walk in the forest. _____

Reading

Read the text. Then answer the question.

    Beavers need a place to live. Beavers use sticks, grass, and mud to build their homes. First, beavers use their sharp front teeth to cut wood. Then they push the wood through the water to the lodge where they stack the wood. Next, they use their claws to scoop up mud and grass. Finally, they pack mud and grass on top of the lodge to hold the sticks together.

7. What do you predict the beavers will do next? Tell why you think so.

   _____

   _____

Language

Read the sentence. Rewrite the sentence using capital letters where needed.

1. We are going to disney world in florida.

   _____

2. We live near myrtle beach, south carolina.

   _____

Math

Write the time that you do each activity. Write the time with **a.m.** or **p.m.**

3.

   _____

4.

   _____

Reading

Read the text. Then answer the question.

   The day is cool and breezy, which is perfect for Emma. She tells her mom that she doesn't need any help and pulls a small table to the sidewalk. She carefully places 10 plates filled with cookies on the table. Soon there is a crowd of people at her table. She has only two plates of cookies left.

5. What do you predict Emma will do next?

   _____

Day 1 | **Week 21**

Language

Read the sentence. Write a synonym for the underlined word.

> pretty   smart   little   scared

1. I have a small cat.

   _____

2. She is so beautiful.

   _____

3. She is afraid of dogs.

   _____

Math

Write the amount shown. Use ¢ or $.

4.

   _____

Reading

Read the text. Then answer the question.

Peanut Butter Apple Slices

Ingredients:
apples
peanut butter
raisins

1. Cut the apples into slices.
2. Spread peanut butter on the slices.
3. Top with raisins.

5. Why did the author include a numbered list?
   - ○ to give facts about apples
   - ○ to tell the steps to follow
   - ○ to list the ingredients

Language

Read the sentence. Write a synonym for the underlined word.

| big   bought   many   built |

1. I have a large dollhouse.

   _____

2. It has several rooms.

   _____

3. My grandpa made it.

   _____

Math

Read the problem. Then answer the item. Show your work.

4. Sally found one quarter, two dimes, and five nickels. How much money did she find?
   - ○ 70¢
   - ○ 75¢
   - ○ 65¢

Reading

Read the text. Then answer the item.

It's snowing! It's snowing!
Let's go out to play.
Put on mittens. Grab your scarf.
We'll have fun today!

5. The author wrote this text to _____.
   - ○ make us smile
   - ○ give us facts

Day 3 — **Week 21**

Name _____

Language

Read the sentence. Write an antonym for the underlined word.

> asleep   sold   got   day

1. We bought a puppy last week.
   _____

2. He cries during the night.
   _____

3. When he is awake, he plays.
   _____

Math

Read the problem. Then answer the item. Show your work.

Ava wants to buy some glitter pens that cost $12. She has saved $8 so far. How much more money does Ava need?

4. Ava needs $_____ more.

Reading

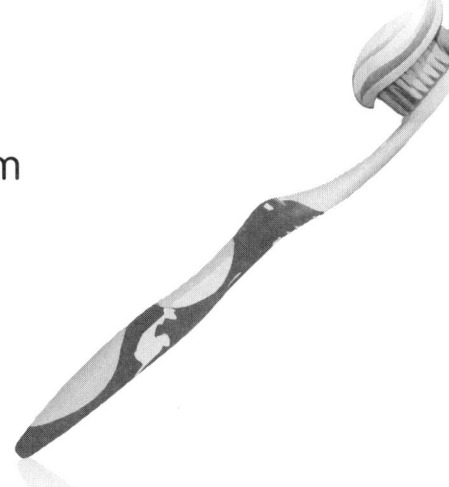

Read the text. Then answer the item.

> You should brush your teeth after breakfast and before bed. Brushing your teeth keeps them clean. Brushing makes your teeth white. This gives you a nice smile. Be good to your teeth.

5. The author wrote this text to _____.
   ○ make us smile
   ○ get us to do something

Name _____

Day 4 | Week 21

Language

Draw a line to match the word to its antonym.

1. sweet • short
2. early • white
3. tall • sour
4. many • late
5. black • few
6. thick • go
7. come • thin

Math

Read the problem. Then answer the item. Show your work.

A marker costs 75¢. Sadie has 2 quarters and 2 dimes. Does she have enough for a marker?

8. ○ yes   ○ no

Reading

Read the text. Then answer the question.

There are several tools to help you know what the weather is like.

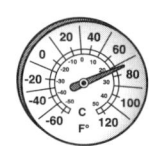 A thermometer tells the temperature.

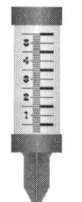 A rain gauge tells how much rain has fallen.

 A windsock shows from which direction the wind blows.

9. Why did the author write this text?

_____

_____

_____

_____

Name _____

Day 5 | **Week 21**

Language

Read the pair of words. Write **S** if they are synonyms. Write **A** if they are antonyms.

1. begin, end _____
2. begin, start _____
3. speak, talk _____
4. full, empty _____
5. wide, narrow _____
6. cheerful, happy _____
7. light, dark _____

Math

Read the problem. Then answer the item.

8. Millie bought a balloon. How much did it cost?

The balloon cost _____.

Reading

Read the text. Then answer the question.

   I was so excited to go to Mason's party. I had two helium balloons to give him. When I opened the door to the car, the balloons slipped out of my hand. Oh no! Through his window, Mason saw what had happened. He ran out and stood next to me. Together, we watched the bright balloons soar toward the sky.

9. Why did the author write this story?

_____

_____

Name _____

Day 1 | **Week 22**

Language

Read the two bold words. Then write the contraction in the sentence. Use an apostrophe.

1. **I am** _____ excited about school today.

2. **We are** _____ making small clay figures.

3. **she will** Miss Lopez says _____ choose the best one.

4. **I have** _____ made lots of clay figures before.

Math

Use the line plot to answer the item.

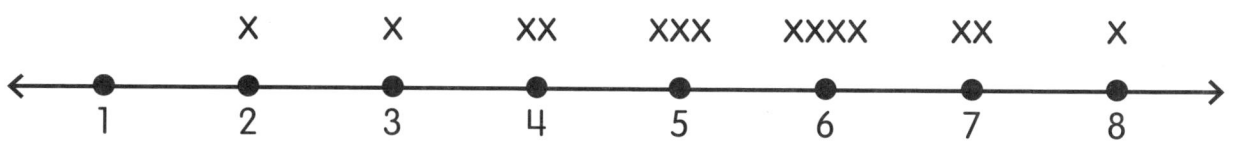

Student Book Orders

number of books ordered

5. Each **x** stands for a _____.   ○ student   ○ book

Reading

Read the text. Then answer the question.

I love riding on the train. It is big and comfy. In one area, the seats face out toward the ocean. As we get closer to Grandma's house, lemon trees line our route. I can almost reach out and pick the bright fruit.

6. Which words tell about the setting on the train?
   ○ **comfortable** and **interesting**
   ○ **crowded** and **dark**

Name _____

Day 2 | **Week 22**

Language

Read the two bold words. Then write the contraction in the sentence. Use an apostrophe.

1. **you are**   Cora, _____ my best friend.

2. **We will**   _____ always be best friends.

3. **You have**   _____ helped me many times.

4. **do not**   Please _____ ever move away.

Math

Use the line plot to answer the item.

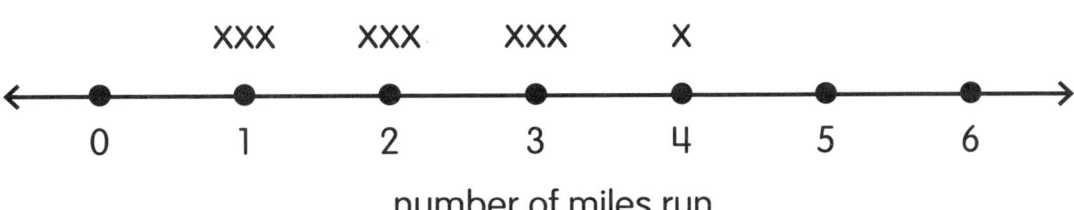

5. Each number stands for how many _____.   ○ runners   ○ miles

Reading

Read the text. Then answer the item.

> Let's review what we know about irregular verbs. Some of the most common verbs are irregular. They do not follow the regular rule of adding **-ed**. For example, we say "I went outside" instead of "I goed outside."

6. The students are in _____.
   ○ a math class
   ○ a language class

Name _____

Day 3 | **Week 22**

Language

Read the sentence. Then write the possessive form of the singular noun.

1. My _____ turtle is so cute.
   brothers   brother's

2. The _____ name is Herman.
   turtles   turtle's

3. It was my _____ gift to him.
   mom's   moms

Math

Use the line plot to answer the item.

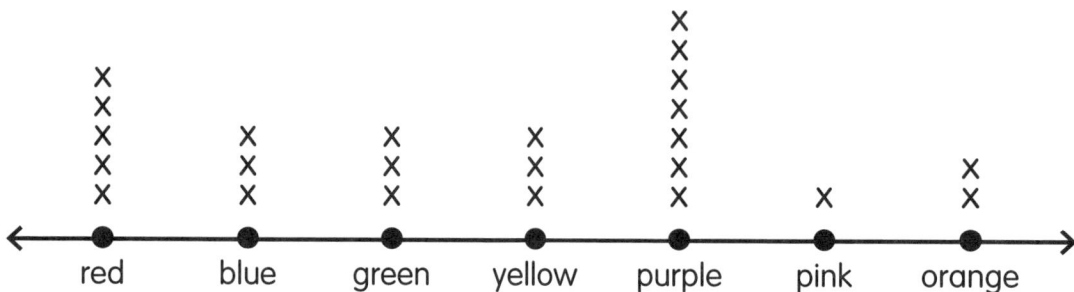

4. How many students answered "blue"? _____

Reading

Read the text. Then answer the question.

   The raft slipped into the water. Right away, the river pulled the group around a bend. The raft lifted and turned. "Oh! Oh! Oh man!" yelled Jared, grabbing on to a raft handle. His grip was so tight that his knuckles turned white.

5. What is the setting of the story? Explain your answer.

_____

_____

Language

Read the sentence pair. Then write the possessive to show who or what owns something. Use an apostrophe.

1. The red lunchbox belongs to Sam. It is _____ lunchbox.

2. The zipper on the backpack broke. The _____ zipper broke.

3. Give this sweater to Jeff. This is _____ sweater.

Math

Use the line plot to answer the item.

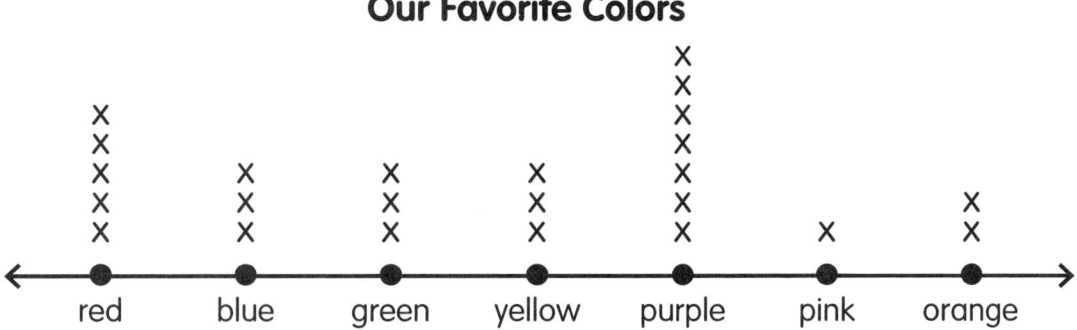

Our Favorite Colors

4. How many students voted for a color? _____

Reading

Read the text. Then answer the item.

    Our canoe drifted along in the sparkling water. Dark green trees lined the shore. In the distance, a black bear was catching a fish with its paws. An eagle soared overhead. We quietly listened to the chatter of frogs and birds.

5. Think about the text. Write adjectives that tell about the setting.

_____

Name _____

Day 5 | **Week 22**

Language

Read the sentence. Then write the possessive form of the plural noun.

1. My two _____ birthdays fall on the same day.
   friend's   friends'

2. The _____ names are Jordan and Austin.
   twins'   twin's

3. All the _____ gifts are on that table.
   guest's   guests'

Math

Use the line plot to answer the item.

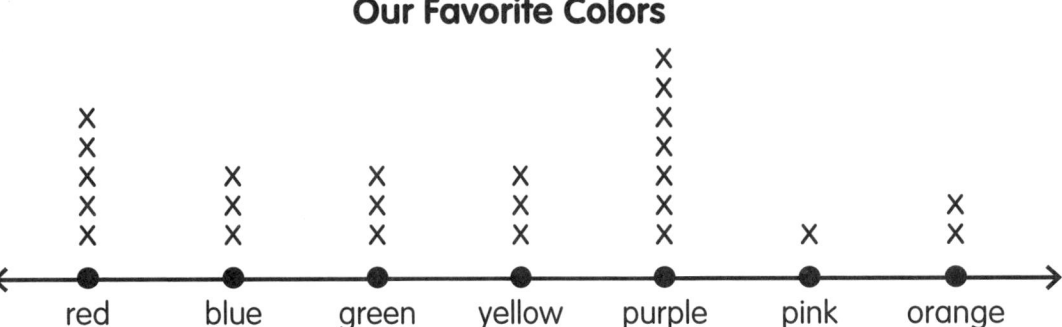

4. Which color received the most votes? _____

Reading

Read the text. Then answer the question.

   We live on a farm and don't get to town much. Last month, the the cobbler came around in his wagon. I was getting new shoes! The cobbler measured my feet with a broom straw. He broke off the straw to the length of my feet. I can't wait until he comes back with my new shoes.

5. Does the story take place in the present or in the past? How do you know?

_____

Language

Read the sentence. Then write the correct word to complete the sentence.

1. I am very _____ at math.
   good   well

2. I did _____ on my math test.
   good   well

3. I had a _____ day at school today.
   good   well

Math

Use the data chart to complete the line plot.

Rope Lengths	
2 yards	II
3 yards	I
4 yards	II
5 yards	III

4. **Rope Lengths**

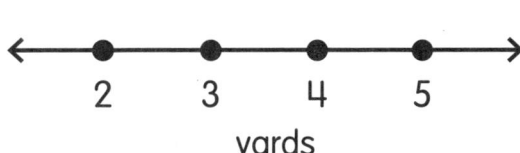

Reading

Read the text. Then answer the item.

    The sun grew hotter and hotter. I took off my cap and wiped my brow. My throat was so dry, and I had no more water. I had to get out of the sun. Finally, I found a big shady tree.

5. The person telling the story wants to _____.
   - ○ enjoy the sun
   - ○ take a nap
   - ○ cool off

Name _____

Day 2 | **Week 23**

Language

Read the sentence. Then write the correct word to complete the sentence.

1. It is _____ to be home.
    good   well

2. I don't feel _____ today.
    good   well

3. The chicken soup tastes _____.
    good   well

Math

Use the data chart to complete the line plot.

Licorice Bits	
1 cm	II
2 cm	I
3 cm	IIII
4 cm	II

4. **Licorice Bits**

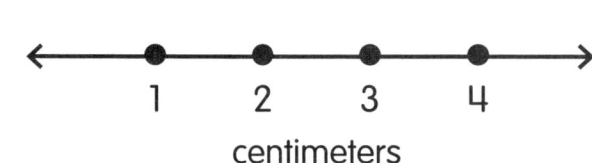

centimeters

Reading

Read the text. Then answer the question.

"Gina! No! Why did you do that?" Neil yelled. He had carefully built a castle using blocks of all shapes and sizes. It even had a bridge. Neil was proud of his work. Then along came his little sister Gina. With one swift kick she had destroyed everything.

5. Do you think Neil is upset? Explain your answer.

_____

_____

Language

Read the sentence. Then write the correct word to complete the sentence.

1. My little brother behaves _____ sometimes.
   bad   badly

2. Mom had a _____ time at the store with him.
   bad   badly

3. There was another boy with _____ manners there, too.
   bad   badly

Math

Use the data chart to complete the line plot.

Paper Strips	
1 inch	II
2 inches	IIII
3 inches	III
4 inches	I

4. **Paper Strips**

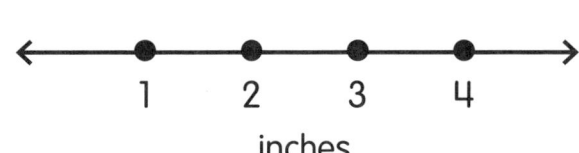

inches

Reading

Read the text. Then answer the question.

   It is our first nice car ride of the season. We drive around town with the windows down. Ears are flapping in the wind, the tongue is hanging out, and the nose is sniffing new smells. For Rusty, a car ride is pure joy.

5. Who is Rusty? Tell how you know.

_____

_____

Name _____

Day 4 **Week 23**

Language

Read the sentence. Then write the correct word to complete the sentence.

1. I have a very _____ cold today.
                     bad   badly

2. My voice sounds _____ when I speak.
                     bad   badly

3. Mom wants me to sing, but I know I will sing _____.
                                                   bad   badly

Math

Use the data chart to complete the line plot.

4. **Student Heights**

Student Heights	
57 inches	II
58 inches	III
59 inches	IIII
60 inches	IIII

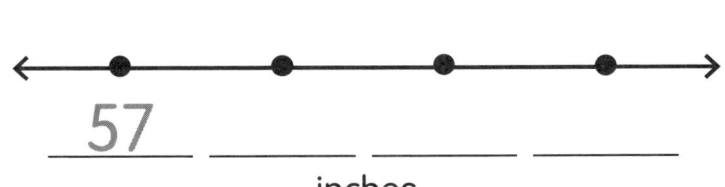

57 _____ _____ _____
inches

Reading

Read the text. Then answer the question.

    What a busy place the shelter was! The kennel had dogs of all types. Each one was yelping, trying to get Jim's attention. A shy, scruffy mutt in the final cage looked up at Jim. It was sitting in the corner, shaking, and Jim knew at once. "Oh, Mom," said Jim. "He's the one!"

5. How does Jim feel about the scruffy dog?
   - ○ He likes the dog.
   - ○ He is afraid of the dog.
   - ○ He thinks the dog is funny.

Language

Read the sentence. Then write the correct word to complete the sentence.

1. The children had a _____ time painting.
   good   well

2. Marta and Marla paint very _____.
   good   well

3. However, the carpet was _____ stained.
   bad   badly

Math

Use the data chart to complete the line plot.

4. **Surfboards**

Surfboards	
7 feet	|||||
8 feet	|||
9 feet	||
10 feet	||||

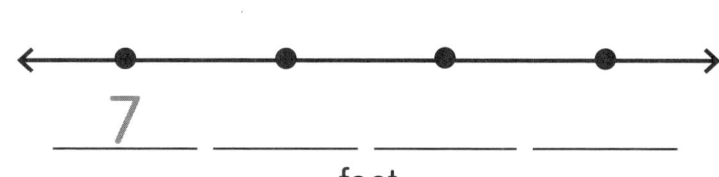

_7_ _____ _____ _____
feet

Reading

Read the text. Then answer the questions.

This is my first time on a skateboard. Maybe I should have practiced at home. Everyone at this park flies by on their boards. How will I keep my balance? What if I fall? Will everyone laugh at me? Okay, here I go!

5. How does the person in the story feel? How do you know?

_____

_____

Name _____

Day 1 | **Week 24**

Language

Write the compound word that is formed by the two smaller words.

1. foot + print _____
2. sun + burn   _____
3. pop + corn   _____
4. mail + box   _____
5. honey + bee _____
6. rain + coat _____

Math

Use the data chart to complete the picture graph.

7.

Reading

Read the text. Then answer the items.

    Goats and sheep are alike and different in many ways. People raise both kinds of animals for food and clothing. Both goats and sheep have two "toes" on each foot. Most goats have a beard, but most sheep do not. A goat's tail sticks up, but a sheep's tail hangs down.

8. How are goats and sheep alike?

   _____

   _____

9. Write a sentence from the text that tells how goats and sheep are different.

   _____

   _____

126   Daily Fundamentals • EMC 3242 • © Evan-Moor Corp.

Language

Complete the sentence. Use two words from the box to make a compound word.

> sun   burn   screen   glasses

1. Wear _____ to protect your eyes.

2. Apply _____ to protect your skin.

3. You don't want to get a _____.

Math

Use the data chart to complete the picture graph.

On the Desk		
pens	pencils	markers
IIII II	III	IIII

4.

On the Desk		
pens	pencils	markers

Reading

Read the text. Then answer the question.

Who makes the rules for people in the United States? A group called Congress does. The rules are called laws. The laws are to protect people. They also make sure that each person is treated fairly. Everyone must follow the laws. Classrooms have rules, too. The teacher makes the rules. Sometimes the teacher meets with the students to help make the rules. The rules protect you and the people in your class. The rules say that each person must always be treated fairly. Everyone must follow the rules.

5. How are the rules in your classroom and the laws of the United States the same?

_____

_____

Language

Complete the sentence. Use two words from the box to make a compound word.

> snow   man   storm   shoes

1. You can walk in the snow with _____.

2. After a big _____, the school was closed.

3. The children ran outside to build a _____.

Math

Use the data chart to complete the bar graph.

Our Birthdays		
June	July	August
III	ЖI	IIII

4.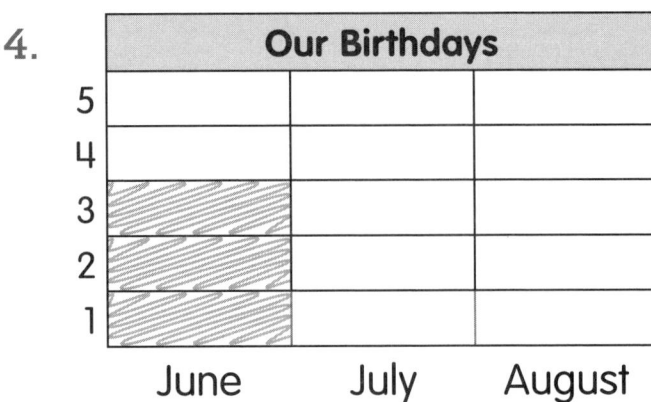

Reading

Read the text. Then answer the question.

　　A proverb is a wise saying. My teacher said that proverbs are useful to us. The proverb today was **practice makes perfect.** At soccer practice, I missed a goal. My coach said, "Keep trying, Lisa. Never give up!" Her words really reminded me of the proverb. I think **practice makes perfect** and **keep trying, never give up** mean almost the same thing.

5. Do you agree with Lisa? Explain why or why not.

_____

_____

Day 4 | **Week 24**

Language

Complete the sentence. Use two words from the box to make a compound word.

> light   sun   stop   bulb

1. We need to change the _____ in the lamp.

2. The warm _____ streams through the window.

3. The car slowed down as it came to the _____.

Math

Use the data chart to complete the bar graph.

Stamps		
Asia	Africa	Europe
IIII	II	IIII I

4.

Stamps		
Asia	Africa	Europe

(y-axis: 1, 2, 3, 4, 5)

Reading

Number the sentences to show the order in a compare-and-contrast paragraph.

5. _____ But chicken feathers are softer than duck feathers.

   _____ Ducks and chickens both lay eggs.

   _____ Ducks and chickens are alike, but they are also different.

   _____ Both kinds of birds have wings and feathers.

6. Now write the sentences to form a paragraph.

_____

_____

_____

_____

Name _____

Day 5 | **Week 24**

Language

Write the two small words that make up the compound word **bathtub**. Then explain the meaning of the word **bathtub**.

1. bathtub = _____ + _____

2. _____
   _____
   _____
   _____

Math

Use the data chart to complete the bar graph.

Get to School		
walk	bus	car
III	ℍ	IIII

3.

Get to School		

5, 4, 3, 2, 1

walk　　bus　　car

Reading

Number the sentences to show the order in a compare-and-contrast paragraph.

4. _____ Boots are warmer and heavier than sandals.

   _____ This means that you wear them on your feet.

   _____ Sandals and boots are types of footwear.

   _____ But sandals and boots are very different.

5. Now write the sentences to form a paragraph.

   _____
   _____
   _____
   _____

Language

Read the sentence. Read the clue below the line.
Then write a word with the suffix -**er**, -**ful**, or -**less**.

1. The rainbow is very _____.
   full of color

2. Mom bought a bag of _____ grapes.
   without seeds

3. The _____ made a beautiful cake.
   one who bakes

Math

Circle the triangle. Then draw the same triangle in the work space.

4.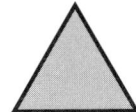

Work Space

Reading

Read the text. Then answer the question.

   Luke watched as Grandma mixed the butter and sugar. Then she added eggs and milk, and last, flour. She poured the batter into round pans and placed them in the oven. "What kind of frosting will you make this time, Grandma?" asked Luke.

5. What do you think Grandma is making? Tell why you think so.

_____

_____

Name _____

Day 2 | **Week 25**

Language

Read the words in the box. Write the words below the correct root word.

> harmful   careful   useless   harmless   useful   careless

use　　　　　　　　**harm**　　　　　　　　**care**

1. _____　3. _____　5. _____

2. _____　4. _____　6. _____

Math

Circle the triangle. Then draw the same triangle in the work space.

Work Space

7.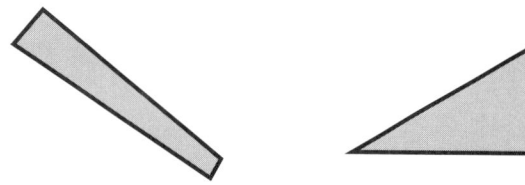

Reading

Read the text. Then answer the questions.

> Mrs. Levitt drove slowly around the neighborhood. "Maxie! Maxie! Come here, girl!" called Brandon, looking up and down the street. Brandon felt awful that he had left the gate open, and now Maxie was gone.

8. Who or what do you think Maxie is? What do you think happened?

_____

_____

Name _____

Day 3 | **Week 25**

Language

Read the meaning. Add **-ful**, **-less**, or **-er** to the root word.

1. without fear — **fear**_____
2. one who sings — **sing**_____
3. one who reads — **read**_____
4. full of joy — **joy**_____
5. one who teaches — **teach**_____
6. full of cheer — **cheer**_____
7. one who paints — **paint**_____
8. without a clue — **clue**_____

Math

Look at the shape. Mark **yes** or **no**. Explain your thinking.

9.

Shape	Is it a triangle?	Explain why or why not.
	○ yes ○ no	

Reading

Read the text. Then answer the question.

Today was Freddy's birthday. Aunt Frida arrived with a brightly wrapped box, about the shape of a video game. Freddy quickly unwrapped the gift, and stopped smiling. The box did not contain a video game at all. "Thank you, Aunt Frida," said Freddy politely.

10. How do you think Freddy felt after he opened the gift? Tell why you think so.

_____

_____

| Name | Day 4 | Week 25 |

Language

Write the meaning of the homophone.

1. **sun**

   meaning: _____

2. **son**

   meaning: _____

Math

Look at the shape. Mark **yes** or **no**. Explain your thinking.

3.

Shape	Is it a triangle?	Explain why or why not.
	○ yes ○ no	_____ _____ _____

Reading

Read the text. Then answer the question.

Tammy was not a picky eater, but she hated the taste of onions. "No onions, please," said Mom each time she ordered for Tammy. One day when her hamburger arrived, Tammy took a huge bite without looking. "Yuck!" cried Tammy, lifting the hamburger bun.

4. What do you think Tammy saw when she lifted the bun? Tell why you think so.

_____

134 Daily Fundamentals • EMC 3242 • © Evan-Moor Corp.

Name _____

Day 5 | **Week 25**

Language

Read the sentence. Then complete the sentence with the correct homophone.

1. I saw a _____ in the forest. **deer**   **dear**
2. The _____ is full of fish. **see**   **sea**
3. Don't fall in the _____! **whole**   **hole**
4. I need _____ to bake the cake. **flour**   **flower**

Math

Draw a closed shape with three straight sides.

5.

Reading

Read the text. Then answer the question.

> Yesterday, all 300 of us stood together on the playground during a fire drill. As we stood talking, the teachers counted to make sure everyone was there. After ten minutes, we lined up and walked back to our classrooms.

6. Where do you think the fire drill is happening? Tell why you think so.

_____

_____

© Evan-Moor Corp. • EMC 3242 • Daily Fundamentals

Name _____   Day 1   Week 26

Language

Read the sentence. Then write the correct verb to complete the sentence.

1. Anton _____ a sandwich from the menu.
   chose   choosed

2. He _____ half the sandwich to Jesse.
   gave   gived

3. He _____ the sandwich was too big for him.
   feeled   felt

Math

Circle the quadrilateral. Then draw the same quadrilateral in the work space.

4.

Work Space

Reading

Read the ad. Then answer the questions.

5. What does the ad show?

   _____

   _____

6. Do you think this store has good prices?

   _____

   _____

136   Daily Fundamentals • EMC 3242 • © Evan-Moor Corp.

Name _____

Day 2 | Week 26

Language

Read the sentence. Then write the correct verb to complete the sentence.

1. Nico _____ the ball to me.
   throwed   threw

2. The ball _____ the table by the sofa.
   hitted   hit

3. A vase _____ onto the floor.
   fell   falled

Math

Circle the quadrilateral. Then draw the same quadrilateral in the work space.

4.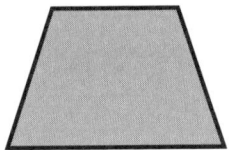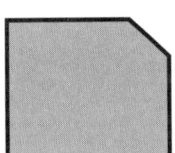

Work Space

Reading

Read the menu. Then answer the questions.

5. What time is breakfast served?
   Ⓐ 5 a.m. to 12 p.m.
   Ⓑ 5 a.m. to 11 a.m.
   Ⓒ 5 a.m. to 10 a.m.

6. What is being offered today only?
   _____

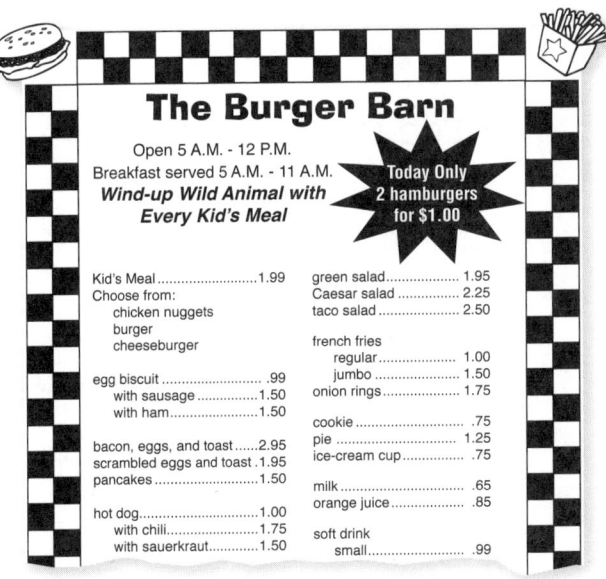

Name _____

Day 3 | **Week 26**

Language

Read the sentence. Then write the correct verb to complete the sentence.

1. We _____ our bikes around the block.
   rided   rode

2. Sela _____ with me on her blue bike.
   came   camed

3. Sela _____ her sweater that day.
   losed   lost

Math

Look at the shape. Mark **yes** or **no**. Explain your thinking.

4.
Shape	Is it a quadrilateral?	Explain why or why not.
△	○ yes ○ no	_____ _____ _____

Reading

Read the recipe. Then answer the question.

5. What do the numbers in this recipe tell you?

   Ⓐ the amount of each soup ingredient

   Ⓑ the steps to make the soup

   Ⓒ how long you should cook the soup

Tom Kha Gai

1. Mix and cook:
   chicken broth
   lime juice
   chopped ginger
   sugar
   coconut milk

2. Add diced, cooked chicken.

3. Spoon over rice.

4. Add cilantro and crushed red pepper.

Language

Read the irregular verb. Write the past tense to complete the sentence.

1. **wake**   I _____ up at 8:00 a.m. today.
2. **drink** I _____ a glass of milk for breakfast.
3. **eat**   I _____ two slices of toast with jam.
4. **run**   Then I _____ to catch the bus.

Math

Look at the shape. Mark **yes** or **no**. Explain your thinking.

5.

Shape	Is it a quadrilateral?	Explain why or why not.
▱	○ yes ○ no	_____

Reading

Read the invitation. Then answer the questions.

6. Where on this invitation would you write your address?
   - Ⓐ Place
   - Ⓑ Day
   - Ⓒ RSVP to

7. What kind of party is it?
   _____

Come to My Party

Place _____
Day _____
Time _____
RSVP to _____

Name _____

Day 5 | **Week 26**

Language

Read the irregular verb. Write the past tense to complete the sentence.

1. **find**   I _____ a box of colored pencils.
2. **make**   I _____ a drawing of a garden.
3. **write**   I _____ my name on the bottom.
4. **give**   Then I _____ the drawing to my teacher.

Math

Draw a closed shape with four straight sides.

5.

6. Write the name of the shape. _____

Reading

Look at the chart. Then answer the questions.

7. What do you think this chart is used for?

   _____

   _____

8. What words helped you know this?

   _____

   _____

Year	What Happened?
1621	_____
1788	_____
1828	_____

Name _____

Day 1 | **Week 27**

Language

Read the sentence. Then write the correct word to complete the sentence.

1. The cat licked _____ paws.

   _____
   its, it's

2. She licked her kittens, _____.

   _____
   to, too

3. The sleeping kittens are _____.

   _____
   quite, quiet

Math

Mark the answer that describes the shape. Then explain your thinking.

4.
   ○ pentagon
   ○ hexagon
   ○ other

   _____
   _____
   _____

Reading

Read the text. Then answer the items.

   A blue whale is one of the largest animals in the world. It is larger than even the largest dinosaurs that once roamed the earth. The tongue of a blue whale can weigh as much as an elephant. The body of a blue whale can measure up to 100 feet long. That's about as long as three school buses.

5. What is the main idea of the text?

   _____
   _____

6. Write one detail from the text that tells about the main idea.

   _____
   _____

Name _____

Day 2 | **Week 27**

Language

Read the sentence. Then write the correct word to complete the sentence.

1. _____ is my book?
   Where, Were

2. I see it over _____.
   their, there

3. That's not my book;

   it's _____ book.
   you're, your

Math

Mark the answer that describes the shape. Then explain your thinking.

4.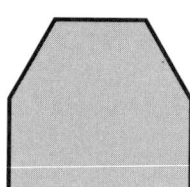
   - ○ pentagon
   - ○ hexagon
   - ○ other

   _____
   _____
   _____

Reading

Read the text. Then answer the items.

Children all over the world enjoy going barefoot, but it is actually important to wear shoes. Shoes help children to stay healthy. Many children play outdoors. They have nothing to keep their bare feet from getting hurt. In some places, children can get sick from not wearing shoes. They can pick up an illness from the soil they walk on.

5. What is the main idea of the text?

_____

6. Write one detail from the text that tells about the main idea.

_____
_____

Day 3 — Week 27

Language

Read the sentence. Then write the correct word to complete the sentence.

1. _____ making so much noise?
   Whose, Who's

2. The _____ of the school wants to know.
   principal, principle

3. She _____ all the students to be quiet.
   accepts, expects

Math

Mark the answer that describes the shape. Then explain your thinking.

4. ○ pentagon
   ○ hexagon
   ○ other

   _____
   _____
   _____

Reading

Read the text. Then answer the items.

Title: _____

Slime makes it easier for snails to move from place to place. Slime helps snails stick to leaves or walls. Slime keeps snails from getting hurt as they move. It lets snails move over rough stones and sharp glass. You may think slime is yucky, but for snails, slime is great!

5. Mark all the details that help you understand why snails need slime.
   ○ Slime makes it easier for snails to move from place to place.
   ○ You may think slime is yucky, but for snails, slime is great!
   ○ Slime keeps snails from getting hurt as they move.

6. Write a title for the text.

Name _____

Day 4 | **Week 27**

Language

Choose the word that correctly completes the sentence.

1. I want _____ get a new
   to, too, two
   backpack.

2. Then I will have _____
   backpacks.   **to, too, two**

3. I will get a new uniform,
   _____.
   to, too, two

Math

Draw a closed shape with five sides.

4.

5. Write the name of the shape.
   _____

Reading

Read the text. Underline the main idea. Circle two details that tell about the main idea.

6.   An octopus might look like a blob with eight arms. But this sea animal is a yummy treat for sharks. So an octopus must use many tricks to hide and stay safe.

   An octopus hides by making itself look like a pile of rocks or sand. An octopus can change its skin color to brown, black, gray, or orange. It can also make its skin look bumpy like a rock. Or it can make its skin look smooth like fine sand. It is hard for sharks to find a hiding octopus.

   An octopus uses ink to stay safe. If a shark comes too close, the octopus squirts ink. The ink makes the water dark, so the shark cannot see. Then the octopus swims away.

Language

Choose the word that correctly completes the sentence.

1. I put my coat _____ the chair. **by, bye, buy**

2. The other kids put _____ **there, they're, their** coats in the closet.

3. I didn't want to _____ a coat. **wear, we're, were**

Math

Draw a closed shape with six sides.

4.

5. Write the name of the shape.

_____

Reading

Read the text. Underline the main idea. Circle two details that tell about the main idea.

6.   Whiting is a small town by the lake. The Fourth of July is a fun day in Whiting. A parade marches down Main Street. People stand and wave little flags. Clowns toss candy and give out balloons. The high school band plays festive songs.

    People look forward to the kiddie portion of the parade. Children ride wagons, bikes, and scooters decorated with streamers and balloons. The smallest children ride in strollers pushed by their mothers. Everyone enjoys the sights and sounds of the parade.

Language

Write **S** if the sentence is a simple sentence.
Write **C** if the sentence is a compound sentence.

1. _____ Aunt Eva visited us today.

2. _____ We ate dinner and the baby slept.

3. _____ Aunt Eva is loud but the baby is quiet.

4. _____ The baby woke up and cried.

Math

Circle the objects shaped like a cube.

5.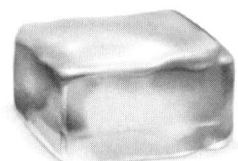

Reading

Read the text. Then answer the question.

    It was lunchtime, and Mom was hungry. She took her basket into the garden. She tore off a bunch of lettuce leaves. She chose a red tomato that smelled good. She snipped off a few pea pods. Then she went back inside to the kitchen.

6. What will Mom probably do next?
   - ○ She will put the veggies away.
   - ○ She will make a salad for lunch.

Language

Write **S** if the sentence is a simple sentence.
Write **C** if the sentence is a compound sentence.

1. _____ We picked three baskets of apples from our tree.

2. _____ Sharon washed the apples and Kate peeled them.

3. _____ Dad baked three apple pies for the bake sale.

4. _____ You can buy a whole pie or you can buy just a slice.

Math

Answer the item.

5. 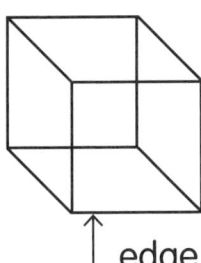 How many edges does a cube have?
   - ○ 8
   - ○ 10
   - ○ 12

↑ edge

Reading

Read the text. Then answer the question.

   Joel likes to save things that he finds in nature. On a shelf in his room, he has bumpy rocks and flat stones. He also has a long white feather. Next to that, there is a tiny nest that he found in the park. Joel made some room on the shelf. Today he is going to the beach!

6. What will Joel probably do at the beach? Tell why you think so.

_____

_____

Name _____

Day 3 | **Week 28**

Language

Combine the two simple sentences to make a compound sentence.

1. Mom came home. We sat down to eat dinner.

   _____

2. Teri made a big salad. Julia baked some bread.

   _____

Math

Answer the item.

3.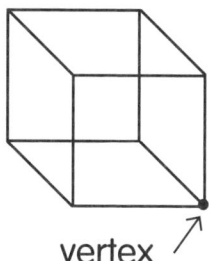
vertex

How many vertices does a cube have?
- ○ 6
- ○ 8
- ○ 10

Reading

Read the text. Then answer the question.

    Izzy hummed as she brushed her teeth. Suddenly, she stopped and gently touched her front tooth. Sure enough, the tooth wiggled. That morning at breakfast, Izzy ate only soft pancakes. She asked her mom to pack only soft foods in her lunch—no apples or chips!

4. How will Izzy probably feel if her mom packs hard foods in her lunch?

   _____

   _____

Name _____

Day 4 | **Week 28**

Language

Combine the two simple sentences to make a compound sentence.

1. I studied for the test. I got a low score.

   _____

2. I can take the test again. I can accept the low score.

   _____

Math

Answer the item.

3. 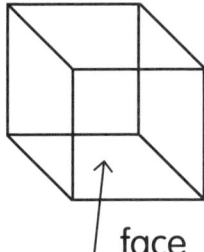 face

   How many faces does a cube have?
   - ○ 6
   - ○ 8
   - ○ 10

Reading

Read the text. Then answer the question.

The house next to Gabe's had been empty for a long time. There weren't any kids in his neighborhood. As he lay on his bed, feeling bored, he heard noises coming from outside. Gabe peeked out the window. A truck was parked in front of the house. Men were unloading furniture and boxes. Gabe wished he knew who was moving in.

4. If kids move into the house next door, what do you predict Gabe will do?

   _____

   _____

Name _____

Day 5 | **Week 28**

Language

Read the sentences. Then combine them to make a compound sentence.

1. Our dog can catch a ball. She can roll over.

   _____

2. Dogs can wait outside. They aren't allowed in the restaurant.

   _____

Math

Follow the steps to draw a cube.

3.
First	Then	Next	Workspace
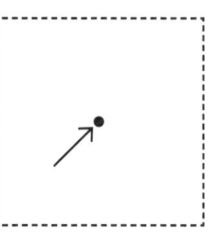	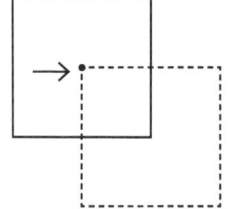	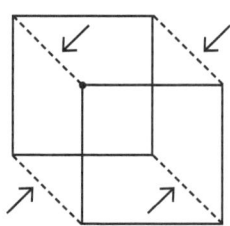	
Draw a square. Draw a dot in the center.	Start at the dot. Draw another square the same size.	Draw straight lines to connect the corners.	

Reading

Read the text. Then answer the questions.

Dad pulls out Sparky's leash and whistles. Sparky hurries over to Dad, wagging her tail. Dad hooks the leash to Sparky's collar, and Sparky runs toward the door. Dad carefully guides Sparky upstairs to give him a bath.

4. Did the story end like you thought it would?   ○ yes   ○ no

5. If you answered **no**, how did you think the story was going to end?

   _____

Language

Read the sentence. Underline the compound word.

1. Hilda's bedroom is pink and purple.
2. Her bookshelf is painted bright yellow.
3. Sunlight comes through the window.
4. Hilda likes all the colors of the rainbow.

Math

Complete the number sentence.

5. 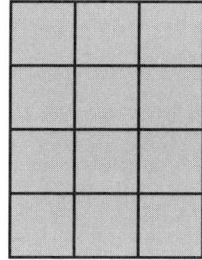 4 rows of 3 = _____ squares

Reading

Read the text. Then answer the question.

    We made a great-looking snowman, all because we worked together. My brother shaped balls of snow for the body. I found the perfect branches for the arms. Mom found a red hat and a scarf. My sister found a crooked carrot for the nose.

6. What was the effect of the family working together?
   - They made a great snowman.
   - The snowman took longer to make.

Name _____

Day 2 | **Week 29**

Language

Read the sentence. Underline the compound word.

1. The ocean is full of jellyfish.

2. The hammerhead shark also lives there.

3. I like to collect seashells on the beach.

4. Will you play in the saltwater with me?

Math

Complete the number sentence.

5. 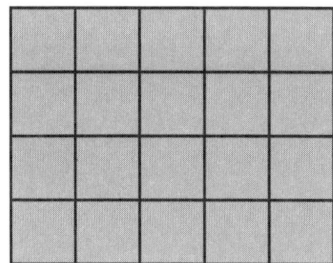 5 columns of 4 = _____ squares

Reading

Read the text. Then answer the question.

    My mom worked hard as a girl because she grew up on a farm. Her life was very different back then. In the morning, she had to milk the cows and feed the pigs before school. Now she just wakes up, eats breakfast, and goes to work. Mom says her life is easier now, but she misses the farm.

6. What caused Mom to feel that life is easier now?

_____

_____

Name _____

Day 3 | **Week 29**

Language

Match the words to make a compound word.

1. snow
2. gold
3. birth
4. air

- fish
- day
- port
- flake

Math

Complete the number sentence.

5.

2 rows of _____ = _____ squares

Reading

Read the text. Then answer the question.

    At the store, you have to pay for grocery bags. That's why Lynne decided to pack all her groceries in one bag. The bag was heavy and full, and Lynne made the mistake of putting the eggs on top. Lynne was sad when the eggs fell onto the sidewalk and broke.

6. What caused Lynne to pack all her groceries in one bag?
   - ○ She wanted the bag to be heavy and full.
   - ○ She didn't want to pay for more than one bag.

Name _____

Day 4 | **Week 29**

Language

Write the two small words that make up the compound word.

1. pan + cake = _____

2. cow + boy = _____

3. sand + box = _____

4. rain + drop = _____

Math

Complete the number sentence.

5. 1 row of _____ = _____ squares

Reading

Read the text. Then answer the question.

    Pam went to Bev's birthday party. She ate some pizza. Then she had cake and ice cream. She also drank a can of soda. Later, Pam ate all the candy that was inside the goodie bag. When Pam got home, her stomach hurt and she didn't feel well.

6. What do you think caused Pam's stomach to hurt?

_____

_____

Name _____

Day 5 | Week 29

Language

Write the two small words that make up the compound word.

1. fish + bowl = _____
2. sea + horse = _____
3. wind + mill = _____
4. sun + shine = _____

Math

Divide the rectangle into 6 columns of 3 squares.

5.

Reading

Read the text. Then answer the question.

    Thousands of wildfires occur each year in the United States. Some people are very careless. They leave campfires burning instead of putting them out. People should be very careful in hot, dry weather. That is when wildfires spread the fastest.

6. What is the effect of hot, dry weather?
   ○ Wildfires spread fast in this weather.
   ○ People leave campfires burning.

© Evan-Moor Corp. • EMC 3242 • Daily Fundamentals

Name _____

Day 1 | **Week 30**

Language

Circle the linking verb in the sentence.

1. This valentine seems pretty.
2. It is pink and red.
3. The cookie feels soft.
4. The cookie smells good.
5. This valentine cookie tastes sweet.
6. You are my best friend!

Math

Look at the shape. Mark the answer that names how much is shaded.

7.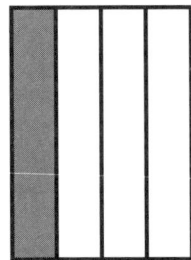

- ○ two thirds
- ○ one fourth
- ○ three fourths

Reading

Read the text. Then answer the questions.

I am helping Grandpa prepare dinner. I wash the carrots and peel the potatoes. Grandpa puts salt on the meat. I check to see if there is any rice made. There's not, so I put three cups of rice and some water into the rice cooker. Grandpa puts the meat, the carrots, and the potatoes in a pan and puts it into the oven to cook.

8. What does **prepare** mean?
   - ○ to put away
   - ○ to get ready

9. What context clues helped you?

_____

Language

Circle the linking verb in the sentence.

1. Dinner was delicious.
2. That sofa seems cozy.
3. This pillow is very soft.
4. The cats are warm.
5. You all look happy together.
6. Everyone is sleepy and quiet.

Math

Look at the shape. Mark the answer that names how much is shaded.

7.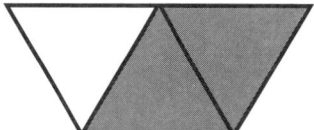

○ two thirds
○ one third
○ one half

Reading

Read the text. Then answer the items.

Mars is one of the planets in our solar system. It is about half the size of Earth. Mars is as dry as a desert except for its ice caps at the north and south poles. Mars has very tall mountains and deep canyons. The soil is full of rust-colored iron dust. This makes Mars look red. Strong winds blow up big storms of red dust.

8. What does **except** mean?   ○ other than   ○ because of

9. Write a sentence using the word **except**.

_____

Name _____

Day 3 | **Week 30**

Language

Circle the linking verb in the sentence.

1. I am a good speller.
2. Mr. Dunn is my spelling teacher.
3. We are a little nervous.
4. Mr. Dunn is very proud of us.
5. I am happy about the test.
6. We are all good spellers.

Math

Look at the shape. Color one third.

7.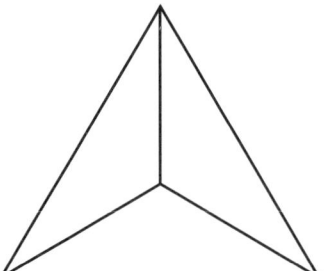

Reading

Read the text. Then answer the items.

    Ginny had been making mud pies in the backyard all afternoon.
    "You're a mess, kiddo!" said her dad. "It's into the bathtub with you."
    "Dad!" screamed Ginny. "Come quickly. There's a spider in the bathtub!"
    Dad came and took a look. "You don't have to be afraid. It won't harm you."
    "I'm not afraid," explained Ginny. "I know it won't hurt me. I don't want it to drown when I turn on the water."

8. What does **harm** mean?

_____

9. Underline the context clues that helped you.

Name _____

Day 4 | **Week 30**

Language

Write **is** or **are** to complete the sentence.

1. The county fair _____ a fun place to visit.
2. There _____ many animals.
3. The chicks _____ the cutest.
4. They _____ soft and fluffy.
5. The fair _____ also fun because of the rides.
6. There _____ a big Ferris wheel.

Math

Look at the shape. Color one fourth.

7.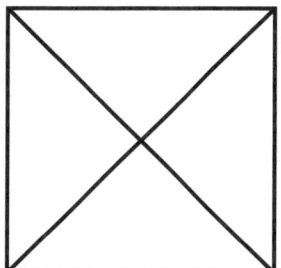

Reading

Read the text. Then answer the questions.

Ethan and Beth flew to Memphis, Tennessee, for a vacation. They got on the plane, buckled their seat belts, and closed their eyes. When they woke up, they saw planes parked beside them, so they knew they had arrived. "That was fast!" said Beth. "I thought the flight would take longer!"

8. What does **arrived** mean?
   ○ to be late to a place
   ○ to get to a place

9. What context clue helped you?

_____

_____

Name _____

Day 5 | **Week 30**

Language

Write **am**, **are**, or **is** to complete the sentence.

1. I _____ 8 years old.
2. Randy _____ 12 years old.
3. The twins _____ 10 years old.
4. I _____ the youngest child.
5. My dad _____ older than my mom.
6. My parents _____ both very busy with us!

Math

Read the problem. Then answer the item.

Jelena ate one third of a round pizza. How much was left over? Draw the pizza. Color the part that was left over.

7.

Reading

Read the text. Then answer the items.

Ishmael and Michelle lived in a big beautiful house in Fort Walton Beach, Florida. They were very wealthy and had many nice things such as cars, boats, and beautiful clothes. One day they decided that they should share their wealth with others. They started to bring food and clothes to people who needed them. They also helped the people find jobs and places to live. Others saw what they were doing and joined them. Now people who are in need in Fort Walton Beach know where to go to get help.

8. What does **wealthy** mean?

_____

9. Write a sentence using the word **wealthy**.

_____

160   Daily Fundamentals • EMC 3242 • © Evan-Moor Corp.

Answer Key

These answers will vary. Examples are given.

Page 11

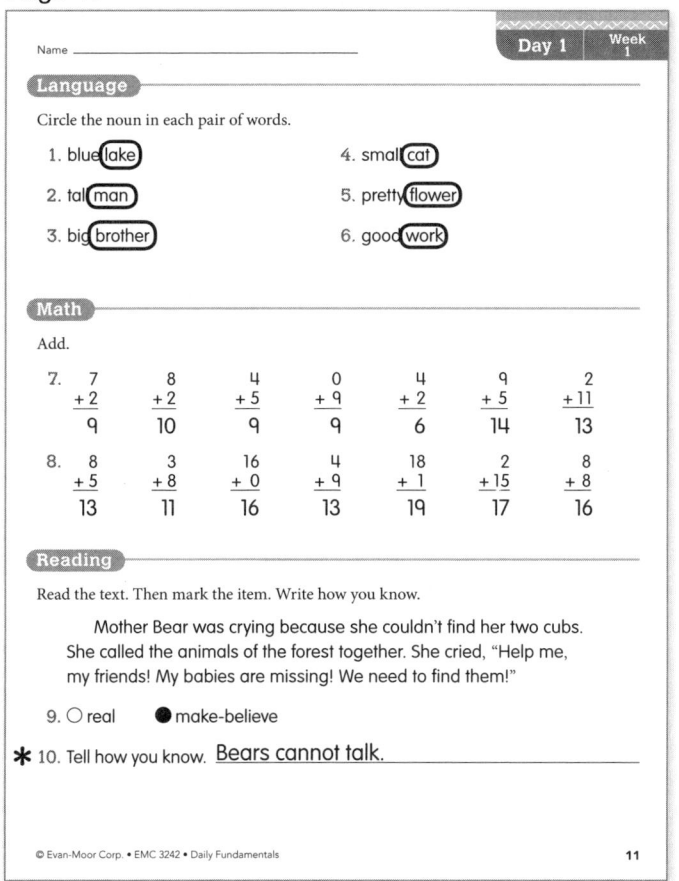

Page 12

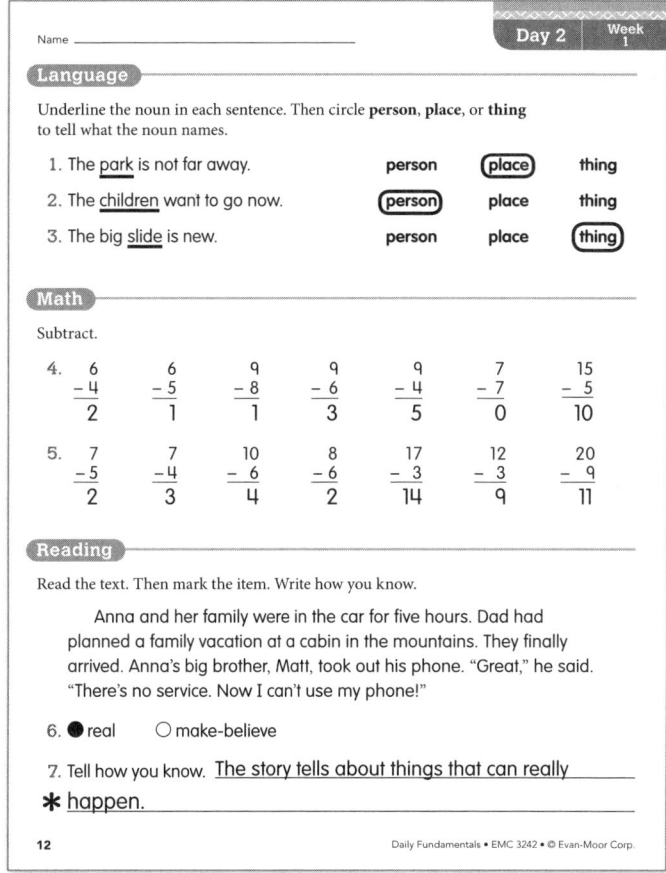

Page 13

Day 3 · Week 1

Language

Write **S** if the underlined noun is **singular**.
Write **P** if the underlined noun is **plural**.

1. My sisters read every day. — P
2. One sister likes chapter books. — P
3. The other sister likes fairy tales. — S

Math

Read the problem. Then answer the items.

20 children were playing soccer. 3 children had to leave early. How many children were still playing?

4. You will find out how many children ____.
   ○ left early   ○ were playing in all   ● were still playing

5. There were __17__ children still playing.

Reading

Read the text. Then answer the items.

A family of rats lived under the chicken coop. All day long they scurried about, eating the chicken feed and hiding from the cat.

6. Mark the sentence that would make this story make-believe.
   ● One day, Father rat said, "It's time to find a new home!"
   ○ The rats under the coop were a problem, so we got another cat.

7. How do you know? __Rats cannot talk.__

*

Page 14

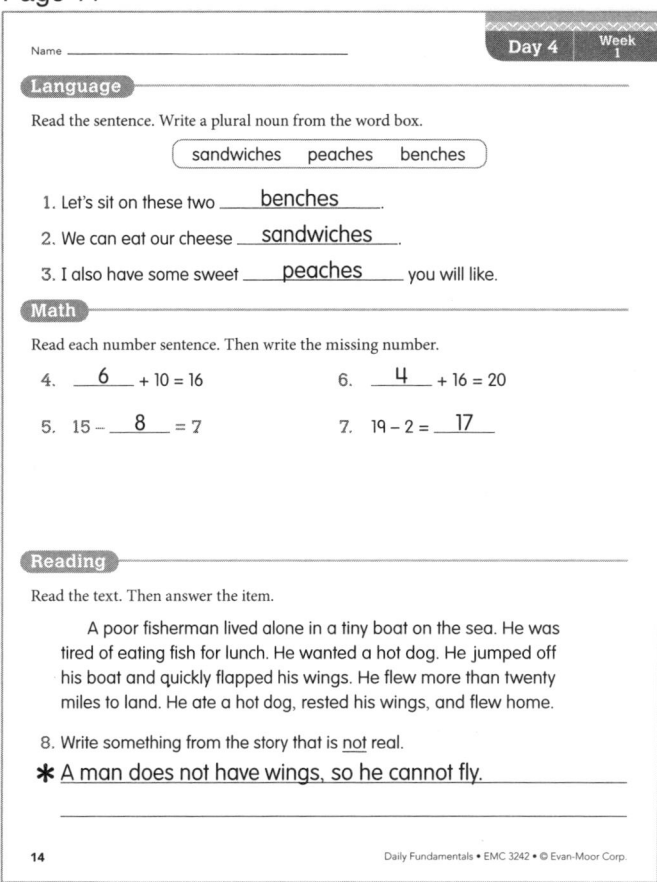

These answers will vary. Examples are given.

Page 15

Day 5 · Week 1

Language

Look at the bold noun. Write the plural form of the noun above it.

1. Many **families** are coming to the party.
   (family)
2. They are all from different **countries**.
   (country)
3. It will be fun to play with the **babies**.
   (baby)

Math

Find the sum or difference. Show a way to think about it.

Drawings may vary.

4. 9 + 8 = **17**
5. 9 − 5 = **4**

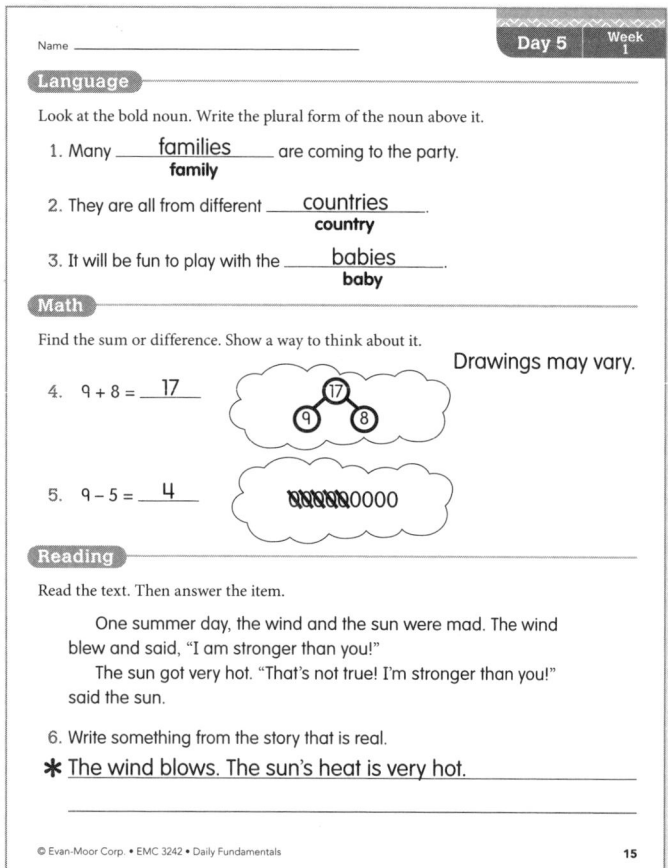

Reading

Read the text. Then answer the item.

One summer day, the wind and the sun were mad. The wind blew and said, "I am stronger than you!"

The sun got very hot. "That's not true! I'm stronger than you!" said the sun.

6. Write something from the story that is real.

 * The wind blows. The sun's heat is very hot.

Page 16

Day 1 · Week 2

Language

Write an adjective to describe the noun.

* 1. **blue** flowers
* 2. **tall** men
* 3. **brick** houses
* 4. **floppy** hats
* 5. **spotted** deer
* 6. **long** dress
* 7. **right** hand
* 8. **twin** bed

Math

Match each digit to its set of cubes. Then write the value below the cubes. One is done for you.

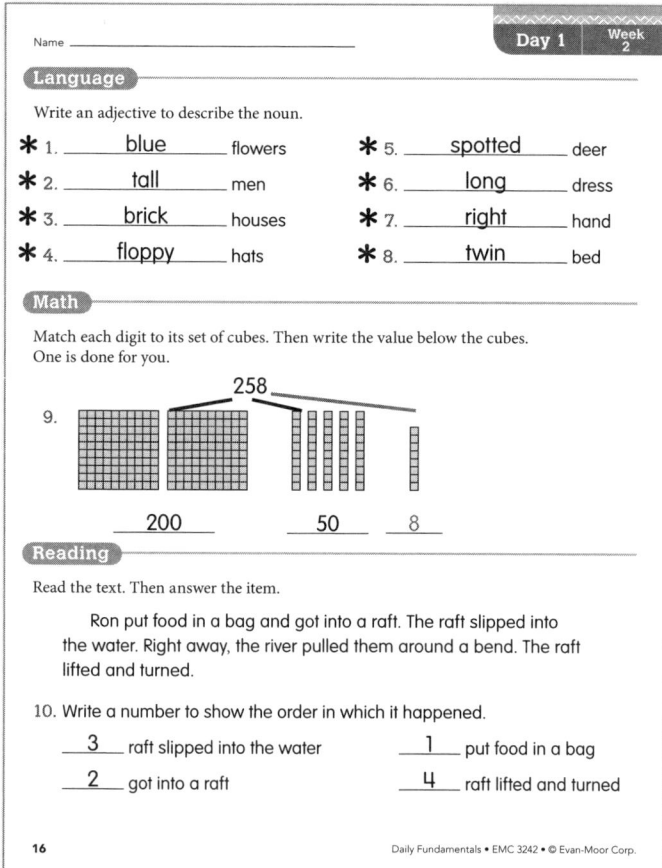

258 → **200**, **50**, **8**

Reading

Read the text. Then answer the item.

Ron put food in a bag and got into a raft. The raft slipped into the water. Right away, the river pulled them around a bend. The raft lifted and turned.

10. Write a number to show the order in which it happened.

3 raft slipped into the water   **1** put food in a bag
2 got into a raft   **4** raft lifted and turned

Page 17

Day 2 · Week 2

Language

Read the sentence. Write an adjective from the word box.

(new   friendly   blue)

1. My house has a **blue/new** rug.
2. My pets are all very **friendly**.
3. I have a **blue/new** backpack this year.

Math

Mark the number that matches the set of cubes.

4. ○ 240
   ● 234
   ○ 232

5. ● 329
   ○ 310
   ○ 320

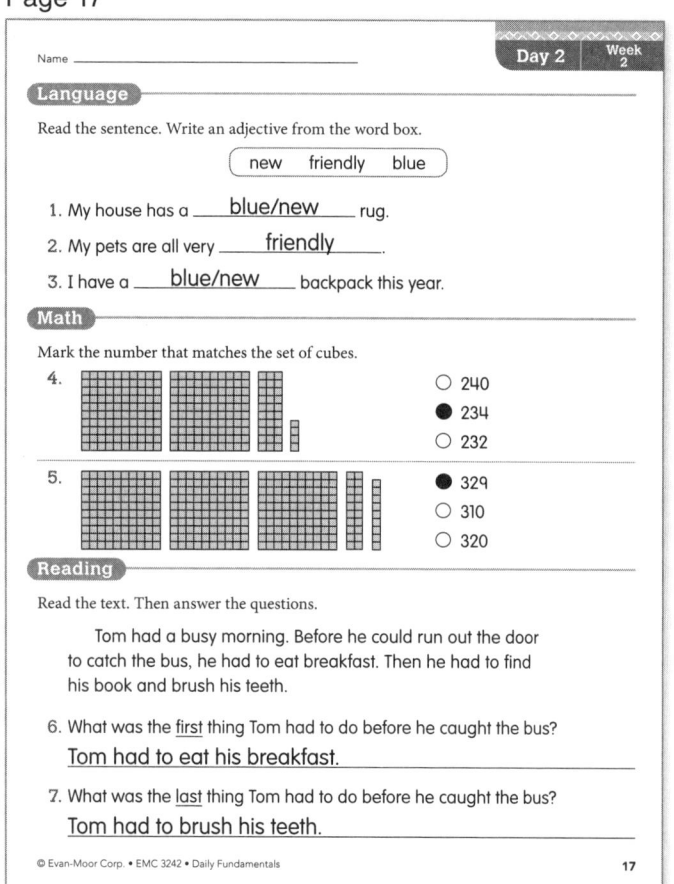

Reading

Read the text. Then answer the questions.

Tom had a busy morning. Before he could run out the door to catch the bus, he had to eat breakfast. Then he had to find his book and brush his teeth.

6. What was the first thing Tom had to do before he caught the bus?
   Tom had to eat his breakfast.

7. What was the last thing Tom had to do before he caught the bus?
   Tom had to brush his teeth.

Page 18

Day 3 · Week 2

Language

Write a noun on the first line. Then write an adjective to tell about it on the next line.

* 1. The **boy** is **bored**.
* 2. The **dog** is **hungry**.
* 3. The **book** is **helpful**.
* 4. The **park** is **huge**.

Math

Complete the table to show each number in three ways.

Base Ten Numeral	Written Form	Expanded Form
5. 118	one hundred eighteen	100 + 10 + 8
6. 436	four hundred thirty-six	400 + 30 + 6

Reading

Read the text. Then answer the item.

It is easy to make lemonade. First, fill a pitcher with water. Add the juice of four lemons. Add a cup of sugar and stir. Finally, add ice and enjoy.

7. Write a number to show the order in which it happened.

1 fill a pitcher with water   **3** add a cup of sugar and stir
4 add ice   **2** add the juice of four lemons

✱ These answers will vary. Examples are given.

Page 19

Language

Write three adjectives that tell about the color, shape, or size of the moon.

✱ 1. white
✱ 2. round
✱ 3. large

Math

Mark the value of the underlined digit.

4. 83<u>4</u>
   ● 4
   ○ 40
   ○ 400

5. 6<u>0</u>7
   ○ 60
   ○ 1
   ● 0 tens

Reading

Read the text. Then answer the question.

Once upon a time there was a poor shoemaker. He measured enough leather to make one pair of shoes. He cut out the leather. He laid it on the table. In the morning, he would sew the shoes.

6. Which one tells about the shoemaker's third step?
   ○ He cut out the leather.
   ● He laid it on the table.

Page 20

Language

Circle the adjective that best completes the sentence. Then write it on the line.

1. The branches are __heavy__ with apples. fun (heavy)
2. Look at all those __beautiful__ apples! (beautiful) noisy
3. Let's put the apples in __strong__ baskets. itchy (strong)

Math

Read the problem. Then answer the items.

The tallest tree in the world is three hundred eighty feet high.

4. Write the height as a number. __380__
5. Write the height using place value.
   __3__ hundreds, __8__ tens, __0__ ones

Reading

Read the text. Then answer the question.

On Saturday mornings, Aaron feeds his dog. First, he gets his dog Spot. Then he makes Spot sit next to his empty bowl. Next, he puts the dog food on the counter. He tells Spot to stay when Spot gets up. Then he pours the food into the bowl. Finally, he tells Spot he can eat.

6. Do you think the steps above are in the right order? Tell why or why not.
✱ No, the steps are not in the right order. I think he should get Spot last instead of first because Spot keeps getting up.

Page 21

Language

Underline the pronoun in the sentence.

1. <u>I</u> have a cheese sandwich.
2. Do <u>you</u> want a bite?
3. <u>I</u> can share the sandwich.
4. <u>She</u> does not have a lunch either.
5. <u>It</u> is a big sandwich.

Math

Answer the item.

6. What number comes next?
   600, 610, 620, 630, ____
   Ⓐ 700
   ● 640
   Ⓒ 631
   Ⓓ 635

Reading

Read the text. Then answer the items.

We put food in the yard for the birds. We put out different kinds of food. Most birds eats seeds. Pigeons and doves eat corn, too. But hummingbirds drink their food. They like the sugar water we put out. The birds come again and again to our yard.

7. Which bird is different from the others?
   ● hummingbird
   ○ dove

8. Tell why the bird you chose is different from the others.
✱ The hummingbird is different because it drinks its food.

Page 22

Language

Write a pronoun to replace the underlined noun or nouns.

1. <u>Dad</u> likes to bake. __He__
2. <u>Dad and I</u> ate some pie. __We__
3. <u>Mom and Jen</u> want some pie, too. __They__
4. Does <u>Rita</u> like pie? __she__
5. <u>The pie</u> is still warm. __It__

Math

Skip count to find the number of cubes.

6.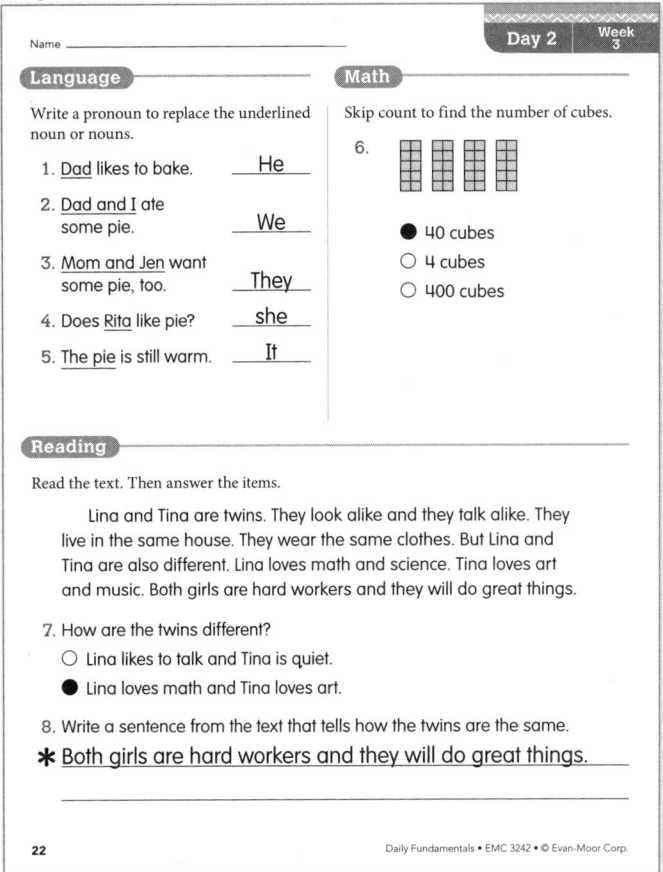
   ● 40 cubes
   ○ 4 cubes
   ○ 400 cubes

Reading

Read the text. Then answer the items.

Lina and Tina are twins. They look alike and they talk alike. They live in the same house. They wear the same clothes. But Lina and Tina are also different. Lina loves math and science. Tina loves art and music. Both girls are hard workers and they will do great things.

7. How are the twins different?
   ○ Lina likes to talk and Tina is quiet.
   ● Lina loves math and Tina loves art.

8. Write a sentence from the text that tells how the twins are the same.
✱ Both girls are hard workers and they will do great things.

These answers will vary. Examples are given.

Page 23

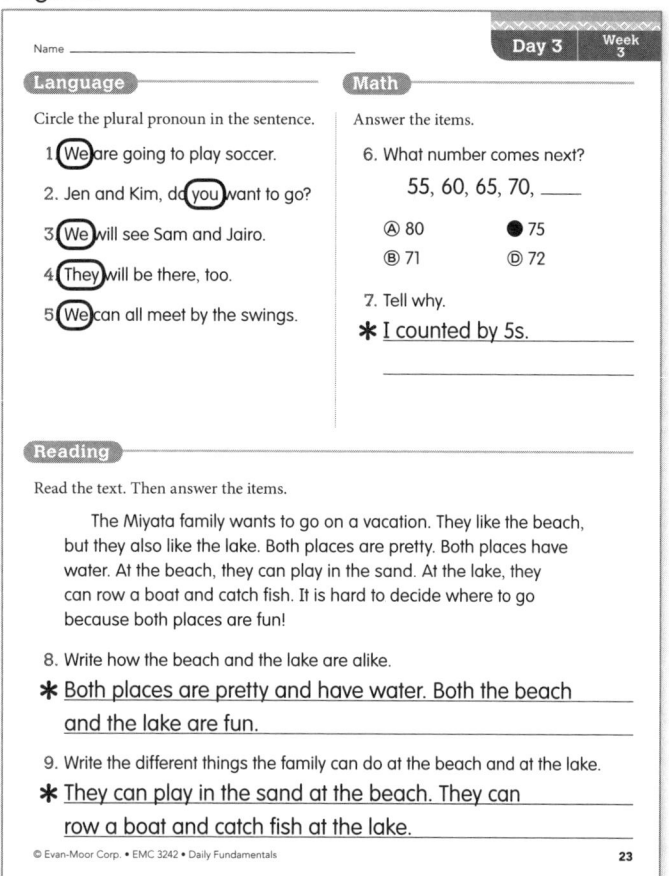

Day 3 Week 3

Language — Circle the plural pronoun in the sentence.
1. (We) are going to play soccer.
2. Jen and Kim, do (you) want to go?
3. (We) will see Sam and Jairo.
4. (They) will be there, too.
5. (We) can all meet by the swings.

Math — Answer the items.
6. What number comes next?
55, 60, 65, 70, ____
Ⓐ 80 ● 75
Ⓑ 71 Ⓓ 72
7. Tell why.
*I counted by 5s.

Reading — Read the text. Then answer the items.

The Miyata family wants to go on a vacation. They like the beach, but they also like the lake. Both places are pretty. Both places have water. At the beach, they can play in the sand. At the lake, they can row a boat and catch fish. It is hard to decide where to go because both places are fun!

8. Write how the beach and the lake are alike.
*Both places are pretty and have water. Both the beach and the lake are fun.
9. Write the different things the family can do at the beach and at the lake.
*They can play in the sand at the beach. They can row a boat and catch fish at the lake.

Page 24

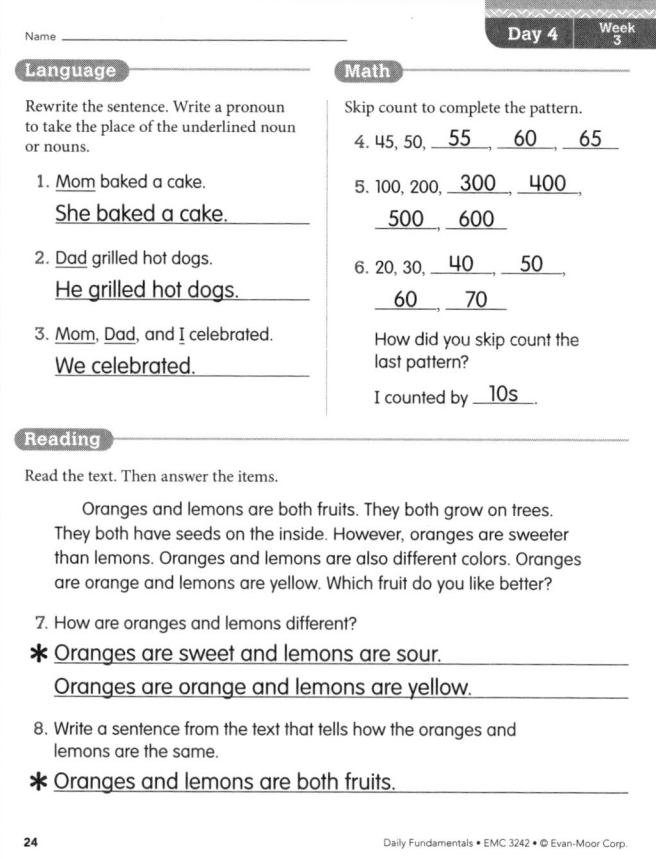

Day 4 Week 3

Language — Rewrite the sentence. Write a pronoun to take the place of the underlined noun or nouns.
1. Mom baked a cake.
   She baked a cake.
2. Dad grilled hot dogs.
   He grilled hot dogs.
3. Mom, Dad, and I celebrated.
   We celebrated.

Math — Skip count to complete the pattern.
4. 45, 50, 55, 60, 65
5. 100, 200, 300, 400, 500, 600
6. 20, 30, 40, 50, 60, 70
How did you skip count the last pattern?
I counted by 10s.

Reading — Read the text. Then answer the items.

Oranges and lemons are both fruits. They both grow on trees. They both have seeds on the inside. However, oranges are sweeter than lemons. Oranges and lemons are also different colors. Oranges are orange and lemons are yellow. Which fruit do you like better?

7. How are oranges and lemons different?
*Oranges are sweet and lemons are sour. Oranges are orange and lemons are yellow.
8. Write a sentence from the text that tells how the oranges and lemons are the same.
*Oranges and lemons are both fruits.

Page 25

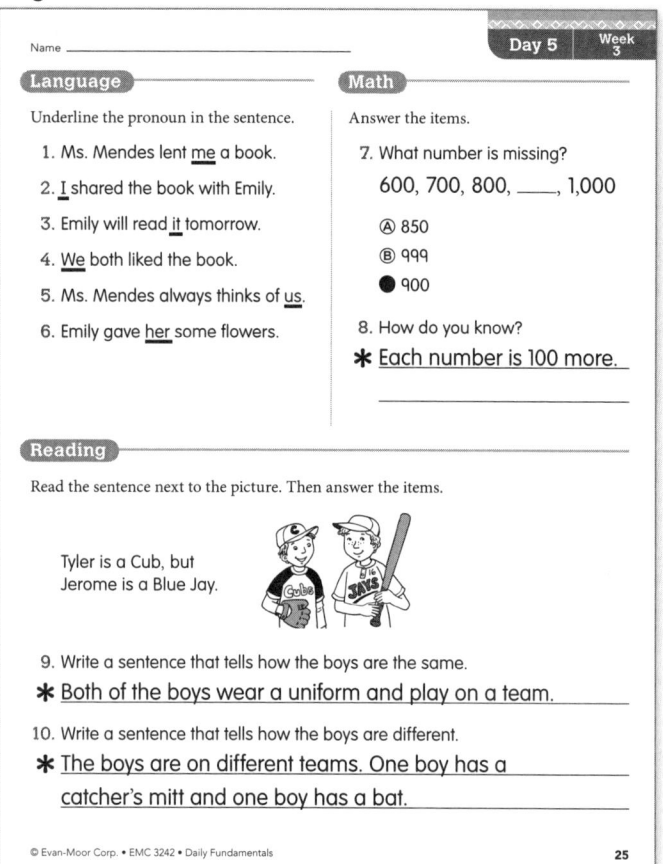

Day 5 Week 3

Language — Underline the pronoun in the sentence.
1. Ms. Mendes lent me a book.
2. I shared the book with Emily.
3. Emily will read it tomorrow.
4. We both liked the book.
5. Ms. Mendes always thinks of us.
6. Emily gave her some flowers.

Math — Answer the items.
7. What number is missing?
600, 700, 800, ____, 1,000
Ⓐ 850
Ⓑ 999
● 900
8. How do you know?
*Each number is 100 more.

Reading — Read the sentence next to the picture. Then answer the items.

Tyler is a Cub, but Jerome is a Blue Jay.

9. Write a sentence that tells how the boys are the same.
*Both of the boys wear a uniform and play on a team.
10. Write a sentence that tells how the boys are different.
*The boys are on different teams. One boy has a catcher's mitt and one boy has a bat.

Page 26

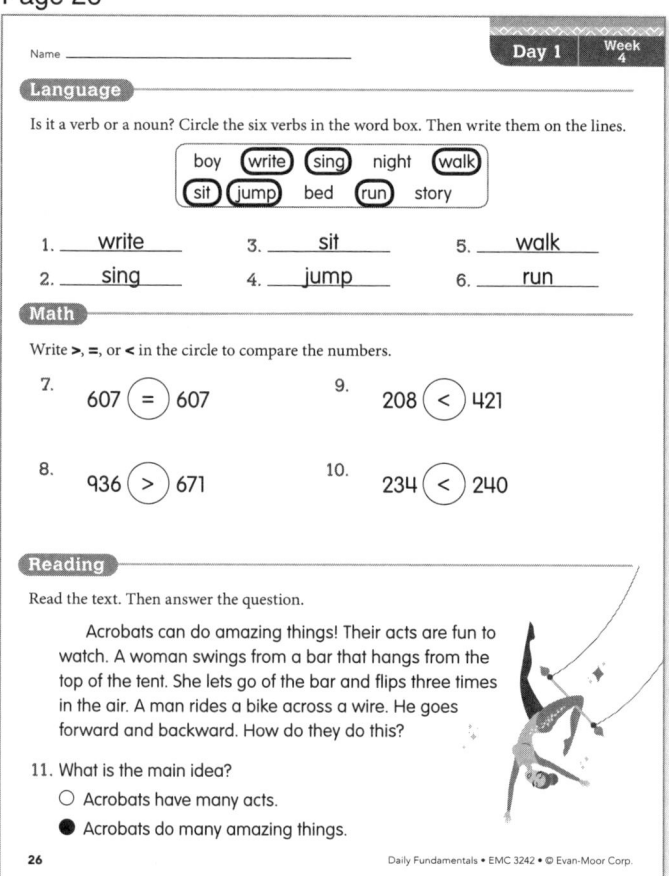

Day 1 Week 4

Language — Is it a verb or a noun? Circle the six verbs in the word box. Then write them on the lines.

boy (write) (sing) night (walk) (sit) (jump) bed (run) story

1. write   3. sit   5. walk
2. sing   4. jump 6. run

Math — Write >, =, or < in the circle to compare the numbers.
7. 607 = 607
8. 936 > 671
9. 208 < 421
10. 234 < 240

Reading — Read the text. Then answer the question.

Acrobats can do amazing things! Their acts are fun to watch. A woman swings from a bar that hangs from the top of the tent. She lets go of the bar and flips three times in the air. A man rides a bike across a wire. He goes forward and backward. How do they do this?

11. What is the main idea?
○ Acrobats have many acts.
● Acrobats do many amazing things.

✱ These answers will vary. Examples are given.

Page 27

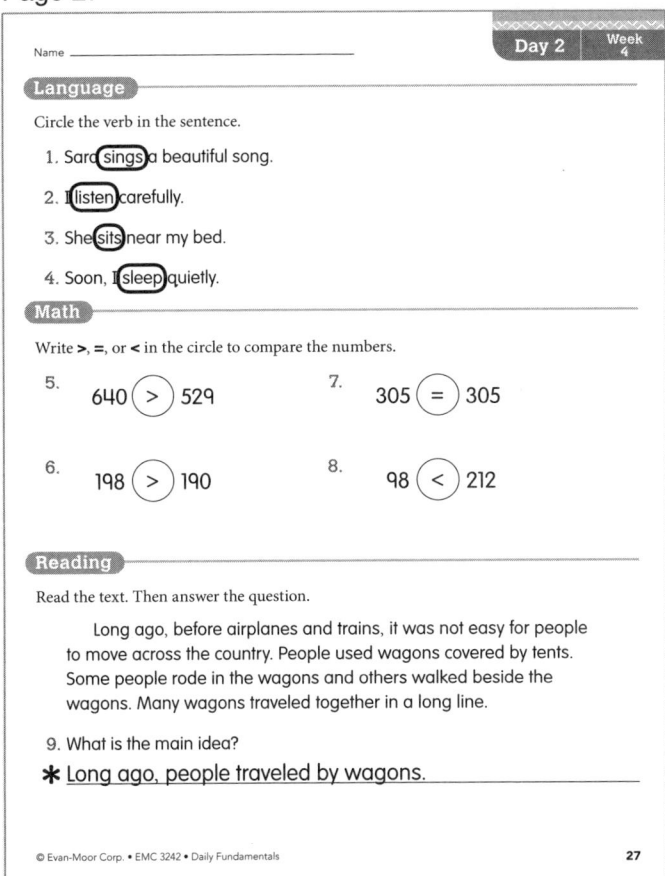

Day 2 — Week 4

Language

Circle the verb in the sentence.
1. Sara (sings) a beautiful song.
2. I (listen) carefully.
3. She (sits) near my bed.
4. Soon, I (sleep) quietly.

Math

Write >, =, or < in the circle to compare the numbers.
5. 640 (>) 529
6. 198 (>) 190
7. 305 (=) 305
8. 98 (<) 212

Reading

Read the text. Then answer the question.

Long ago, before airplanes and trains, it was not easy for people to move across the country. People used wagons covered by tents. Some people rode in the wagons and others walked beside the wagons. Many wagons traveled together in a long line.

9. What is the main idea?
✱ Long ago, people traveled by wagons.

Page 28

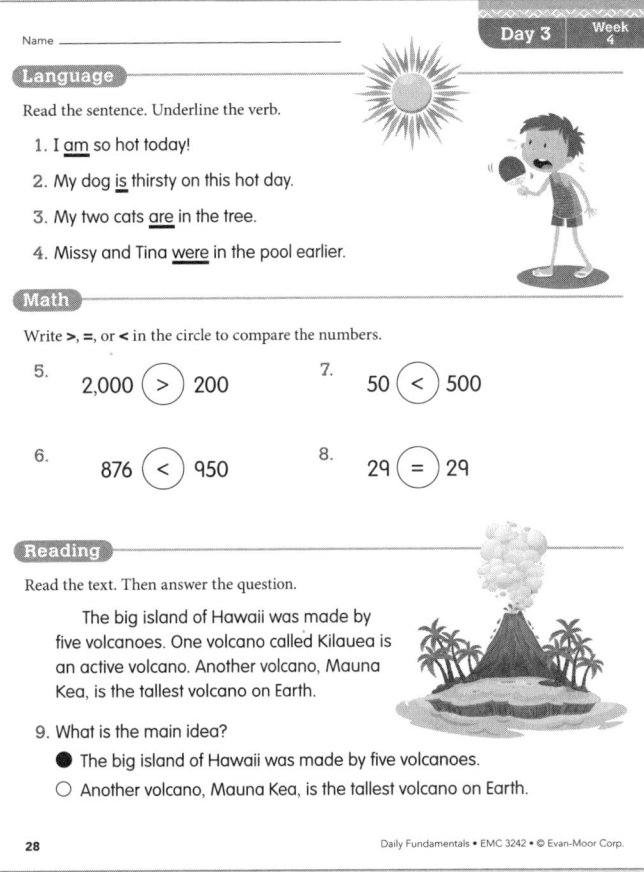

Day 3 — Week 4

Language

Read the sentence. Underline the verb.
1. I <u>am</u> so hot today!
2. My dog <u>is</u> thirsty on this hot day.
3. My two cats <u>are</u> in the tree.
4. Missy and Tina <u>were</u> in the pool earlier.

Math

Write >, =, or < in the circle to compare the numbers.
5. 2,000 (>) 200
6. 876 (<) 950
7. 50 (<) 500
8. 29 (=) 29

Reading

Read the text. Then answer the question.

The big island of Hawaii was made by five volcanoes. One volcano called Kilauea is an active volcano. Another volcano, Mauna Kea, is the tallest volcano on Earth.

9. What is the main idea?
● The big island of Hawaii was made by five volcanoes.
○ Another volcano, Mauna Kea, is the tallest volcano on Earth.

Page 29

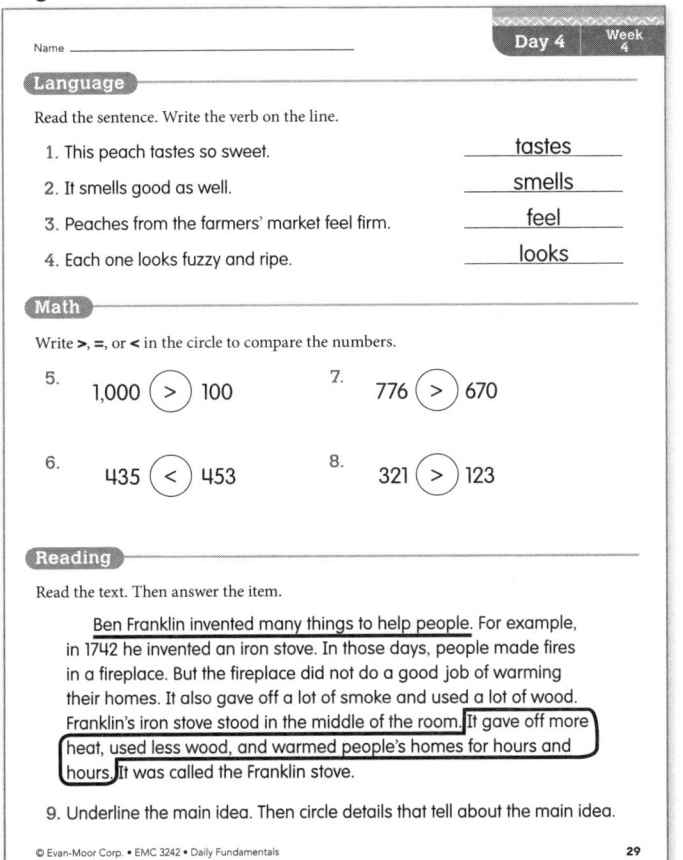

Day 4 — Week 4

Language

Read the sentence. Write the verb on the line.
1. This peach tastes so sweet. — tastes
2. It smells good as well. — smells
3. Peaches from the farmers' market feel firm. — feel
4. Each one looks fuzzy and ripe. — looks

Math

Write >, =, or < in the circle to compare the numbers.
5. 1,000 (>) 100
6. 435 (<) 453
7. 776 (>) 670
8. 321 (>) 123

Reading

Read the text. Then answer the item.

Ben Franklin invented many things to help people. For example, in 1742 he invented an iron stove. In those days, people made fires in a fireplace. But the fireplace did not do a good job of warming their homes. It also gave off a lot of smoke and used a lot of wood. Franklin's iron stove stood in the middle of the room. [It gave off more heat, used less wood, and warmed people's homes for hours and hours.] It was called the Franklin stove.

9. Underline the main idea. Then circle details that tell about the main idea.

Page 30

Day 5 — Week 4

Language

Write two sentences about school. Use verbs that tell what is happening **now**.
✱ 1. My school is having a carnival.
✱ 2. My friends are cleaning the playground.

Math

Write >, =, or < in the circle to compare the numbers.
3. 344 (<) 444
4. 1,000 (>) 999
5. 67 (=) 67
6. 325 (<) 355

Reading

Read the text. Then write the main idea.

The stem holds the apple to the tree. The leaf uses water, sunlight, and air to make food for the tree. The core holds the seeds. The skin protects the apple. The flesh is the part of the apple that tastes good.

✱ 7. The main idea tells what the parts of an apple do.

These answers will vary. Examples are given.

Page 31

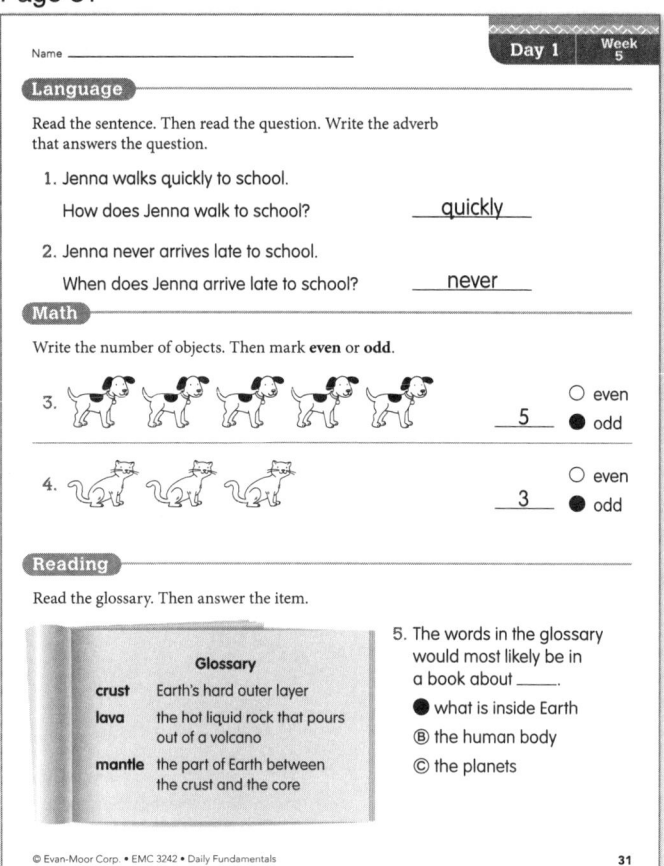

Page 32

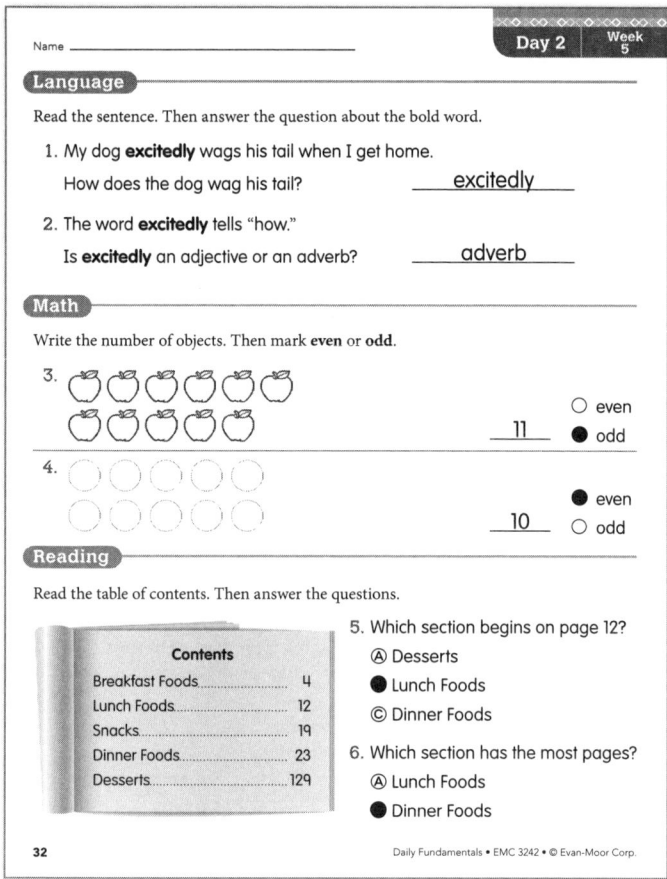

Page 33

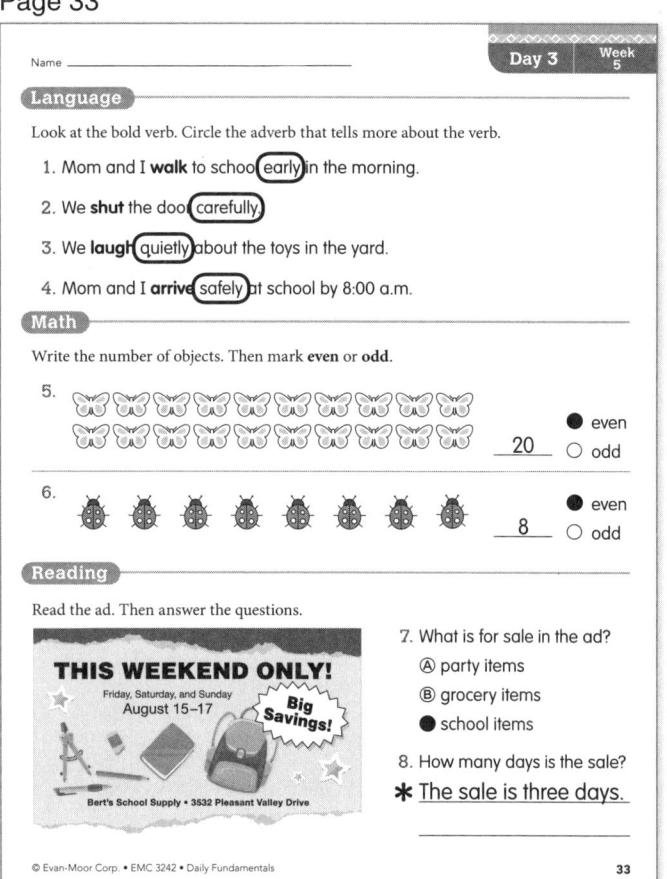

Page 34

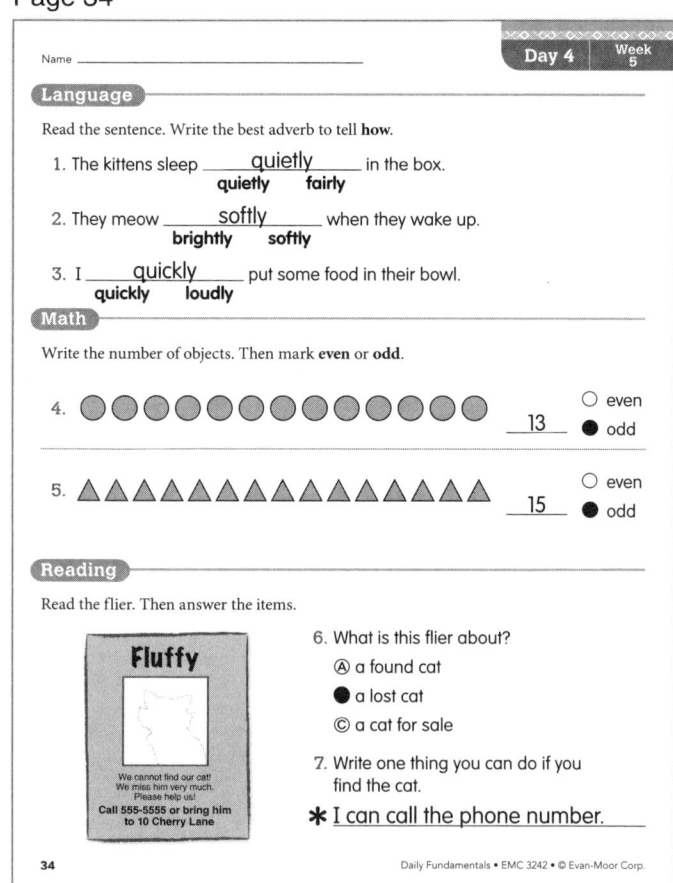

* These answers will vary. Examples are given.

Page 35
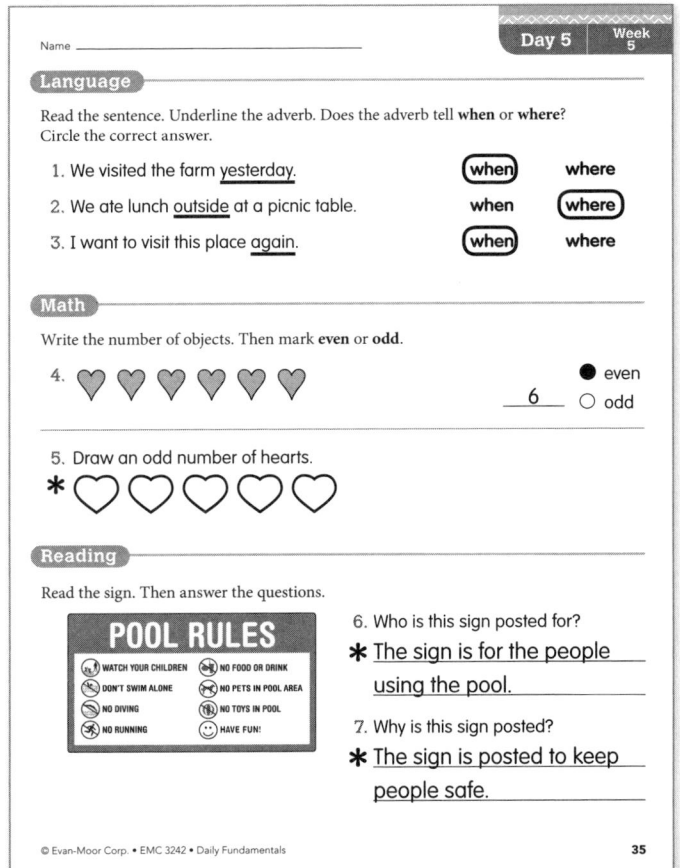

Page 36
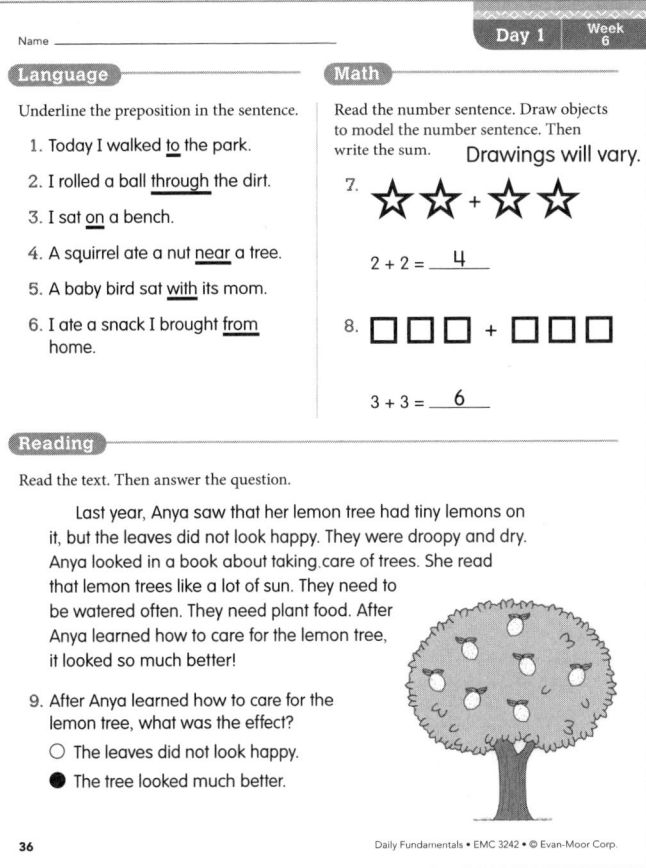

Page 37
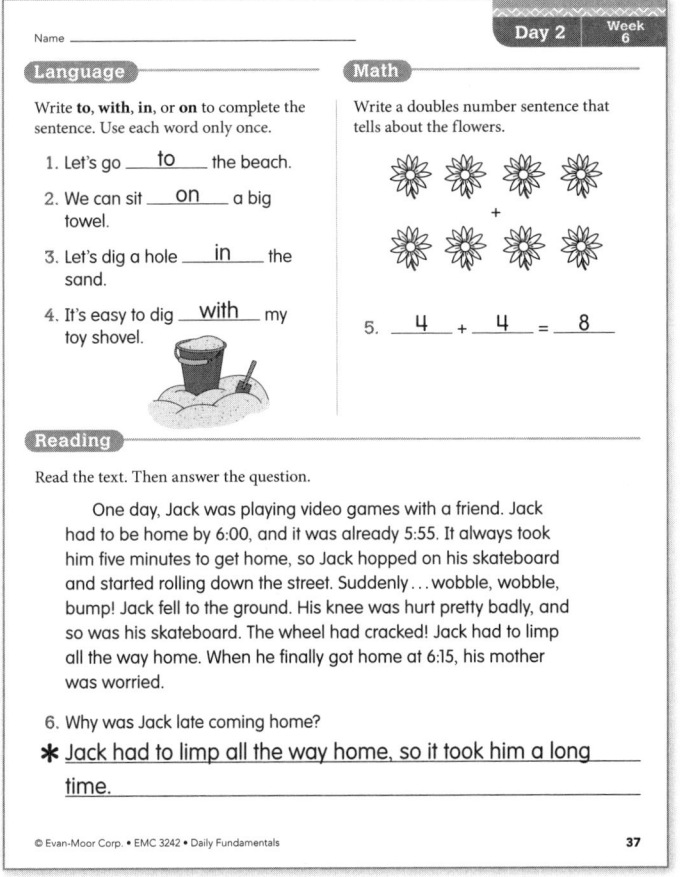

Page 38
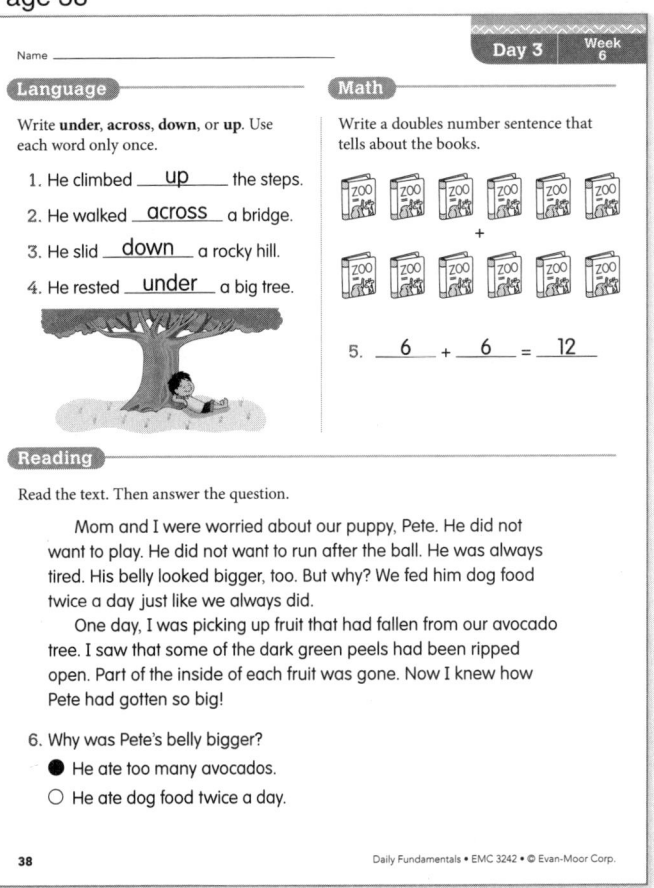

These answers will vary. Examples are given.

Page 39

Day 4 — Week 6

Language

Underline the preposition in the sentence.

1. Come <u>to</u> my birthday party.
2. It will be <u>at</u> Albany Park.
3. We will be <u>by</u> the playground.
4. Walk <u>across</u> the parking lot.
5. Find the tree <u>with</u> balloons.
6. We will wait <u>for</u> you!

Math

Read the problem. Then answer the item.

Each box has 18 cookies. The cookies look like this:

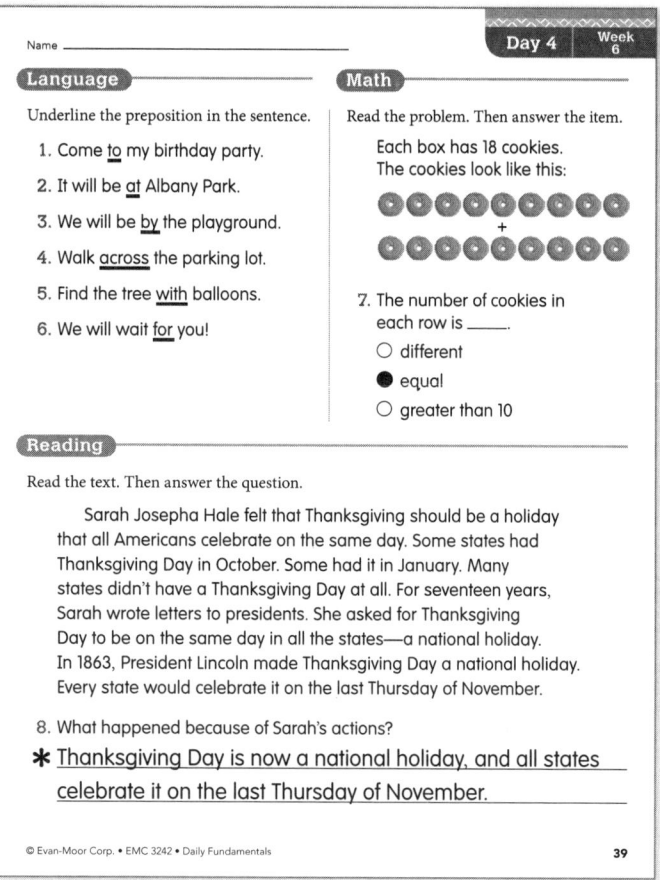

7. The number of cookies in each row is ____.
   ○ different
   ● equal
   ○ greater than 10

Reading

Read the text. Then answer the question.

Sarah Josepha Hale felt that Thanksgiving should be a holiday that all Americans celebrate on the same day. Some states had Thanksgiving Day in October. Some had it in January. Many states didn't have a Thanksgiving Day at all. For seventeen years, Sarah wrote letters to presidents. She asked for Thanksgiving Day to be on the same day in all the states—a national holiday. In 1863, President Lincoln made Thanksgiving Day a national holiday. Every state would celebrate it on the last Thursday of November.

8. What happened because of Sarah's actions?
* <u>Thanksgiving Day is now a national holiday, and all states celebrate it on the last Thursday of November.</u>

Page 40

Day 5 — Week 6

Language

Underline the preposition in the sentence.

1. Mom and I sit <u>on</u> a bench.
2. We like sitting <u>near</u> the pond.
3. Five little ducks are swimming <u>in</u> the pond.
4. We take a few pictures <u>with</u> Mom's phone.
5. We walk <u>around</u> the park.
6. Tomorrow we will come back <u>to</u> this same spot.

Math

Write a doubles number sentence that tells about the marbles.

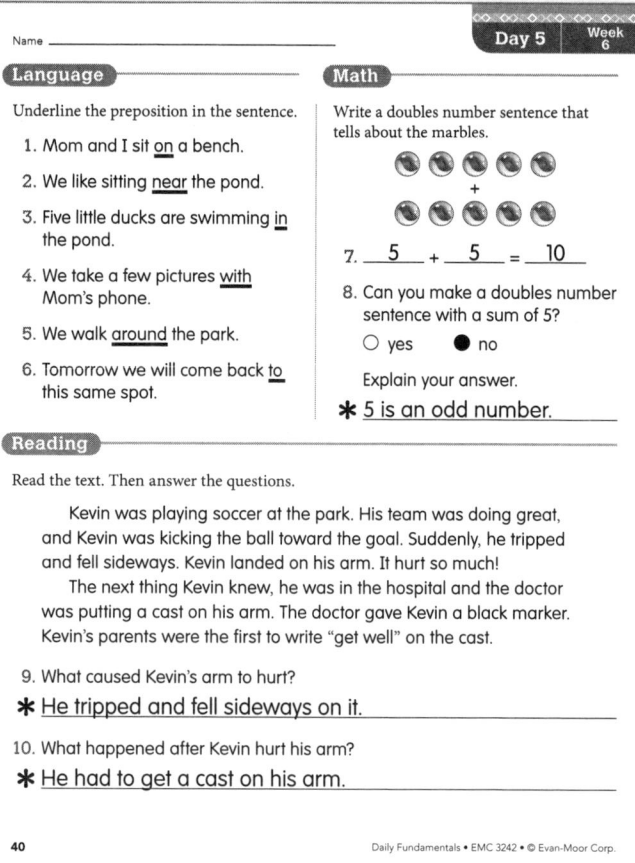

7. <u>5</u> + <u>5</u> = <u>10</u>

8. Can you make a doubles number sentence with a sum of 5?
   ○ yes   ● no

   Explain your answer.
   * <u>5 is an odd number.</u>

Reading

Read the text. Then answer the questions.

Kevin was playing soccer at the park. His team was doing great, and Kevin was kicking the ball toward the goal. Suddenly, he tripped and fell sideways. Kevin landed on his arm. It hurt so much! The next thing Kevin knew, he was in the hospital and the doctor was putting a cast on his arm. The doctor gave Kevin a black marker. Kevin's parents were the first to write "get well" on the cast.

9. What caused Kevin's arm to hurt?
* <u>He tripped and fell sideways on it.</u>

10. What happened after Kevin hurt his arm?
* <u>He had to get a cast on his arm.</u>

Page 41

Day 1 — Week 7

Language

What kind of sentence is it? Write **telling**, **asking**, or **exclamation** on the line.

1. It's time to pick the apples from our tree. — telling
2. Look at all those big green apples! — exclamation
3. Let's put the biggest ones in this basket. — telling
4. Will you bake a pie for us? — asking

Math

Write how many bugs are in each **column**. Then complete the number sentence.

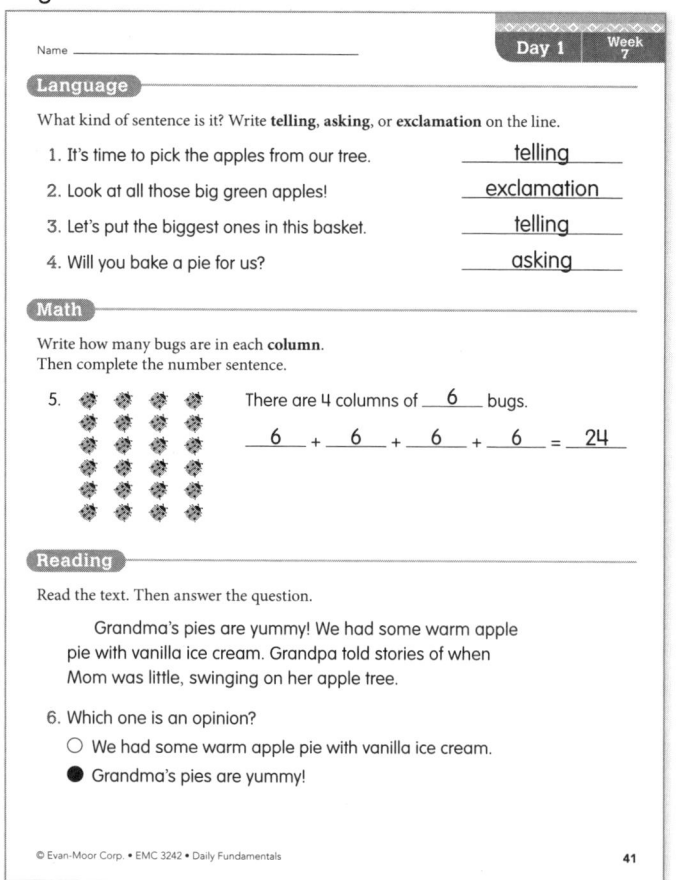

5. There are 4 columns of <u>6</u> bugs.
   <u>6</u> + <u>6</u> + <u>6</u> + <u>6</u> = <u>24</u>

Reading

Read the text. Then answer the question.

Grandma's pies are yummy! We had some warm apple pie with vanilla ice cream. Grandpa told stories of when Mom was little, swinging on her apple tree.

6. Which one is an opinion?
   ○ We had some warm apple pie with vanilla ice cream.
   ● Grandma's pies are yummy!

Page 42

Day 2 — Week 7

Language

Answer the question with a statement.

1. What is your favorite lunch? <u>My favorite lunch is a turkey and</u>
* <u>cheese sandwich with chips and grapes.</u>

2. What is your favorite color? <u>My favorite color is green.</u>
* _____

Math

Write how many hearts are in each **column**. Then complete the number sentence.

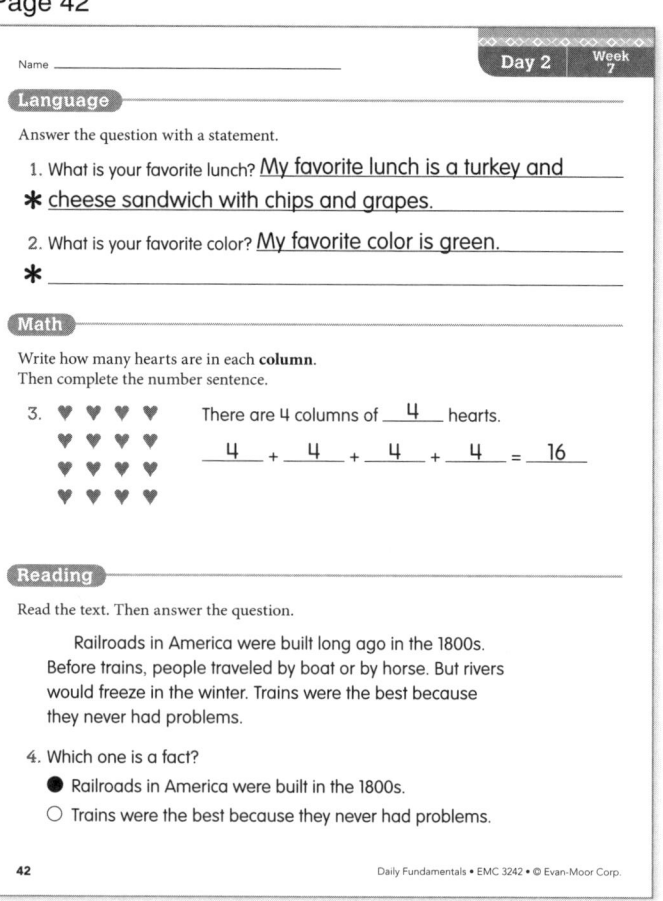

3. There are 4 columns of <u>4</u> hearts.
   <u>4</u> + <u>4</u> + <u>4</u> + <u>4</u> = <u>16</u>

Reading

Read the text. Then answer the question.

Railroads in America were built long ago in the 1800s. Before trains, people traveled by boat or by horse. But rivers would freeze in the winter. Trains were the best because they never had problems.

4. Which one is a fact?
   ● Railroads in America were built in the 1800s.
   ○ Trains were the best because they never had problems.

* These answers will vary. Examples are given.

Page 43

Day 3 — Week 7

Language
Write a period or a question mark to end each sentence.
Circle **S** if it is a statement or **Q** if it is a question.

1. I have a new puppy named Buddy. — **S** Q
2. Would you like to meet him? — S **Q**
3. When can you come over? — S **Q**

Math
Write how many stars are in each **row**.
Then complete the number sentence.

4. There are 3 rows of __5__ stars.
   __5__ + __5__ + __5__ = __15__

Reading
Read the text. Then answer the item.

César Chavéz was born in Arizona in 1927. Arizona is the greatest state. His family had a farm and a grocery store. When César was ten years old, there was not enough water for the plants on the farm. Most of the plants died.

5. Write a sentence from the text that is an opinion.
   Arizona is the greatest state.

Page 44

Day 4 — Week 7

Language
Circle the question word. Then rewrite the sentence with an end mark.

1. (When) is the first day of school
2. When is the first day of school?
3. (Who) will be your teacher
4. Who will be your teacher?

Math
Mark the number sentence that tells about the array.

5. ● ● ● ● ●
   ● ● ● ● ●

   ● 2 + 2 + 2 + 2 + 2 = ?
   ○ 2 + 2 + 2 + 2 = ?
   ○ 5 + 5 + 5 = ?

Reading
Read the text. Then answer the item.

A magnet will attract some things made of steel. Many refrigerators are made of steel. So are things like paper clips, pins, nails, and cars. Magnets are fun.

6. Write a sentence from the text that is a fact.
* A magnet will attract some things made of steel.

Page 45

Day 5 — Week 7

Language
Read the sentence. Look at the picture.
Then write two sentences with ! that go with the picture.

There's water all over the floor!

* 1. Be careful!
* 2. Hurry up and mop the floor!

Math
Write a number sentence that tells about the array.

3. There are 5 rows of __3__.
   __3__ + __3__ + __3__ + __3__ + __3__ = __15__

Reading
Read the text. Then answer the question.

A family of rats lived near a rice field. They visited the rice field every day to see if the rice had grown. There wasn't much rain, so the rice did not grow. Rice fields need to be flooded with water in order for the rice to grow. I think rats like to live near rice fields.

4. Does this text have both a fact and an opinion? Explain your answer.
* Yes, this text has both. The fact is rice needs a lot of water to grow. The opinion is rats like to live near rice fields.

Page 46

Day 1 — Week 8

Language
Read the sentence. Then rewrite it using capital letters for the holidays.

1. We will take Mom out to lunch on mother's day.
   We will take Mom out to lunch on Mother's Day.
2. On valentine's day, we made cards for our friends.
   On Valentine's Day, we made cards for our friends.

Math
Solve the problem. Draw or write to show your thinking.

3. 62 + 24 = __86__
4. 42 + 36 = __78__

Work/models will vary.

Reading
Read the text. Then answer the question.

After school, my friend and I ride our bikes to the park. We sit on the bench and watch the ducks in the pond. After a while, it's time to go home, but first we ride slowly on the bike path around the pond.

5. After reading the story, what do you know about the park? Write about it.
* The park has a duck pond, a bench, and a bike path.

© Evan-Moor Corp. • EMC 3242 • Daily Fundamentals

⁕ These answers will vary. Examples are given.

Page 47

Day 2 — Week 8

Language

Read the sentence. Then rewrite it using capital letters where they are needed.

1. On monday and wednesday I go to swimming class.
   On Monday and Wednesday I go to swimming class.
2. Paul's birthday party is this saturday.
   Paul's birthday party is this Saturday.

Math

Solve the problem. Draw or write to show your thinking.

3. 33 + 44 = 77
4. 23 + 62 = 85

Work/models will vary.

Reading

Read the text. Then answer the item.

One summer day, in a village in Mexico, Sergio and Lupe were married. They had no family and no money, so they had no party and no cake. Still, they were happy.

5. Tell when and where the story takes place.
   ⁕ It takes place in the summer in a village in Mexico.

Page 48

Day 3 — Week 8

Language

Read the sentence. Then rewrite it using capital letters where they are needed.

1. My sister's birthday is in june.
   My sister's birthday is in June.
2. Thanksgiving is in november.
   Thanksgiving is in November.

Math

Solve the problem. Draw or write to show your thinking.

3. 15 + 75 = 90 (80, 10)
4. 12 + 76 = 88 (80, 8)

Work/models will vary.

Reading

Read the text. Then answer the questions.

One cool autumn day, a young hunter went out to find food for his family. He saw deer tracks and followed them. Before he knew it, the sky was dark and he was far from home. So he wrapped himself in his fur blanket and laid down to sleep under the tall trees.

5. Does the story take place in a city or in a forest? How do you know?
   ⁕ The story takes place in a forest because there are deer tracks and he sleeps under trees.

Page 49

Day 4 — Week 8

Language

Read the sentence. Then rewrite it using capital letters where they are needed.

1. sara lopez and mike anderson are my best friends.
   Sara Lopez and Mike Anderson are my best friends.
2. sally ford has a cousin named richard.
   Sally Ford has a cousin named Richard.

Math

Read the problem. Then answer the item. Show your work.

Tyson has 26 students in his class.
Jordy has 30 students in his class.
Allen has 27 students in his class.
How many students are in all three classes?

Work/models will vary.

3. 83 students in all three classes

Reading

Read the text. Then answer the questions.

Hank looked out over the wide plains. He saw some folks coming on a wagon train, probably on their way out west. Hank rode out on his horse to meet them. He waved his hat and said, "Hello there! I reckon you are looking for a place to settle down?"

4. Does the story take place now or long ago? How do you know?
   ⁕ The story takes place long ago because there is a wagon train and they are going west.

Page 50

Day 5 — Week 8

Language

Read the sentence. Then rewrite it using capital letters where they are needed.

1. bill, mary, and keith will visit us on thanksgiving.
   Bill, Mary, and Keith will visit us on Thanksgiving.
2. They will stay until tuesday, december 5.
   They will stay until Tuesday, December 5.

Math

Read the problem. Then answer the item. Show your work.

On Monday, Bree rode 12 miles.
On Tuesday, she rode 17 miles.
On Wednesday, she rode 8 miles.
On Thursday, she rode 13 miles.
How many miles did Bree ride altogether?

Work/models will vary.

3. 50 miles altogether

Reading

Read the text. Then answer the questions.

The smell of candy drifted down the hall. The machines went cha-gug, cha-gug, cha-gug as they spat little yellow drops onto the long black belt. Workers with white caps and blue gloves checked every piece of candy to make sure it was soft and perfectly round.

4. Where does the story take place? How do you know?
   ⁕ It takes place in a candy factory because there are machines and workers.

✱ These answers will vary. Examples are given.

Page 51

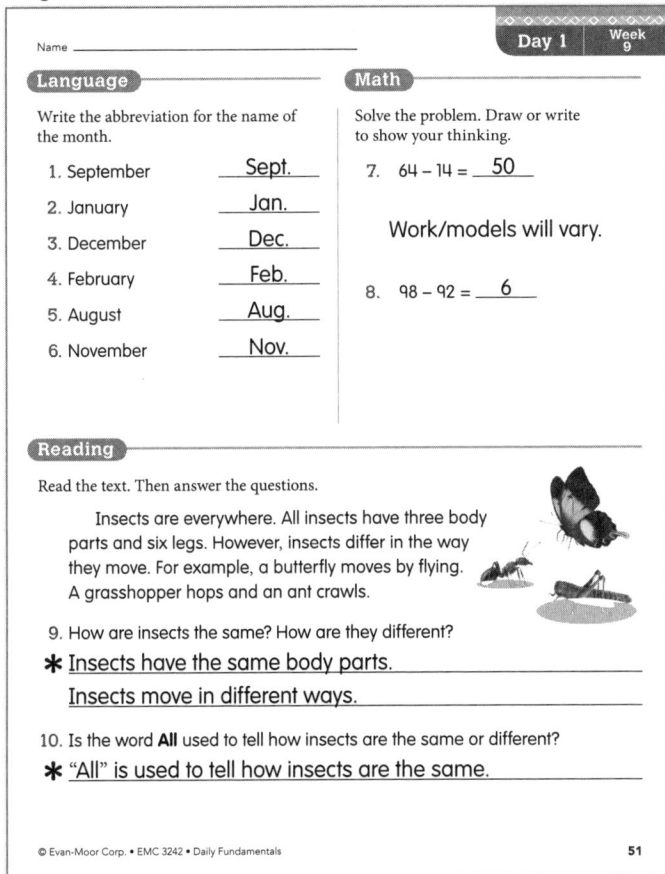

Page 52

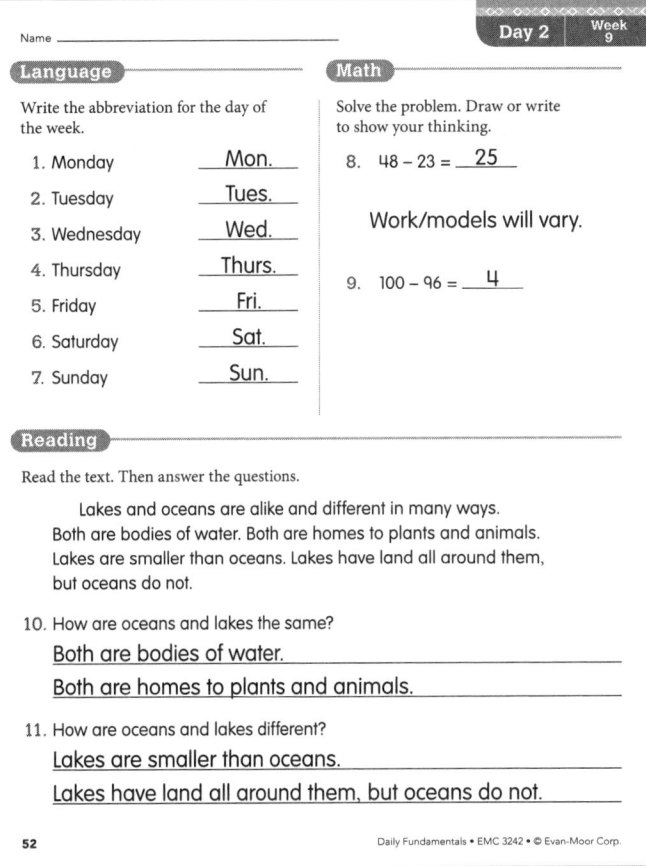

Page 53

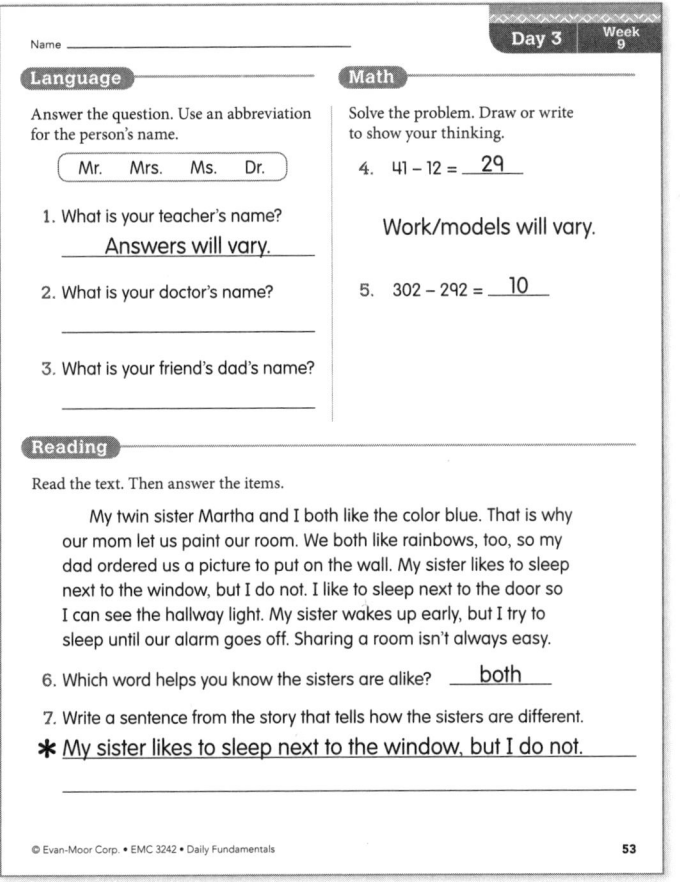

Page 54

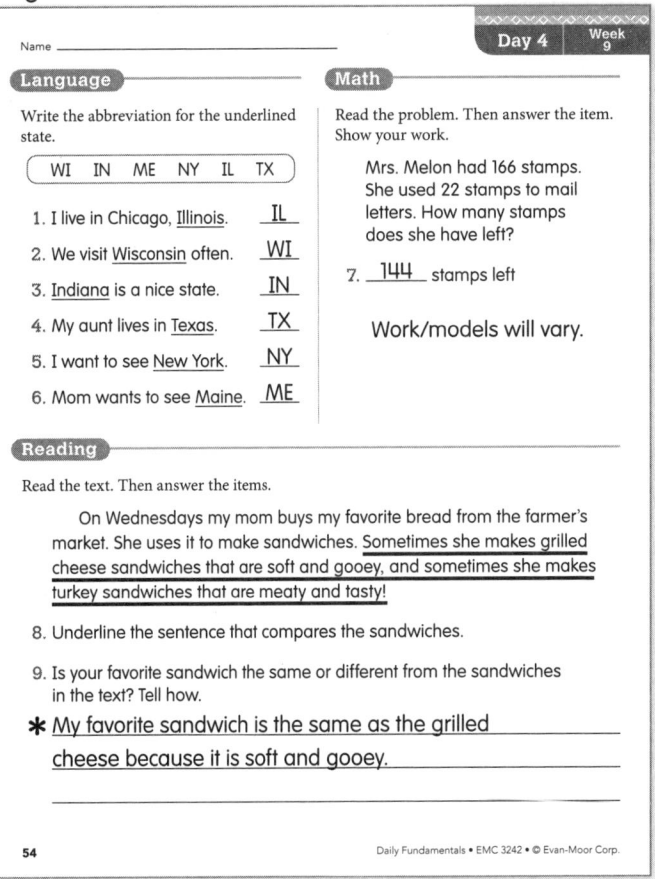

* These answers will vary. Examples are given.

Page 55

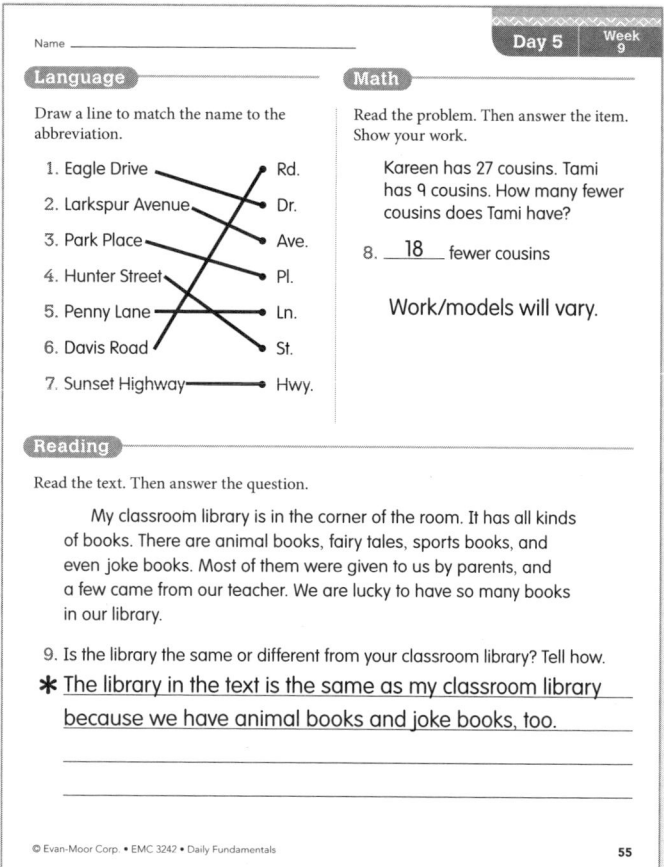

Page 56

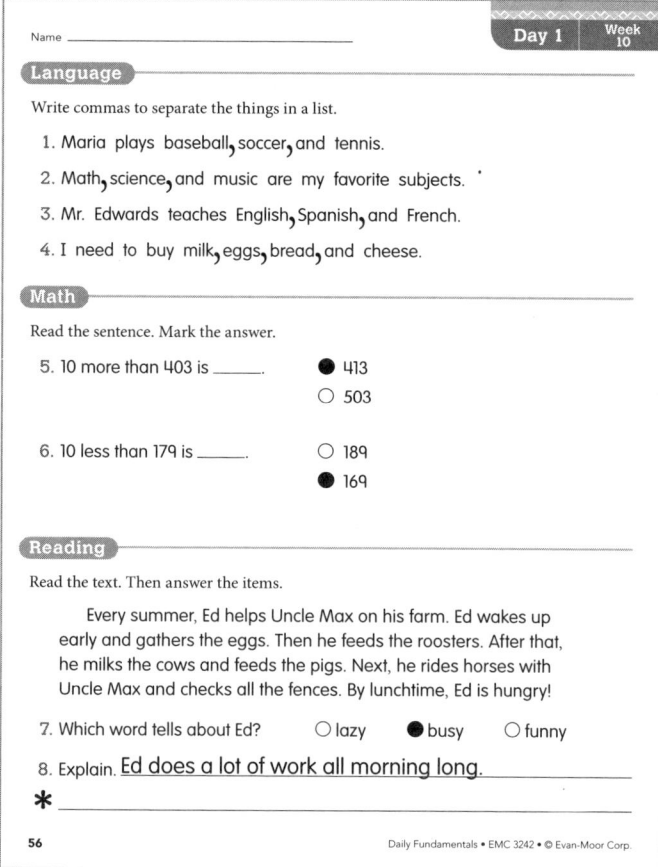

Page 57

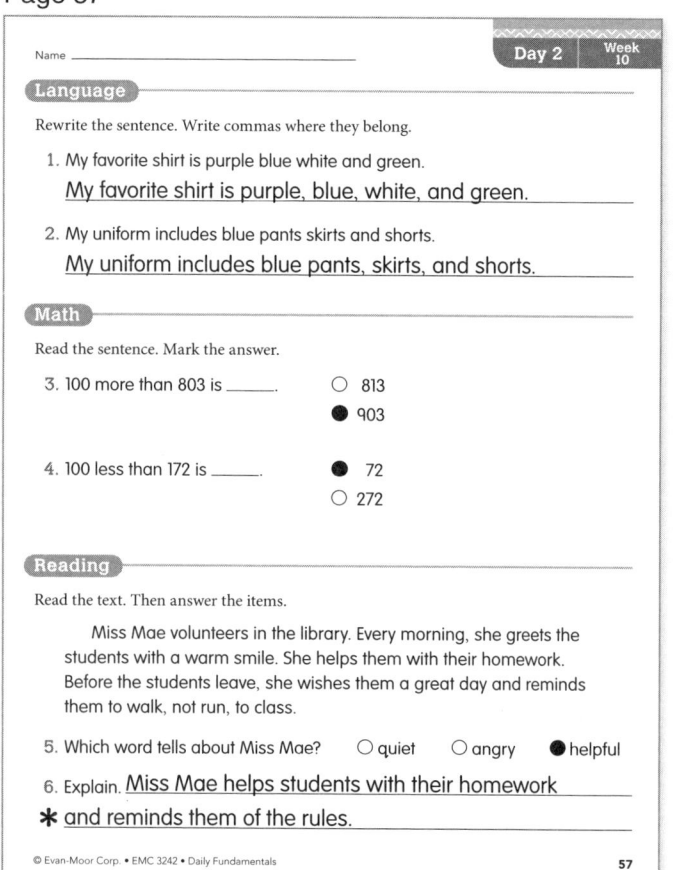

Page 58

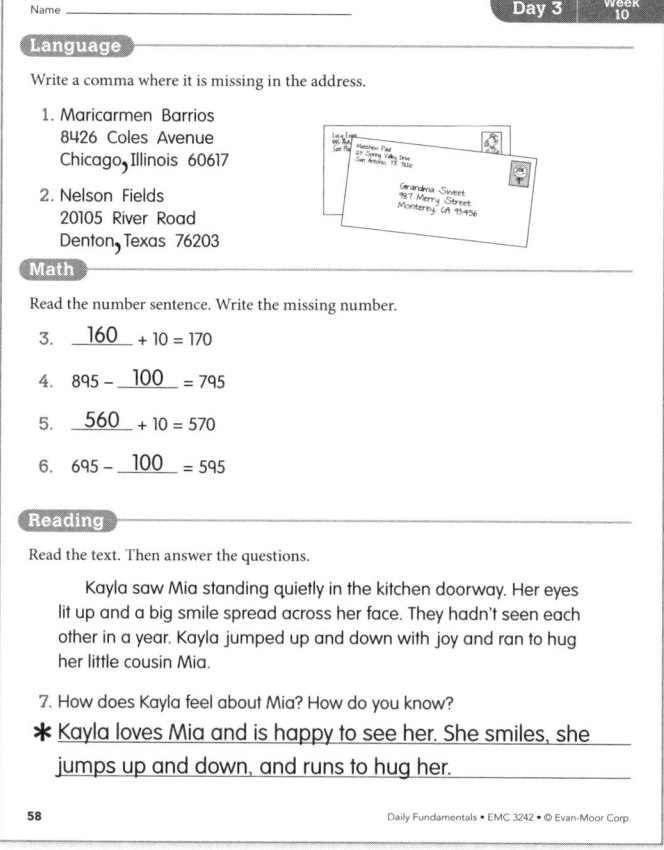

* These answers will vary. Examples are given.

Page 59

Day 4 — Week 10

Language
Write a comma where it belongs in the sentence.
1. Molly asked**,** "May I borrow a pencil?"
2. Anthony answered**,** "I have an extra pencil."
3. "Thank you. I will return it soon**,**" said Molly.
4. "You can keep it**,**" said Anthony.

Math
Read the number sentence. Write the missing number.
5. __470__ + 10 = 480
6. 475 − __100__ = 375
7. __860__ + 10 = 870
8. 472 − __10__ = 462

Reading
Read the text. Then answer the questions.

It was the first day at a new school. Henry waited, shifting from one foot to the other. What if the bus driver missed his stop? What if he couldn't find his classroom? What if no one liked him?

9. How does Henry feel on the first day of school? How do you know?

* __Henry is nervous and scared. He has many questions.__

Page 60

Day 5 — Week 10

Language
Read the letter. Write commas where they belong.

1. Dear Grandpa**,**
   When will you come to Texas? We miss you very much.
   Your grandson**,**
   Marco

2. Dear Emmy**,**
   Thank you for coming to my party. It was nice to see you.
   Love**,**
   Belinda

Math
Read the number sentence. Write the missing number.
3. __432__ + 100 = 532
4. 352 − __10__ = 342
5. __755__ + 10 = 765
6. 847 − __10__ = 837

Reading
Read the text. Then answer the question.

Tomorrow was Grandma's birthday. Joey and Grandpa were shopping for a card. "How about this one?" asked Joey. "Or this one? It has pink roses, her favorite. No, wait. This one's better. It has pink and yellow roses. Come here, Grandpa! Here's another one!"

7. What does the story tell you about Joey?

* __Joey is happy and excited to buy his grandma a card.__
__He notices the things he thinks his grandma will like.__

Page 61

Day 1 — Week 11

Language
Write **a** or **an** to complete the sentence.
1. Do you have __a__ banana in your lunchbox?
2. I usually eat __an__ apple at lunchtime.
3. But this time I have __an__ orange.
4. Would you like __a__ piece of my orange?

Math
Read the problem. Then answer the item.

225 kids played at the park on Monday. 10 fewer kids played at the park on Tuesday. How many kids played at the park on Tuesday?

5. __215__ kids played on Tuesday.

Mark the value in **225** that changes when you find **10** fewer.
6. ○ 5   ● 20   ○ 200

Reading
Look at the chart. Read the text. Then answer the item.

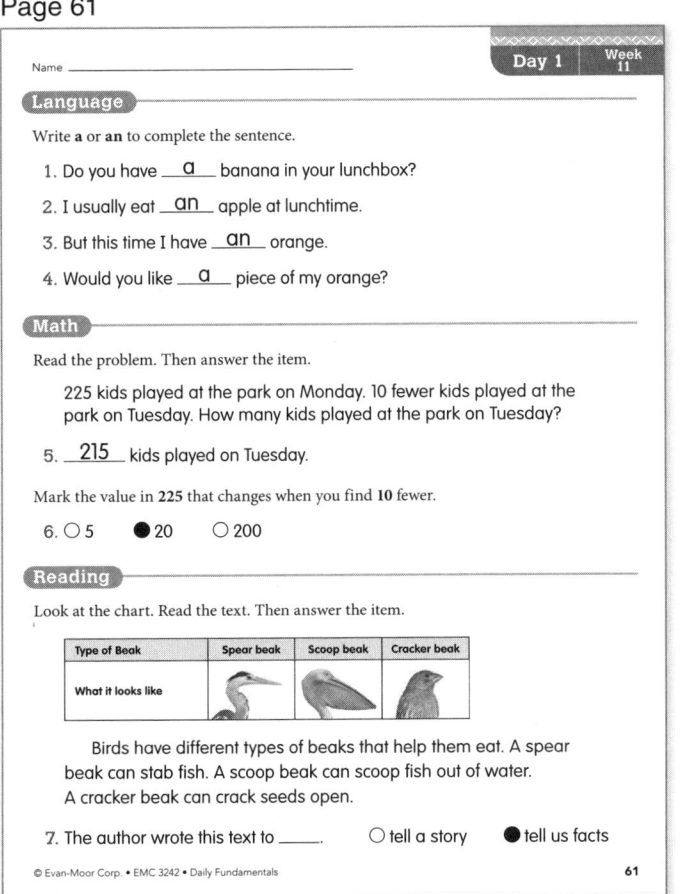

Birds have different types of beaks that help them eat. A spear beak can stab fish. A scoop beak can scoop fish out of water. A cracker beak can crack seeds open.

7. The author wrote this text to ____.   ○ tell a story   ● tell us facts

Page 62

Day 2 — Week 11

Language
Write **a** or **an** to complete the sentence.
1. Tomorrow my class will have __a__ bake sale.
2. Aunt Cathy will bake __a__ lemon cake.
3. Grandma will bake __an__ angel food cake.
4. I will buy __an__ oatmeal cookie from Miss Sanders.

Math
Read the problem. Then answer the item.

Blake has 132 rocks in his collection. Kalia gave him 10 rocks from her collection. How many rocks does Blake have now?

5. __142__ rocks

Mark the value in **132** that changes when you add **10** more.
6. ○ 2   ● 30   ○ 100

Reading
Read the text. Then answer the items.

Some things are not easy to recycle or reuse, but that doesn't mean you should throw them away. Think of how to use them in a different way. When we recycle, we make less garbage and that is good for Earth.

7. The author wrote this text to ____.
   ○ make us laugh   ● get us to do something

8. Tell how you know. __The author wants us to think about__
* __how to reuse things to make less garbage on Earth.__

These answers will vary. Examples are given.

Page 63

Day 3 | Week 11

Language
Write **I** or **me** to complete the sentence.
1. __I__ like to write stories about my life.
2. Grandma gave __me__ a blue notebook.
3. __I__ write in it almost every day.
4. Grandma always tells __me__ to keep on writing!

Math
Read the problem. Then answer the item.

On Saturday, 468 planes flew out of the airport. On Sunday, 100 more planes flew out of the airport. How many planes flew out on Sunday?

5. __568__ planes flew out on Sunday.

Mark the value in **468** that changes when you find **100** more.

6. ○ 8   ○ 60   ● 400

Reading
Read the text. Then answer the items.

One day Mama Bear said, "It's time to have a party! Baby Bear, tell our friends that we are having a party today. Sister Bear, make the honey cakes and pick the berries. Oh, and Baby Bear…Baby Bear? Did he already leave?" Mama Bear went outside and saw all their friends. Baby Bear spread his arms and said, "I told them!"

7. The author wrote this story to ____. ● make us smile ○ tell us facts

✱ 8. Tell how you know. __This story is about bears that act like people.__

Page 64

Day 4 | Week 11

Language
Write **Gil and I** on the line in the *naming* part of the sentence.
Write **Gil and me** on the line in the *telling* part of the sentence.

1. __Gil and I__ went to the park on Saturday.
2. Some kids asked __Gil and me__ to play catch with them.
3. __Gil and I__ played with them for a long time.

Math
Read the problem. Then answer the item.

Last month, my dad drove his truck 236 miles. This month, my dad drove his truck 100 miles. How many miles did he drive in both months?

4. __336__ miles

Mark the value in **236** that changes when you find **100** more.

5. ○ 6   ○ 30   ● 200

Reading
Read the text. Then answer the question.

The sun warms the land, air, and water. Sunlight warms the earth for people, animals, and plants to live. Sunlight makes plants grow. People and animals need plants for food. Without the sun, nothing could live on Earth.

6. What does the author want you to know?
✱ __The author wants me to know what sunlight does.__

Page 65

Day 5 | Week 11

Language
Write three sentences about your friend and you. Use **my friend and I** or **my friend and me**.

1. __Sentences will vary.__
2.
3.

Math
Read the problem. Then answer the item.

Muds 'n' Suds washed 151 dogs last month. They want to wash 10 fewer dogs this month. How many dogs do they want to wash this month?

4. __141__ dogs

Mark the value in **151** that changes when you find **10** fewer.

5. ○ 1   ● 50   ○ 100

Reading
Read the text. Then answer the question.

Chocolate-granola apple slices make a yummy snack. To make this snack, melt chocolate chips in the microwave. Dip slices of apple in the melted chocolate. Then dip the slices in the granola. Enjoy!

6. What does the author want you to know?
✱ __The author wants me to know how to make chocolate-granola apple slices.__

Page 66

Day 1 | Week 12

Language
Write the prefix **un-** to make a new word.
1. The family __un__packed their bags in the hotel.
2. Dad __un__folded his pants and hung them up.
3. Zack was __un__able to lift a huge bag.
4. So Dad lifted the bag onto the bed and __un__zipped the top.

Math
Read the problem. Then answer the item.

8 children arrived at Hector's party. 5 minutes later, 3 more arrived. How many children were at the party altogether?

5. ● 8 + 3 = 11
   ○ 11 − 3 = 8
   ○ 8 − 3 = 5

Reading
Read the text. Then answer the question.

After loading his truck, Mr. Walker begins his work. He parks his truck and puts his bag over his shoulder. He walks up one side of the street, stopping at every house. Then he walks down the other side of the street. Many people say hello to Mr. Walker, and some even wait for him by the curb to give him their mail.

6. What is Mr. Walker's job? Tell why you think so.
✱ __Mr. Walker is a letter carrier. I think so because he carries a bag and stops at every house.__

✱ These answers will vary. Examples are given.

Page 67

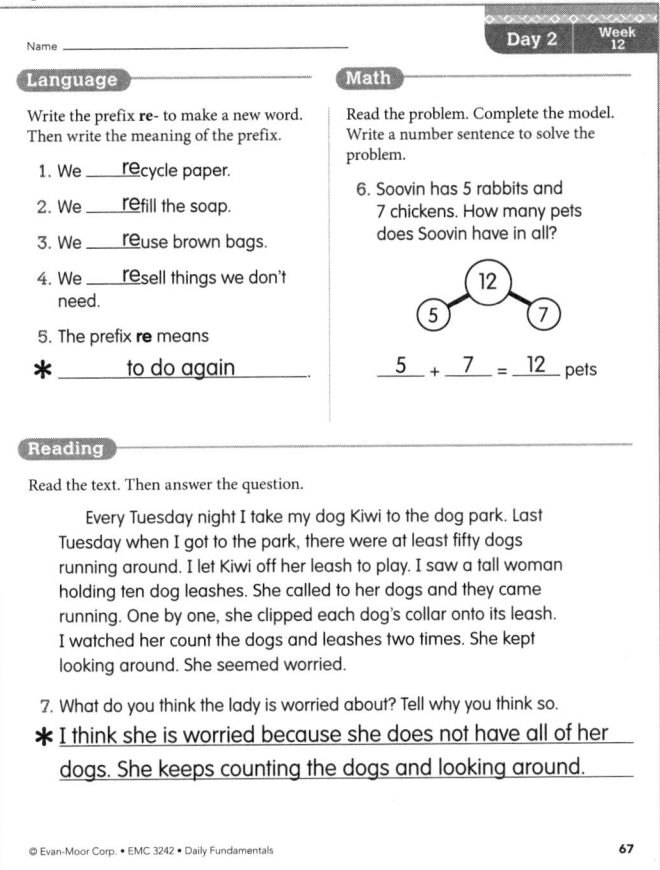

Day 2 — Week 12

Language

Write the prefix **re-** to make a new word. Then write the meaning of the prefix.

1. We __re__cycle paper.
2. We __re__fill the soap.
3. We __re__use brown bags.
4. We __re__sell things we don't need.
5. The prefix **re** means
✱ __to do again__.

Math

Read the problem. Complete the model. Write a number sentence to solve the problem.

6. Soovin has 5 rabbits and 7 chickens. How many pets does Soovin have in all?

(12) / (5) (7)

__5__ + __7__ = __12__ pets

Reading

Read the text. Then answer the question.

Every Tuesday night I take my dog Kiwi to the dog park. Last Tuesday when I got to the park, there were at least fifty dogs running around. I let Kiwi off her leash to play. I saw a tall woman holding ten dog leashes. She called to her dogs and they came running. One by one, she clipped each dog's collar onto its leash. I watched her count the dogs and leashes two times. She kept looking around. She seemed worried.

7. What do you think the lady is worried about? Tell why you think so.
✱ I think she is worried because she does not have all of her dogs. She keeps counting the dogs and looking around.

Page 68

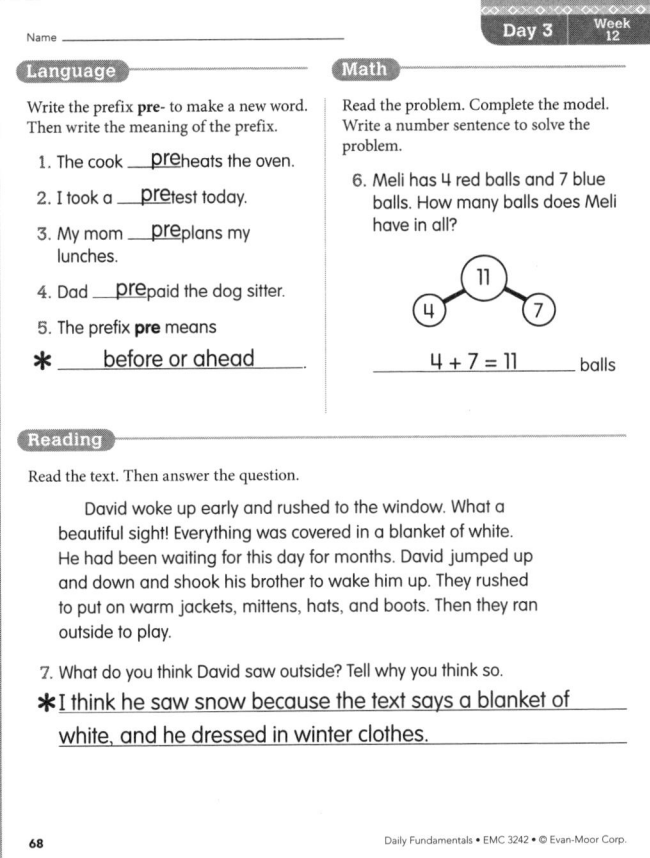

Day 3 — Week 12

Language

Write the prefix **pre-** to make a new word. Then write the meaning of the prefix.

1. The cook __pre__heats the oven.
2. I took a __pre__test today.
3. My mom __pre__plans my lunches.
4. Dad __pre__paid the dog sitter.
5. The prefix **pre** means
✱ __before or ahead__.

Math

Read the problem. Complete the model. Write a number sentence to solve the problem.

6. Meli has 4 red balls and 7 blue balls. How many balls does Meli have in all?

(11) / (4) (7)

__4 + 7 = 11__ balls

Reading

Read the text. Then answer the question.

David woke up early and rushed to the window. What a beautiful sight! Everything was covered in a blanket of white. He had been waiting for this day for months. David jumped up and down and shook his brother to wake him up. They rushed to put on warm jackets, mittens, hats, and boots. Then they ran outside to play.

7. What do you think David saw outside? Tell why you think so.
✱ I think he saw snow because the text says a blanket of white, and he dressed in winter clothes.

Page 69

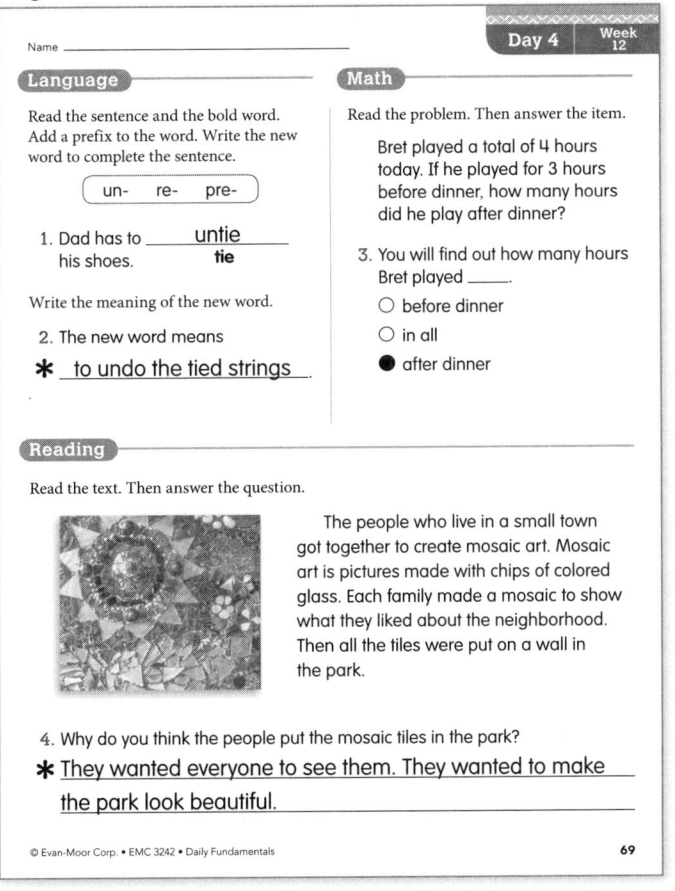

Day 4 — Week 12

Language

Read the sentence and the bold word. Add a prefix to the word. Write the new word to complete the sentence.

[un-   re-   pre-]

1. Dad has to __untie__ his shoes. **tie**

Write the meaning of the new word.

2. The new word means
✱ __to undo the tied strings__.

Math

Read the problem. Then answer the item.

Bret played a total of 4 hours today. If he played for 3 hours before dinner, how many hours did he play after dinner?

3. You will find out how many hours Bret played ___.
○ before dinner
○ in all
● after dinner

Reading

Read the text. Then answer the question.

The people who live in a small town got together to create mosaic art. Mosaic art is pictures made with chips of colored glass. Each family made a mosaic to show what they liked about the neighborhood. Then all the tiles were put on a wall in the park.

4. Why do you think the people put the mosaic tiles in the park?
✱ They wanted everyone to see them. They wanted to make the park look beautiful.

Page 70

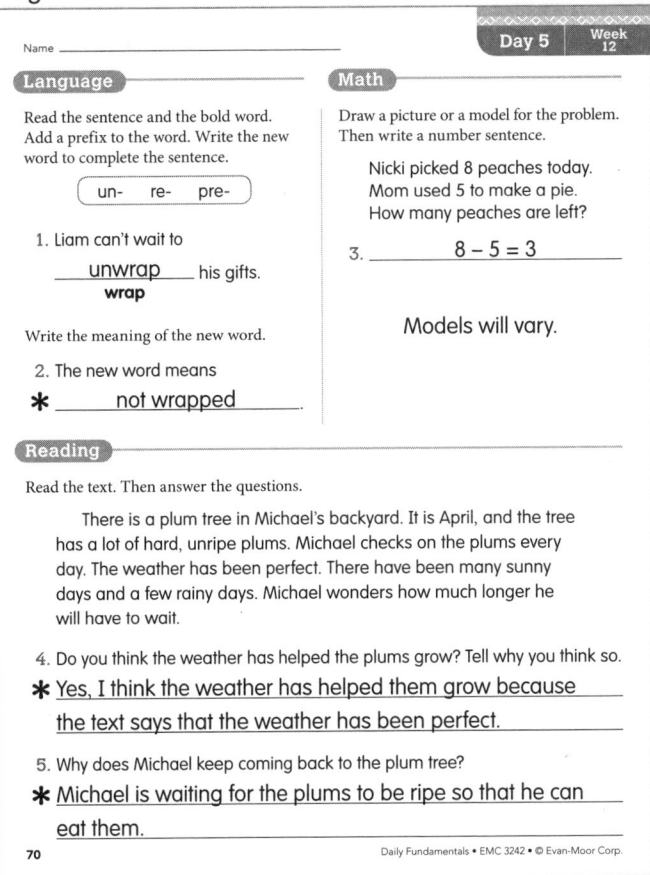

Day 5 — Week 12

Language

Read the sentence and the bold word. Add a prefix to the word. Write the new word to complete the sentence.

[un-   re-   pre-]

1. Liam can't wait to __unwrap__ his gifts. **wrap**

Write the meaning of the new word.

2. The new word means
✱ __not wrapped__.

Math

Draw a picture or a model for the problem. Then write a number sentence.

Nicki picked 8 peaches today. Mom used 5 to make a pie. How many peaches are left?

3. __8 − 5 = 3__

Models will vary.

Reading

Read the text. Then answer the questions.

There is a plum tree in Michael's backyard. It is April, and the tree has a lot of hard, unripe plums. Michael checks on the plums every day. The weather has been perfect. There have been many sunny days and a few rainy days. Michael wonders how much longer he will have to wait.

4. Do you think the weather has helped the plums grow? Tell why you think so.
✱ Yes, I think the weather has helped them grow because the text says that the weather has been perfect.

5. Why does Michael keep coming back to the plum tree?
✱ Michael is waiting for the plums to be ripe so that he can eat them.

✳ These answers will vary. Examples are given.

Page 71

Day 1 — Week 13

Language
Write the word. Then add the ending given. The first one is done for you.
1. happy **(er)**   happier
2. cry **(ed)**   cried
3. cherry **(es)**   cherries
4. funny **(est)**   funniest

Math
Read the problem. Mark the pair of number sentences that can help you solve it. Then write the answer.

Dori ate 12 red grapes and 7 green grapes. Grace ate 14 purple grapes. How many more grapes did Dori eat than Grace?

5. ● 12 + 7 = ? and 19 − 14 = ?   6. __5__ more grapes
   ○ 12 − 7 = ? and 14 − 7 = ?

Reading
Read the text. Then answer the question.

It was a warm spring day, and Jaimee was outside drawing a yellow rose. Suddenly, dark clouds appeared and it began to rain. "Oh no!" said Jaimee. "My drawing is getting wet!"

7. What will Jaimee probably do next?
   ○ She will keep drawing and enjoy the rain.
   ● She will run inside and start a new drawing.

Page 72

Day 2 — Week 13

Language
Read the sentence. Then write the correct word to complete the sentence.
1. I like __writing__ short stories about animals.
   writing   writeing   writting
2. My __latest__ story is about a funny rabbit.
   latist   latest   lattest
3. This story is much __funnier__ than my other story.
   funnyer   funier   funnier

Math
Read the problem. Then answer the item. Show your work.

Roy has 64 crayons. Jerry has 6 fewer than Roy. How many crayons do they have altogether?

4. __122__ crayons

Reading
Read the text. Then answer the question.

One summer day, Lori and Tim decided to sell cold lemonade. They set up a table in front of their house and put up a sign. Mom made a big pitcher of lemonade. In no time at all, the pitcher was empty. Thirsty customers were still coming. Lori and Tim had to act fast!

5. What will Lori and Tim probably do next?
   ○ They will take down the sign and go inside.
   ● They will ask Mom to make another pitcher of lemonade.

Page 73

Day 3 — Week 13

Language
Read the sentence. Underline the misspelled words. Then write the sentence correctly.

1. I <u>thougt</u> vanilla was your favorite flavor of ice <u>crem</u>.
   I thought vanilla was your favorite flavor of ice cream.

2. You <u>allways</u> get vanilla, but today you got a <u>difrent</u> flavor.
   You always get vanilla, but today you got a different flavor.

Math
Read the problem. Then answer the item. Show your work.

52 dads went to back-to-school night. 12 more moms went than dads. How many parents went in all?

3. __116__ parents

Reading
Read the text. Then answer the question.

The children have lots of fun during recess. They run, climb, and swing. After 20 minutes, the bell rings. The children quickly form a line.

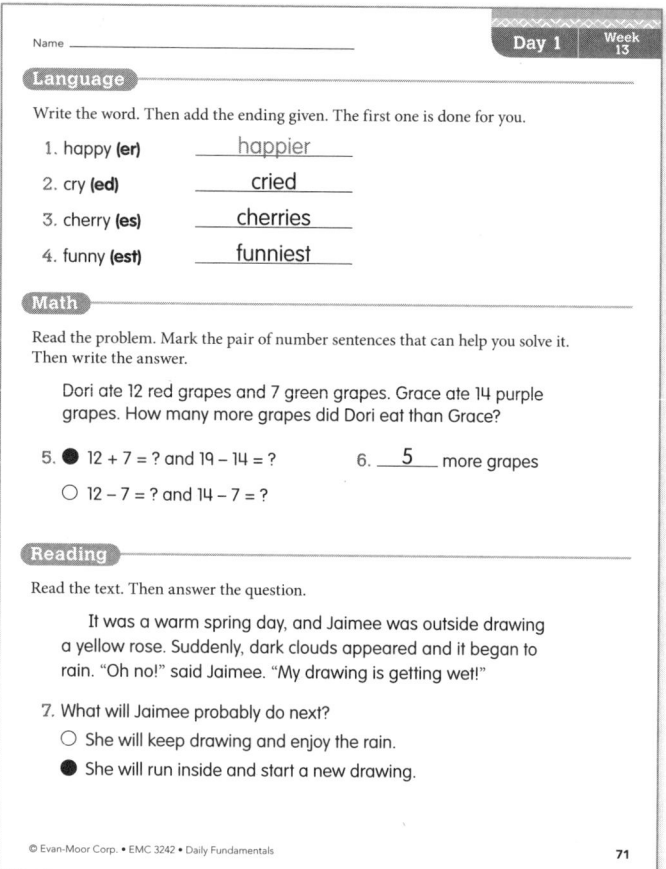

4. What do you think the children will do next?
   ✳ The children will go back into their classrooms.

Page 74

Day 4 — Week 13

Language
Read the sentence. Underline the misspelled words. Then write the sentence correctly.

1. I like to play <u>owtside</u> with my best <u>freind</u>.
   I like to play outside with my best friend.

2. <u>Woud</u> you like to play with us, <u>to</u>?
   Would you like to play with us, too?

Math
Read the problem. Then answer the item. Show your work.

13 children were playing. 8 more children joined them. Then 3 children left. How many children are still playing?

3. __18__ children

Reading
Read the text. Then answer the questions.

Kendra was sitting at the table eating breakfast. Toby, her dog, had just finished eating his food. Now he sat at the back door. Then he raised his paw and touched the door. "What's wrong, boy?" asked Kendra. "Do you need to go out?"

4. What do you predict will happen next? Why do you think so?
   ✳ Kendra will open the door for Toby. I think she will open the door because Toby acted like he needed to go outside.

These answers will vary. Examples are given.

Page 75

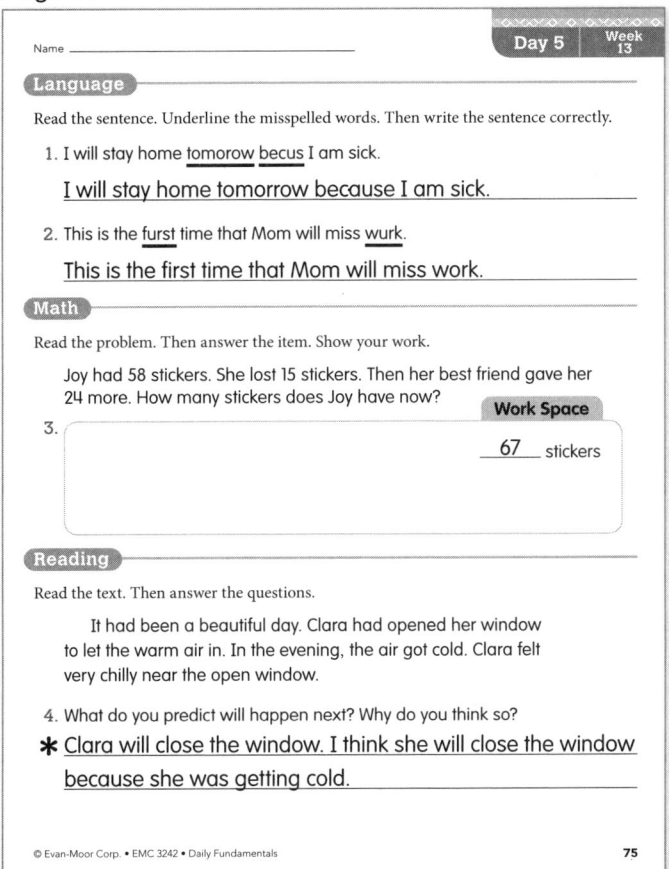

Page 76

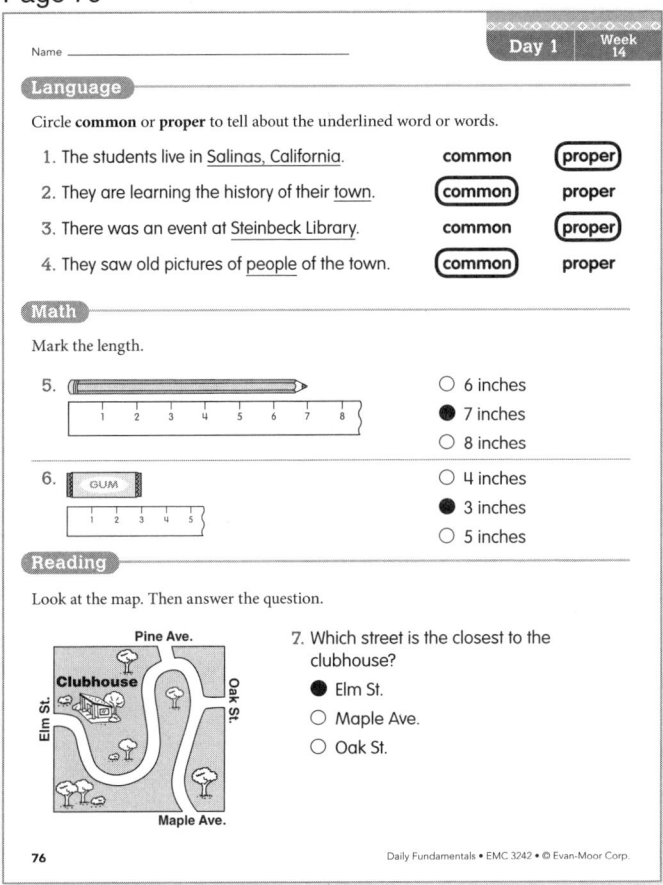

Page 77

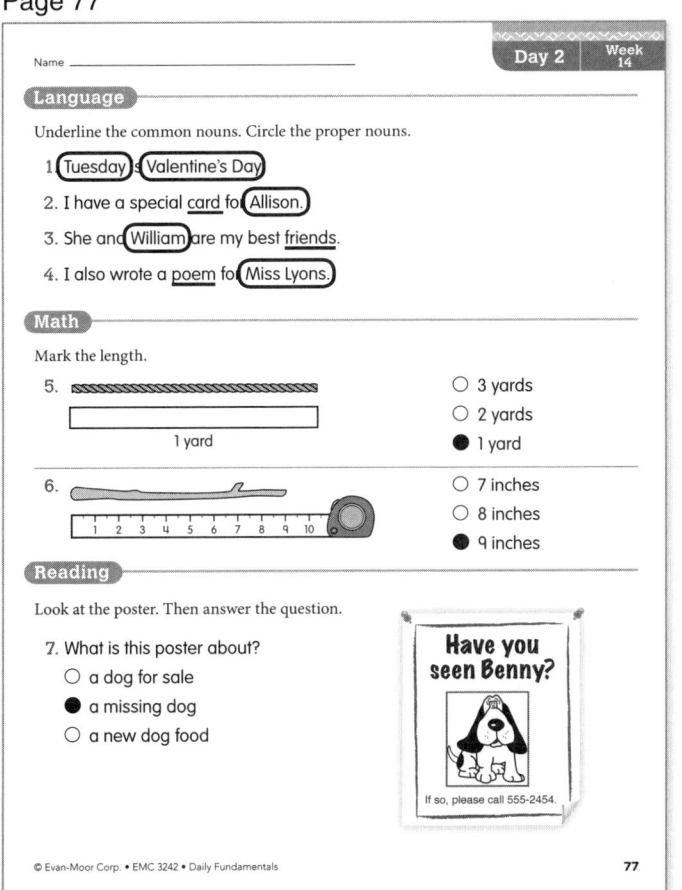

Page 78

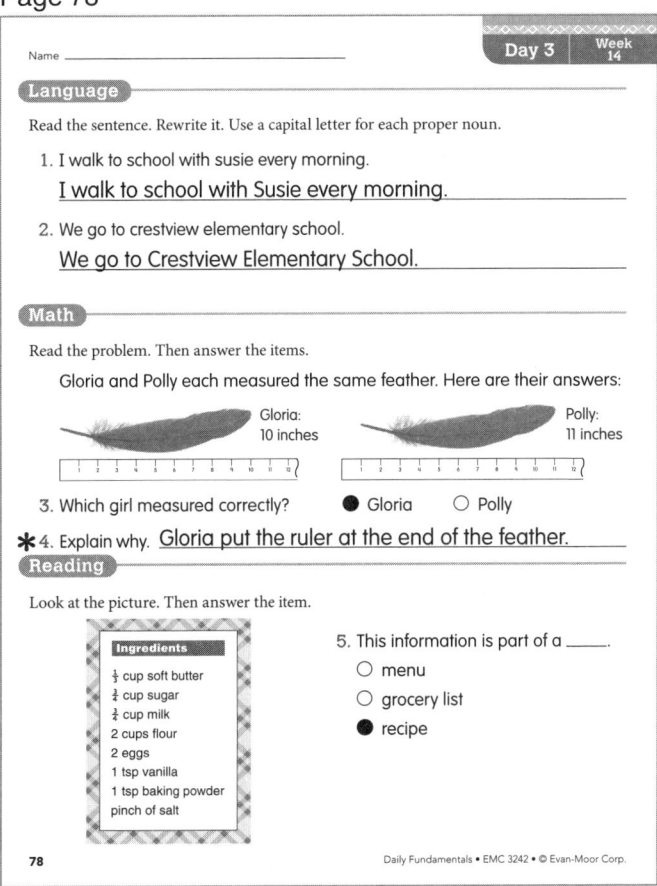

✱ These answers will vary. Examples are given.

Page 79

Day 4 — Week 14

Language

Read the sentence. Rewrite it. Use a capital letter for each proper noun.

1. Monday, wednesday, and friday I have swimming class.
   Monday, Wednesday, and Friday I have swimming class.
2. My swimming teacher's name is mr. longman.
   My swimming teacher's name is Mr. Longman.

Math

Use your inch ruler to measure the scissors.

3. 5 inches

Reading

Look at the graph. Then answer the question.

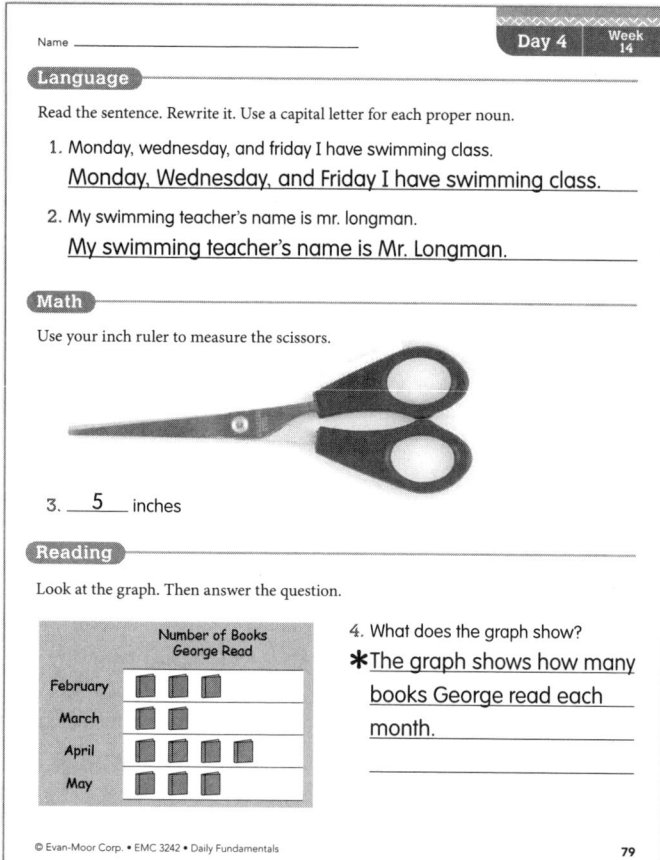

4. What does the graph show?
   ✱ The graph shows how many books George read each month.

Page 80

Day 5 — Week 14

Language

Write two sentences about your school. Use proper nouns.

1. Sentences will vary.
2. Sentences will vary.

Math

Answer the items.

3. What can you measure with an inch ruler?
   ✱ a book
4. What can you measure with a yardstick?
   ✱ a window

Reading

Look at the graph. Then answer the question.

5. What does the graph show?
   ✱ The graph shows how many people like each kind of pie.

Page 81

Day 1 — Week 15

Language

Circle the adjective that tells about the underlined noun.

1. Sunday is our (last) day at the lake.
2. It was a (short) vacation.
3. I want to stay (another) week.
4. (Two) kids from school are here.
5. Our (tiny) cabin is near the lake.
6. I hope we can visit (next) month.

Math

Mark the height.

7.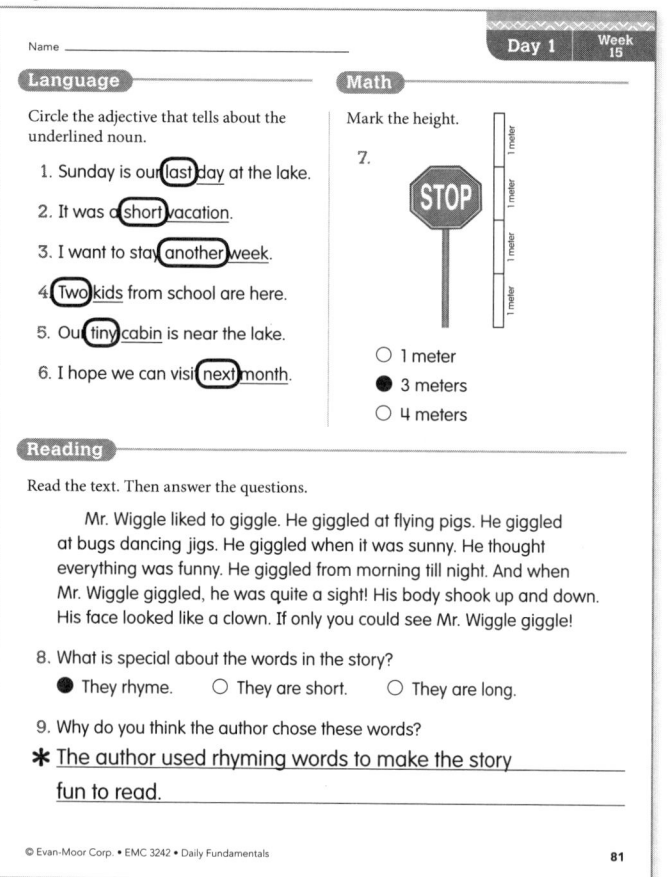
   ○ 1 meter
   ● 3 meters
   ○ 4 meters

Reading

Read the text. Then answer the questions.

Mr. Wiggle liked to giggle. He giggled at flying pigs. He giggled at bugs dancing jigs. He giggled when it was sunny. He thought everything was funny. He giggled from morning till night. And when Mr. Wiggle giggled, he was quite a sight! His body shook up and down. His face looked like a clown. If only you could see Mr. Wiggle giggle!

8. What is special about the words in the story?
   ● They rhyme.   ○ They are short.   ○ They are long.
9. Why do you think the author chose these words?
   ✱ The author used rhyming words to make the story fun to read.

Page 82

Day 2 — Week 15

Language

Underline the adjective that is comparing two people, places, or things.

1. Annie is younger than me.
2. I am taller than Annie.
3. Her house is bigger than a castle.
4. The grass looks greener on that side.
5. This summer is hotter than last summer.
6. Maybe this winter will be colder than last winter.

Math

Mark the length.

7.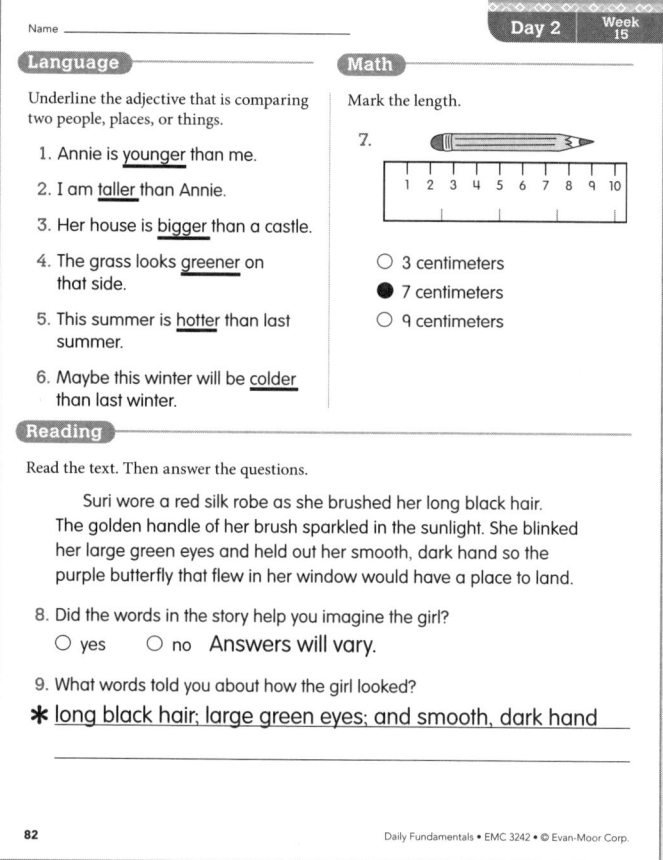
   ○ 3 centimeters
   ● 7 centimeters
   ○ 9 centimeters

Reading

Read the text. Then answer the questions.

Suri wore a red silk robe as she brushed her long black hair. The golden handle of her brush sparkled in the sunlight. She blinked her large green eyes and held out her smooth, dark hand so the purple butterfly that flew in her window would have a place to land.

8. Did the words in the story help you imagine the girl?
   ○ yes   ○ no   Answers will vary.
9. What words told you about how the girl looked?
   ✱ long black hair; large green eyes; and smooth, dark hand

These answers will vary. Examples are given.

Page 83

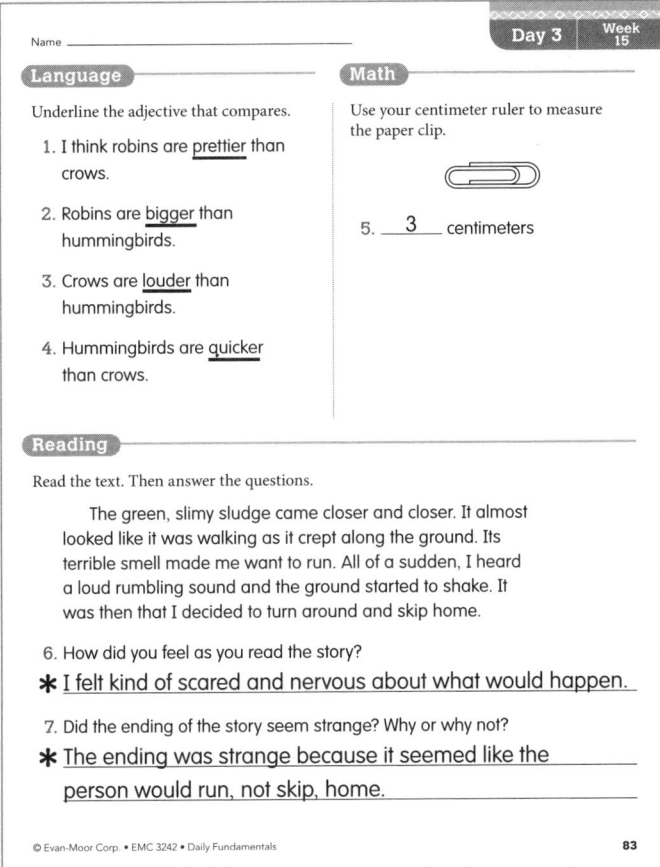

Page 84

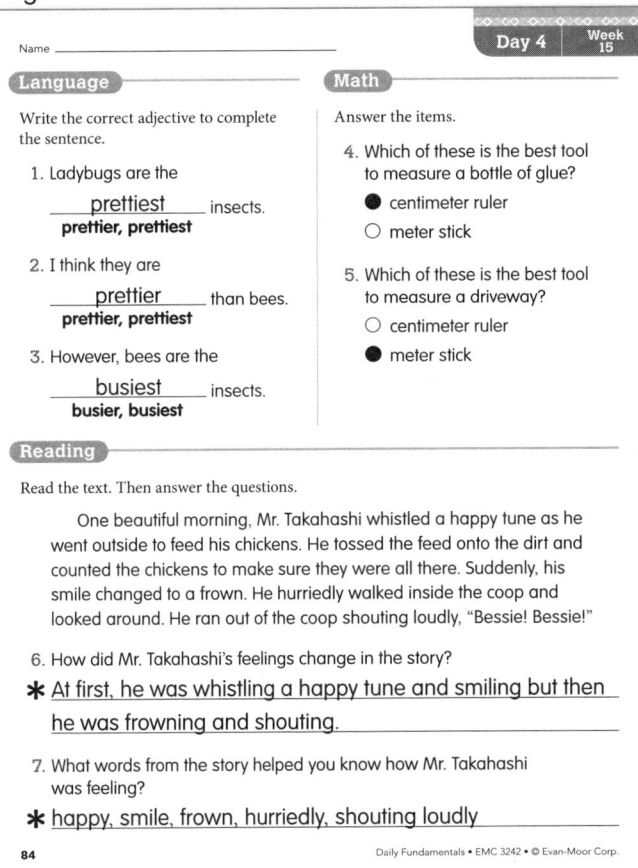

Page 85

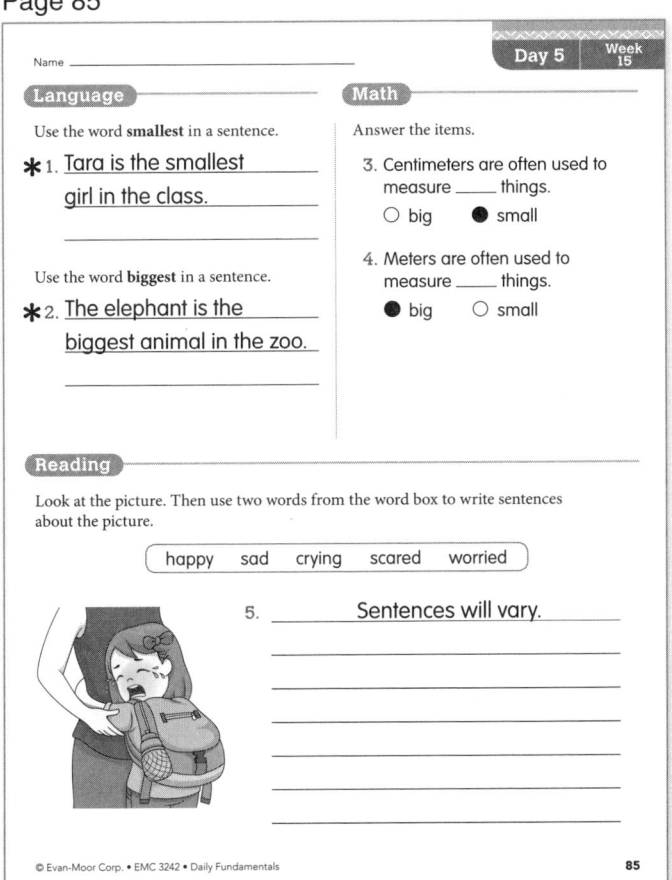

Page 86

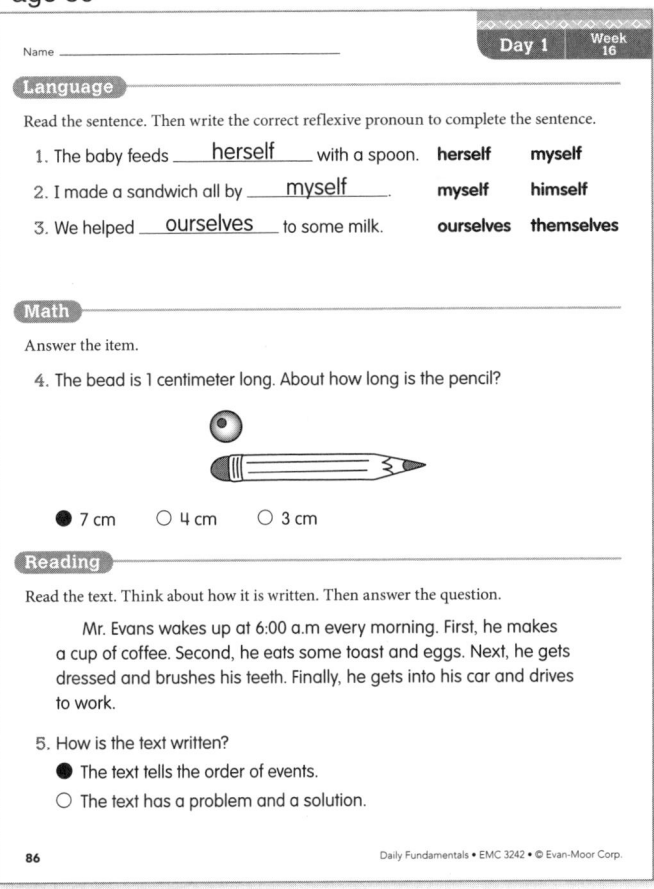

⁎ These answers will vary. Examples are given.

Page 87

Day 2 — Week 16

Language

Read the sentence. Then write the correct reflexive pronoun to complete the sentence.

1. David photographed __himself__ at the farm.
2. At this farm, you can pick strawberries __yourself__.
3. Dad almost bought a strawberry pie, but Mom said we should bake one __ourselves__ instead.

Math

Answer the item.

4. The bat is 1 yard long. About how long is the rope?

○ 3 yards   ○ 3 feet   ● 2 yards

Reading

Read the text. Think about how it is written. Then answer the question.

Last year, my family moved from California to Florida. These states are alike in many ways. Both California and Florida have a lot of sunny days. Both states also have a lot of trees, wild animals, and bugs!

5. How is the text written?
   ○ The text tells the order of events.
   ● The text compares two states.

Page 88

Day 3 — Week 16

Language

Look at the underlined word or words. Write the correct possessive pronoun to complete the sentence.

1. That red bike is Billy's. That red bike is __his__.
2. The blue bikes are the twins'. The blue bikes are __theirs__.
3. The yellow bike is Mom's. The yellow bike is __hers__.

Math

Answer the item.

4. The ruler is 1 foot long. About how long is the log?

○ 3 yards   ● 3 feet   ○ 2 feet

Reading

Read the text. Think about how it is written. Then answer the question.

Simone had a problem. She kept losing her jackets! She left them on the bus, on the playground, and at her friends' houses! Her parents were not happy about this. Finally, Simone thought of a solution. She decided to tie her jacket around her waist when she took it off. So far, it's worked!

5. How is the text written?
   ○ The text tells the order of events.
   ● The text has a problem and a solution.

Page 89

Day 4 — Week 16

Language

Read the sentence. Look at the underlined word or words. Then circle the possessive pronoun that refers to them.

1. Sandra's swimsuit is purple. She wears (hers) all summer long.
2. The twins' suits are blue. (Theirs) were on sale last month.
3. Lena, your suit looks comfortable. Where did you get (yours)?

Math

Answer the item.

4. The stick is 8 centimeters long. About how long is the bug?

○ 1 centimeter   ○ 4 centimeters   ● 2 centimeters

Reading

Look at the picture. Read the text. Then answer the questions.

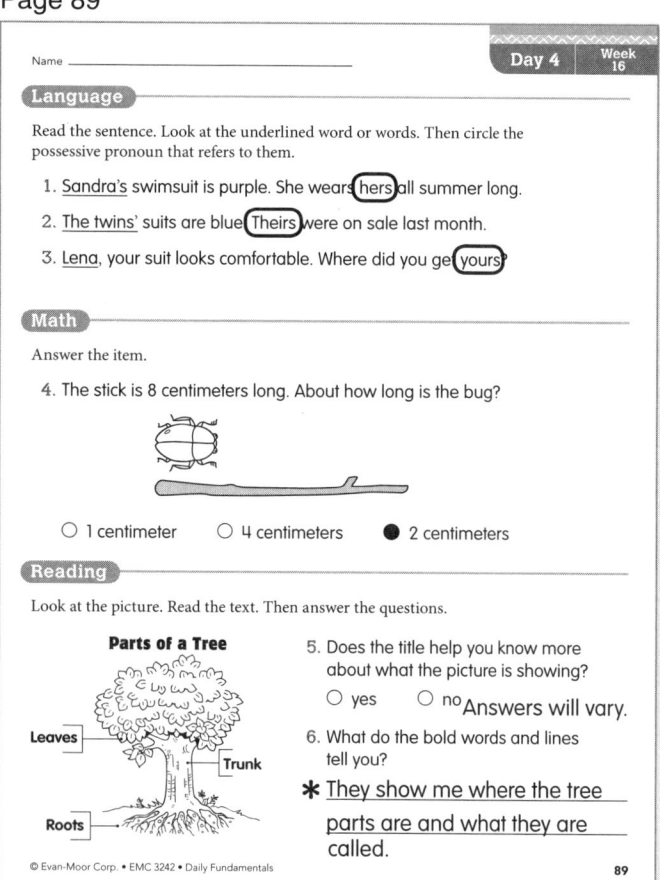

Parts of a Tree — Leaves, Trunk, Roots

5. Does the title help you know more about what the picture is showing?
   ● yes   ○ no   Answers will vary.

6. What do the bold words and lines tell you?
⁎ __They show me where the tree parts are and what they are called.__

Page 90

Day 5 — Week 16

Language

Write two sentences using a pronoun from the word box.

| theirs | his | yours | hers | ours | mine |

1. __Sentences will vary.__
2. __Sentences will vary.__

Math

Answer the item.

3. The broom is 1 meter long. About how long is the ladder?

● 2 meters   ○ 3 meters   ○ 1 meter

Reading

Look at the chart. Read the text. Then answer the question.

☀ Summer Months	Winter Months ❄
July	January
August	February

4. Why are the titles above the names of the months important?
⁎ __They tell me what the chart is for.__

✱ These answers will vary. Examples are given.

Page 91

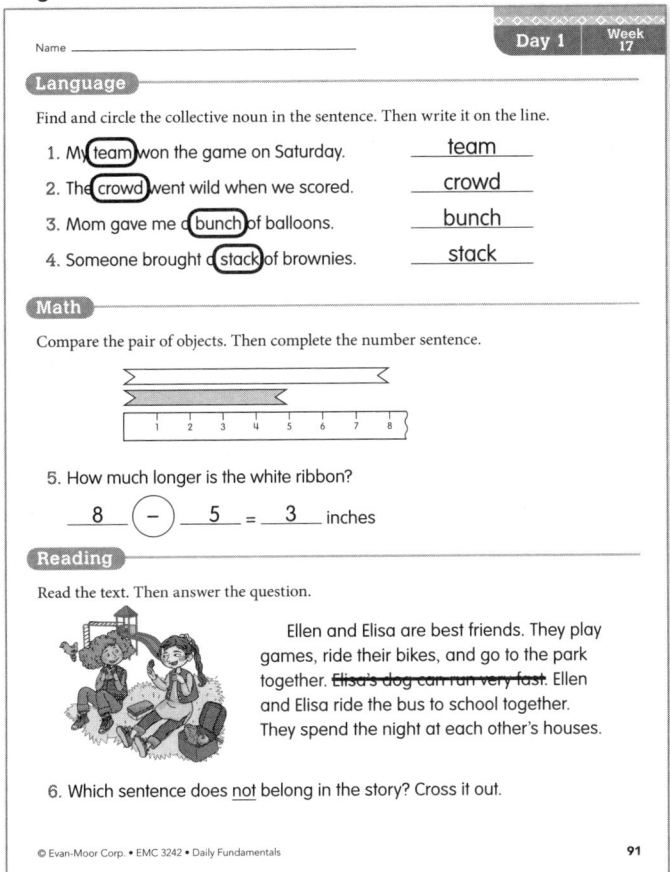

Page 92

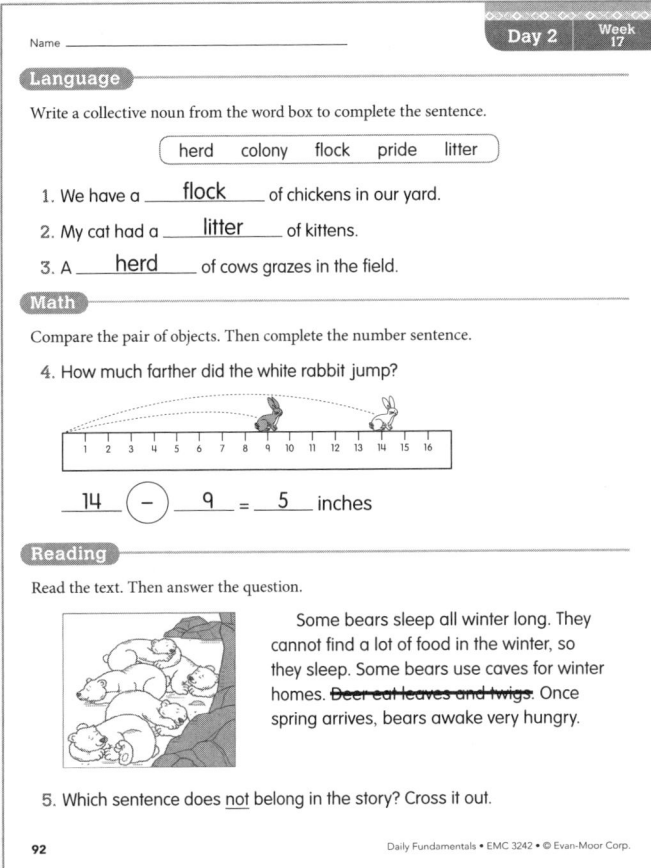

Page 93

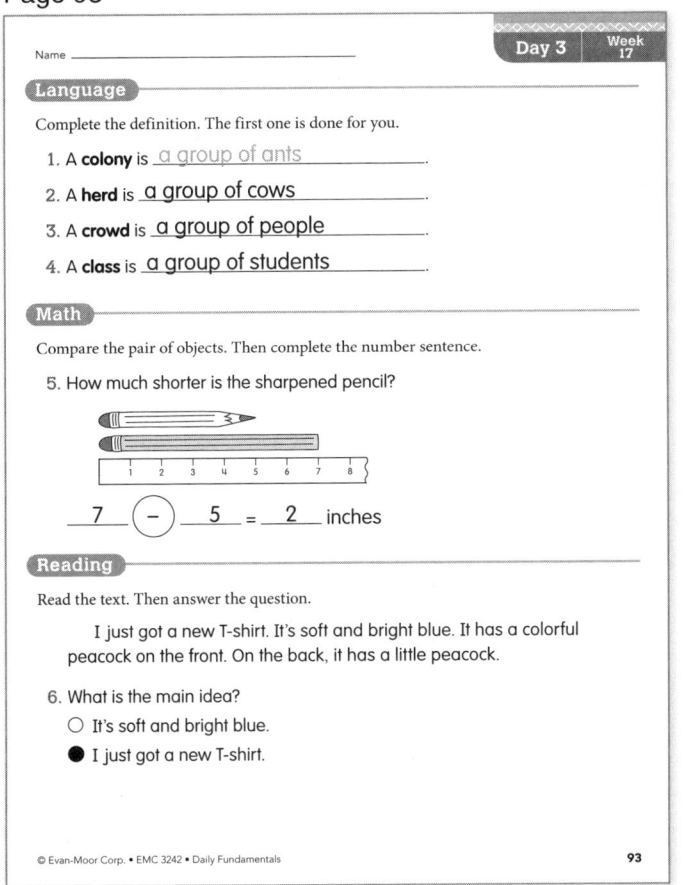

Page 94

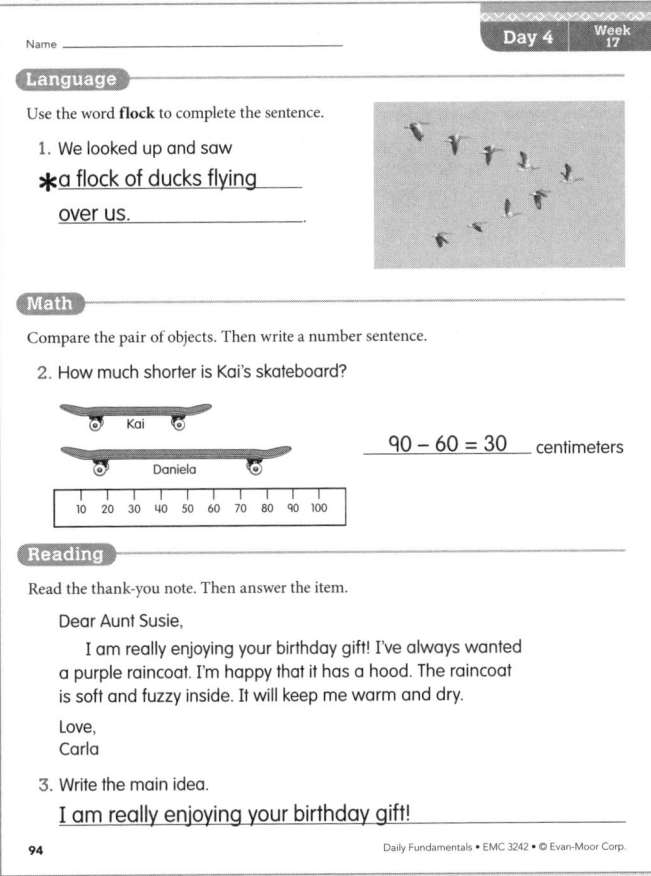

✳ These answers will vary. Examples are given.

Page 95

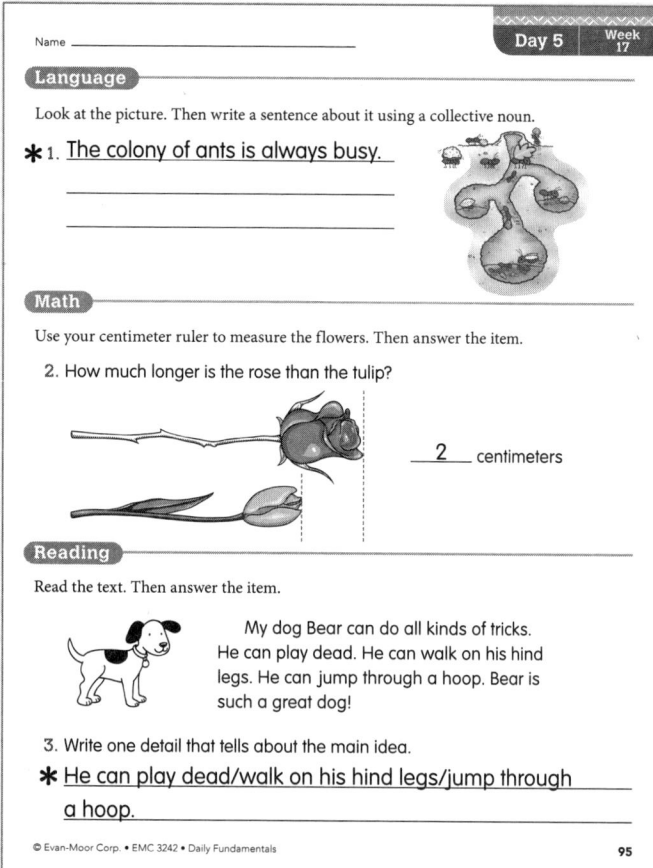

Language

Look at the picture. Then write a sentence about it using a collective noun.

✳ 1. The colony of ants is always busy.

Math

Use your centimeter ruler to measure the flowers. Then answer the item.

2. How much longer is the rose than the tulip?

_2_ centimeters

Reading

Read the text. Then answer the item.

My dog Bear can do all kinds of tricks. He can play dead. He can walk on his hind legs. He can jump through a hoop. Bear is such a great dog!

3. Write one detail that tells about the main idea.

✳ He can play dead/walk on his hind legs/jump through a hoop.

Page 96

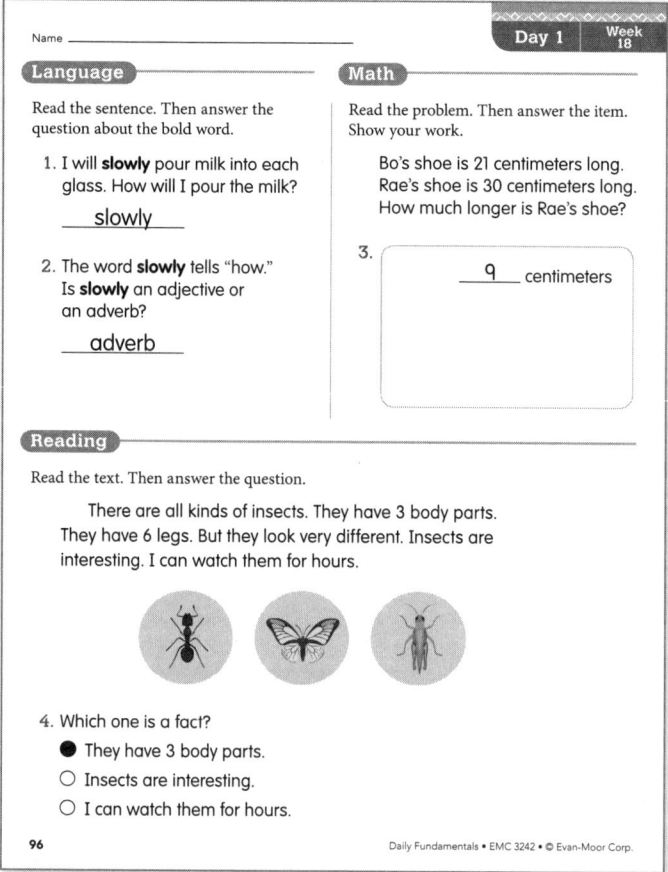

Language

Read the sentence. Then answer the question about the bold word.

1. I will **slowly** pour milk into each glass. How will I pour the milk?

slowly

2. The word **slowly** tells "how." Is **slowly** an adjective or an adverb?

adverb

Math

Read the problem. Then answer the item. Show your work.

Bo's shoe is 21 centimeters long. Rae's shoe is 30 centimeters long. How much longer is Rae's shoe?

3. _9_ centimeters

Reading

Read the text. Then answer the question.

There are all kinds of insects. They have 3 body parts. They have 6 legs. But they look very different. Insects are interesting. I can watch them for hours.

4. Which one is a fact?
● They have 3 body parts.
○ Insects are interesting.
○ I can watch them for hours.

Page 97

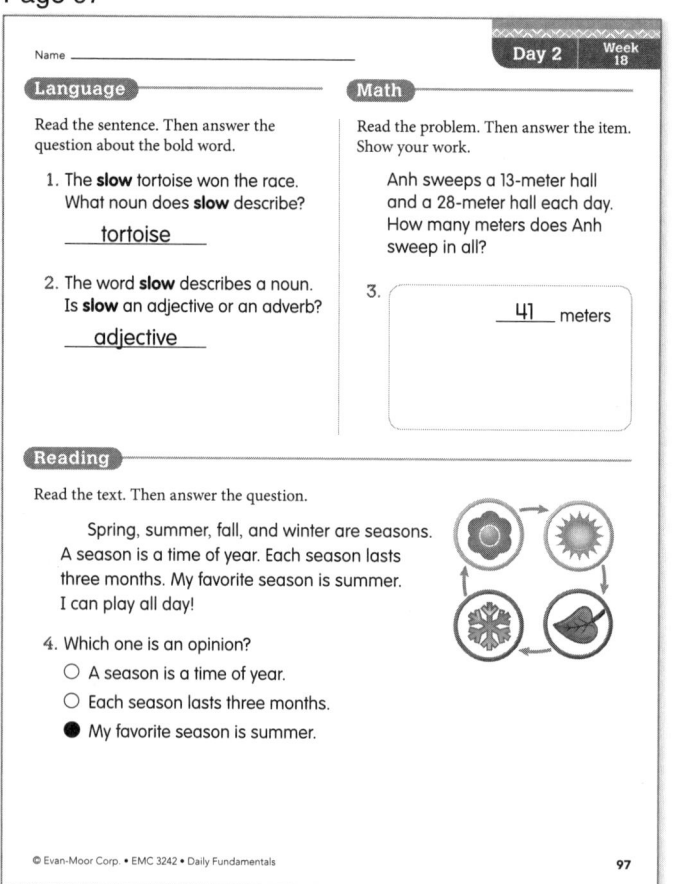

Language

Read the sentence. Then answer the question about the bold word.

1. The **slow** tortoise won the race. What noun does **slow** describe?

tortoise

2. The word **slow** describes a noun. Is **slow** an adjective or an adverb?

adjective

Math

Read the problem. Then answer the item. Show your work.

Anh sweeps a 13-meter hall and a 28-meter hall each day. How many meters does Anh sweep in all?

3. _41_ meters

Reading

Read the text. Then answer the question.

Spring, summer, fall, and winter are seasons. A season is a time of year. Each season lasts three months. My favorite season is summer. I can play all day!

4. Which one is an opinion?
○ A season is a time of year.
○ Each season lasts three months.
● My favorite season is summer.

Page 98

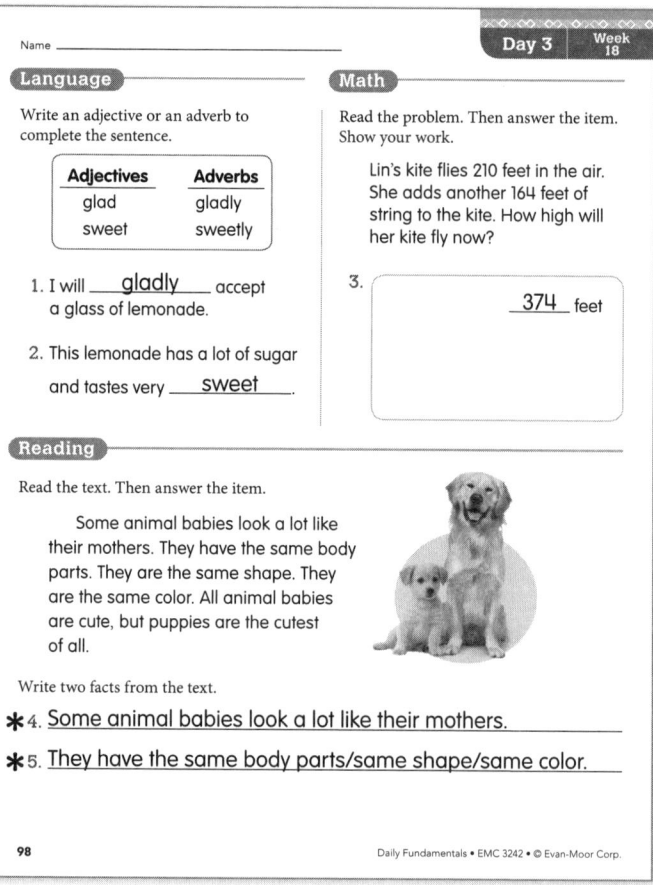

Language

Write an adjective or an adverb to complete the sentence.

Adjectives	Adverbs
glad	gladly
sweet	sweetly

1. I will _gladly_ accept a glass of lemonade.

2. This lemonade has a lot of sugar and tastes very _sweet_.

Math

Read the problem. Then answer the item. Show your work.

Lin's kite flies 210 feet in the air. She adds another 164 feet of string to the kite. How high will her kite fly now?

3. _374_ feet

Reading

Read the text. Then answer the item.

Some animal babies look a lot like their mothers. They have the same body parts. They are the same shape. They are the same color. All animal babies are cute, but puppies are the cutest of all.

Write two facts from the text.

✳ 4. Some animal babies look a lot like their mothers.

✳ 5. They have the same body parts/same shape/same color.

* These answers will vary. Examples are given.

Page 99

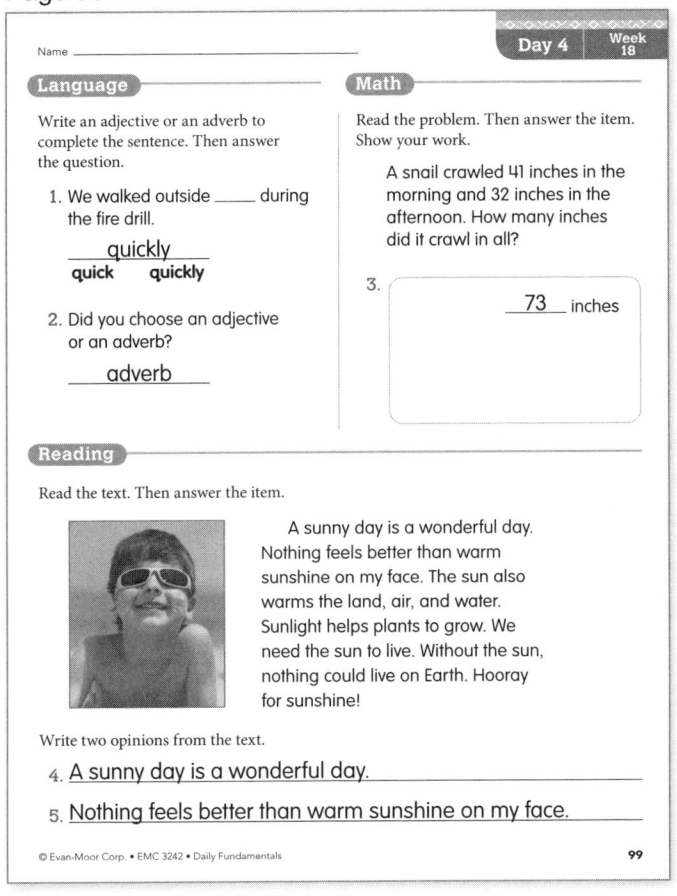

Page 100

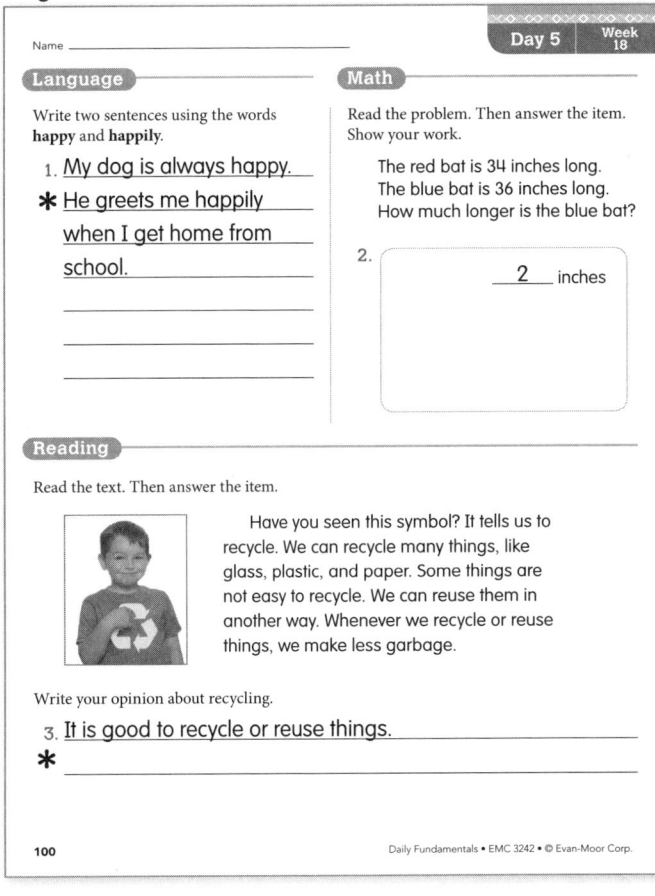

Page 101

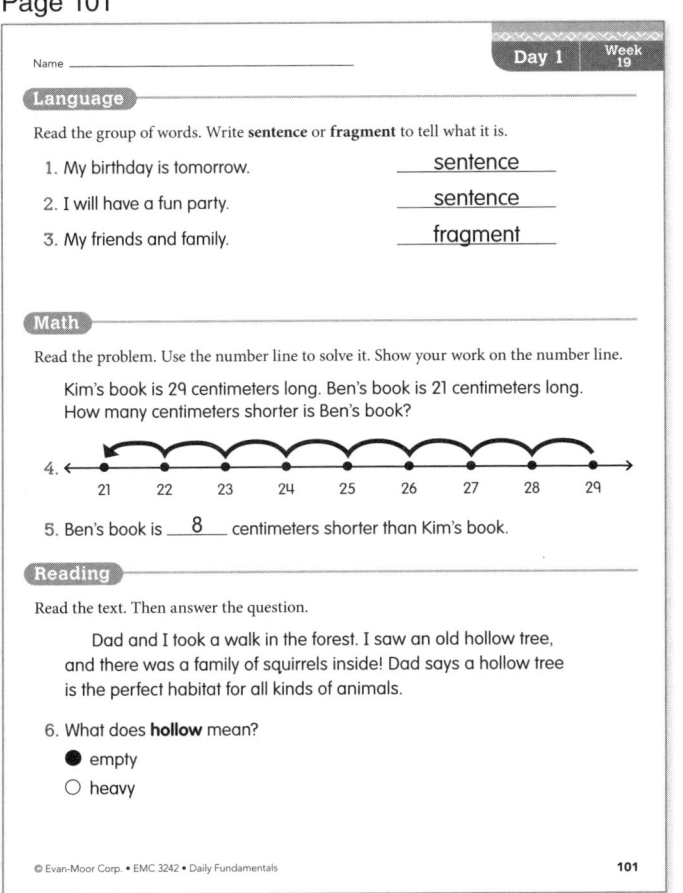

Page 102

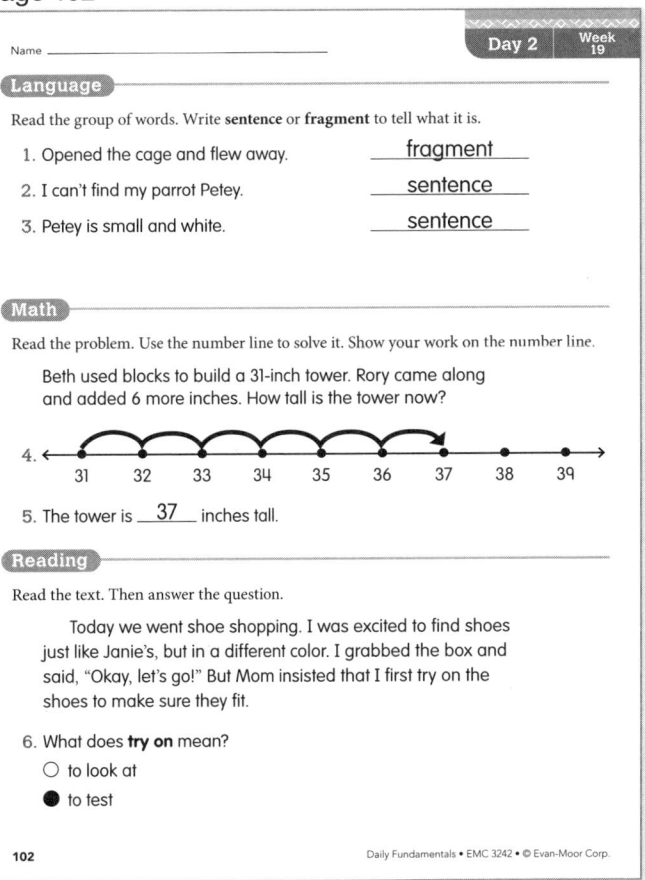

These answers will vary. Examples are given.

Page 103

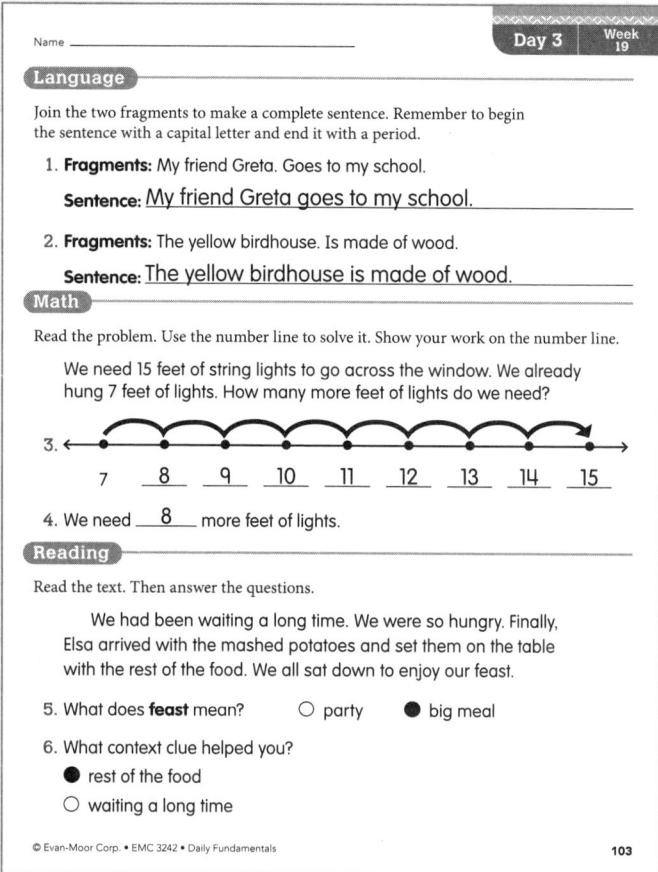

Page 104

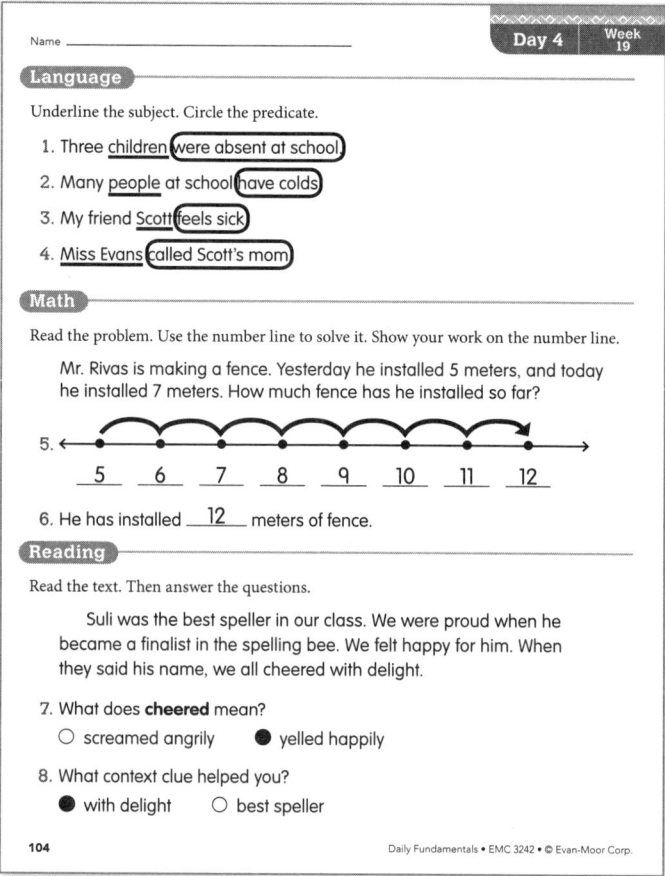

Page 105

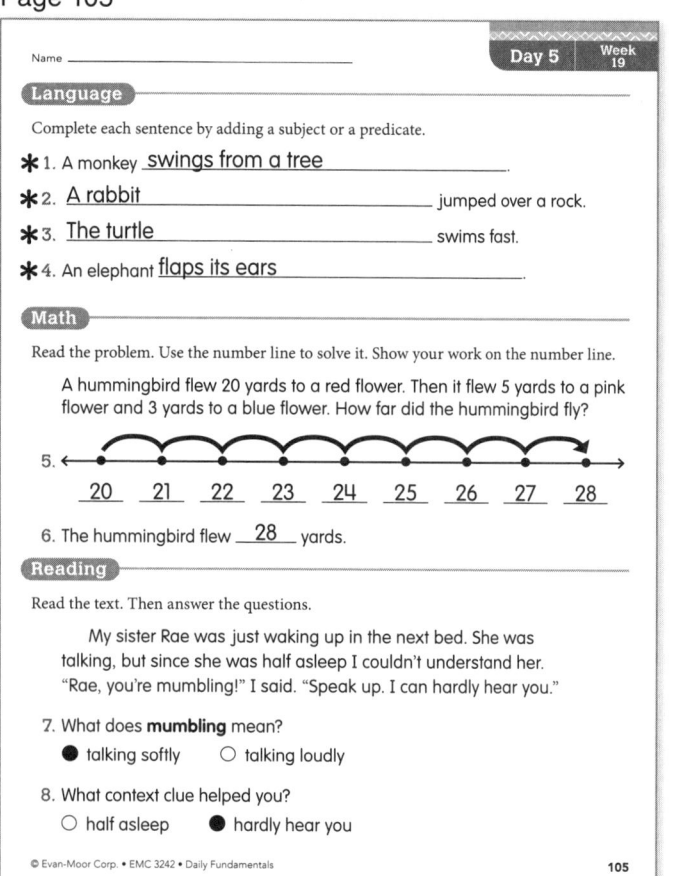

Page 106

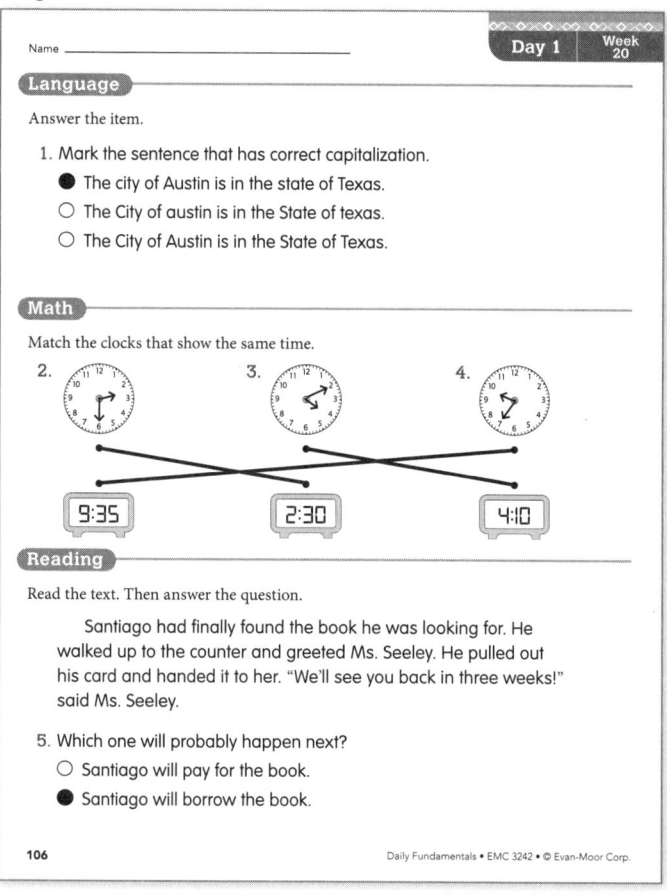

These answers will vary. Examples are given.

Page 107

Day 2 — Week 20

Language
Rewrite the sentence. Use a capital letter where needed.

1. Our house in chicago was close to lake michigan.
   Our house in Chicago was close to Lake Michigan.
2. Aunt mary lives in washington near the city of seattle.
   Aunt Mary lives in Washington near the city of Seattle.

Math
Write the time.

3. 12:45
4. 3:55
5. 8:05

Reading
Read the text. Then answer the question.

My name is Jerome. I have a dog named Hoover. If you drop any food—poof!—he eats it. I don't mind because it is my job to wipe the table and sweep the floor after dinner. I hardly have any work to do with Hoover around! I just wipe the food onto the floor. But Dad doesn't like it when Hoover eats food off the floor, so he started putting him outside.

6. How will Hoover being outside change Jerome's job?
   * I think Jerome will have more work to do because Hoover will not be there to eat the food off the floor.

Page 108

Day 3 — Week 20

Language
Read the sentence. Rewrite the sentence using capital letters where needed.

1. We rafted along the colorado river.
   We rafted along the Colorado River.
2. We drove six hours to the state of arizona.
   We drove six hours to the state of Arizona.

Math
Mark the matching time.

3. 7 o'clock in the evening — ● 7 p.m.
4. 2 o'clock in the afternoon — ● 2 p.m.
5. 8 o'clock in the morning — ● 8 a.m.
6. 10 o'clock at night — ● 10 p.m.

Reading
Read the text. Then answer the question.

This summer, Jada has a piano class that meets at 8:00 a.m. It's very early, but she really wants to learn to play. Jada has been late to class twice, and she doesn't want to be late again. Jada and her mom went to the store and bought an alarm clock.

7. What do you predict will happen next? Tell why you think so.
   * I think Jada will be on time for class because the alarm clock will ring and wake her up.

Page 109

Day 4 — Week 20

Language
Read the sentence. Rewrite the sentence using capital letters where needed.

1. Death valley national park is very hot.
   Death Valley National Park is very hot.
2. The park is in the states of california and nevada.
   The park is in the states of California and Nevada.

Math
Write **a.m.** or **p.m.** to tell when each action likely happened.

3. Dad picked me up after school. — p.m.
4. My brother and I got dressed for school. — a.m.
5. We sat around the campfire after dinner. — p.m.
6. After lunch, we went for a walk in the forest. — p.m.

Reading
Read the text. Then answer the question.

Beavers need a place to live. Beavers use sticks, grass, and mud to build their homes. First, beavers use their sharp front teeth to cut wood. Then they push the wood through the water to the lodge where they stack the wood. Next, they use their claws to scoop up mud and grass. Finally, they pack mud and grass on top of the lodge to hold the sticks together.

7. What do you predict the beavers will do next? Tell why you think so.
   * I think they will live in the lodge because they have finished building their home.

Page 110

Day 5 — Week 20

Language
Read the sentence. Rewrite the sentence using capital letters where needed.

1. We are going to disney world in florida.
   We are going to Disney World in Florida.
2. We live near myrtle beach, south carolina.
   We live near Myrtle Beach, South Carolina.

Math
Write the time that you do each activity. Write the time with **a.m.** or **p.m.**

3. * 7:00 a.m.
4. * 8:30 p.m.

Reading
Read the text. Then answer the question.

The day is cool and breezy, which is perfect for Emma. She tells her mom that she doesn't need any help and pulls a small table to the sidewalk. She carefully places 10 plates filled with cookies on the table. Soon there is a crowd of people at her table. She has only two plates of cookies left.

5. What do you predict Emma will do next?
   * She will ask her mom to bring her more plates of cookies.

These answers will vary. Examples are given.

Page 111

Day 1 — Week 21

Language

Read the sentence. Write a synonym for the underlined word.

pretty   smart   little   scared

1. I have a small cat. **little**
2. She is so beautiful. **pretty**
3. She is afraid of dogs. **scared**

Math

Write the amount shown. Use ¢ or $.

4. $3.60

Reading

Read the text. Then answer the question.

Peanut Butter Apple Slices
Ingredients: apples, peanut butter, raisins
1. Cut the apples into slices.
2. Spread peanut butter on the slices.
3. Top with raisins.

5. Why did the author include a numbered list?
- ○ to give facts about apples
- ● to tell the steps to follow
- ○ to list the ingredients

Page 112

Day 2 — Week 21

Language

Read the sentence. Write a synonym for the underlined word.

big   bought   many   built

1. I have a large dollhouse. **big**
2. It has several rooms. **many**
3. My grandpa made it. **built**

Math

Read the problem. Then answer the item. Show your work.

4. Sally found one quarter, two dimes, and five nickels. How much money did she find?
- ● 70¢
- ○ 75¢
- ○ 65¢

Reading

Read the text. Then answer the item.

It's snowing! It's snowing!
Let's go out to play.
Put on mittens. Grab your scarf.
We'll have fun today!

5. The author wrote this text to ___.
- ● make us smile
- ○ give us facts

Page 113

Day 3 — Week 21

Language

Read the sentence. Write an antonym for the underlined word.

asleep   sold   got   day

1. We bought a puppy last week. **sold**
2. He cries during the night. **day**
3. When he is awake, he plays. **asleep**

Math

Read the problem. Then answer the item. Show your work.

Ava wants to buy some glitter pens that cost $12. She has saved $8 so far. How much more money does Ava need?

4. Ava needs $ **4** more.

Reading

Read the text. Then answer the item.

You should brush your teeth after breakfast and before bed. Brushing your teeth keeps them clean. Brushing makes your teeth white. This gives you a nice smile. Be good to your teeth.

5. The author wrote this text to ___.
- ○ make us smile
- ● get us to do something

Page 114

Day 4 — Week 21

Language

Draw a line to match the word to its antonym.

1. sweet — sour
2. early — late
3. tall — short
4. many — few
5. black — white
6. thick — thin
7. come — go

Math

Read the problem. Then answer the item. Show your work.

A marker costs 75¢. Sadie has 2 quarters and 2 dimes. Does she have enough for a marker?

8. ○ yes   ● no

Reading

Read the text. Then answer the question.

There are several tools to help you know what the weather is like.

- A thermometer tells the temperature.
- A rain gauge tells how much rain has fallen.
- A windsock shows from which direction the wind blows.

9. Why did the author write this text?
* to tell us something; to give us facts

These answers will vary. Examples are given.

Page 115

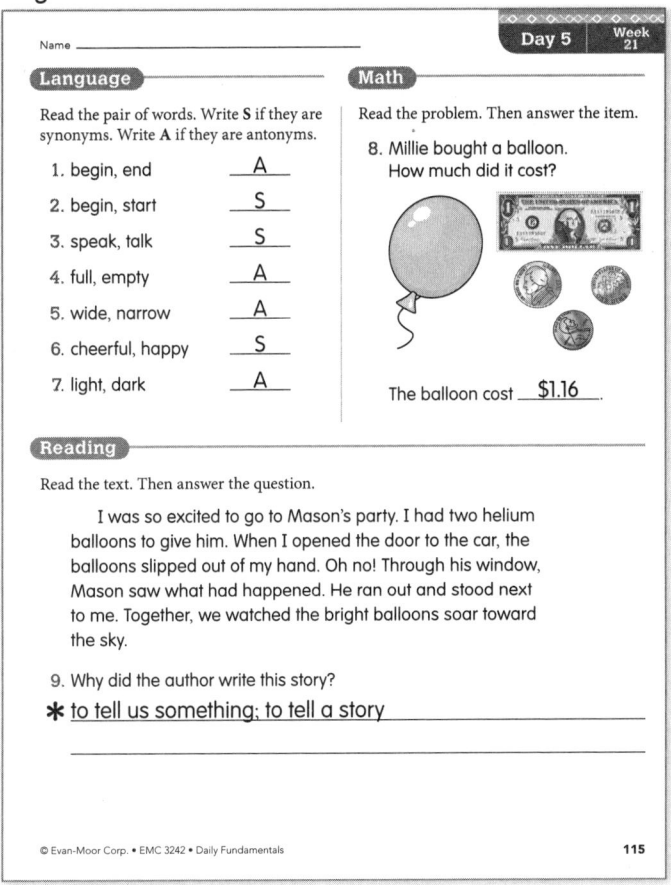

Page 116

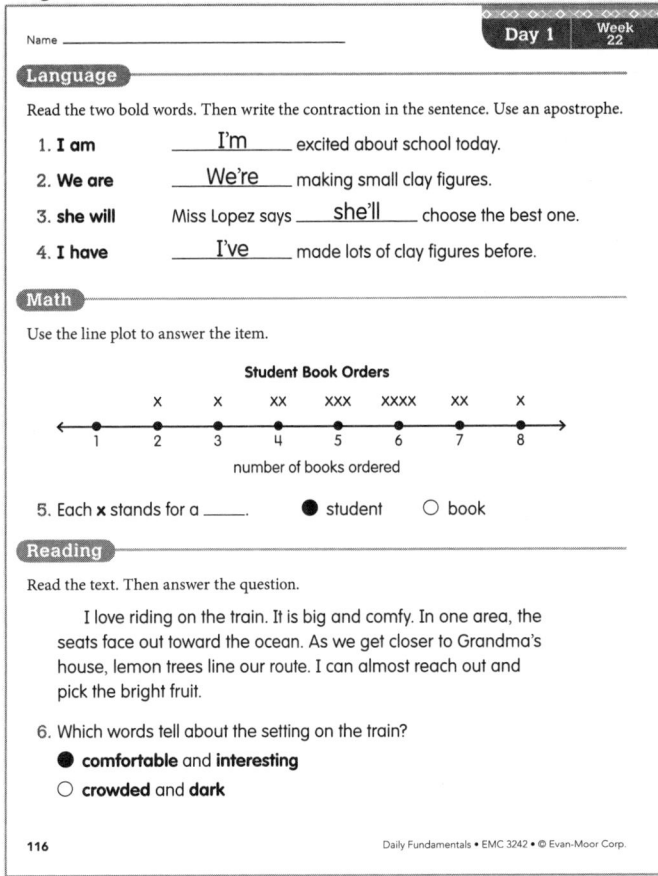

Page 117

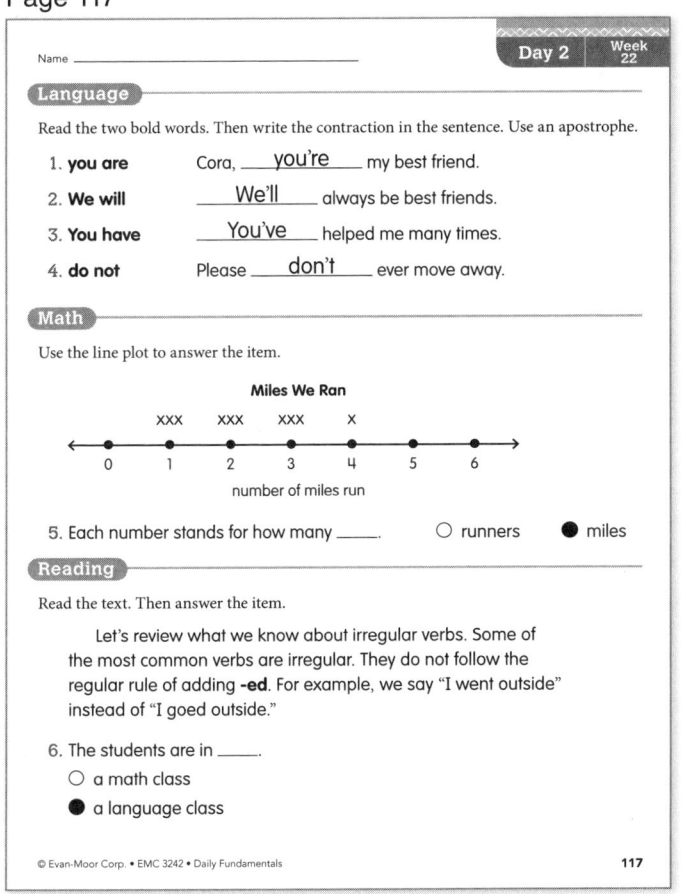

Page 118

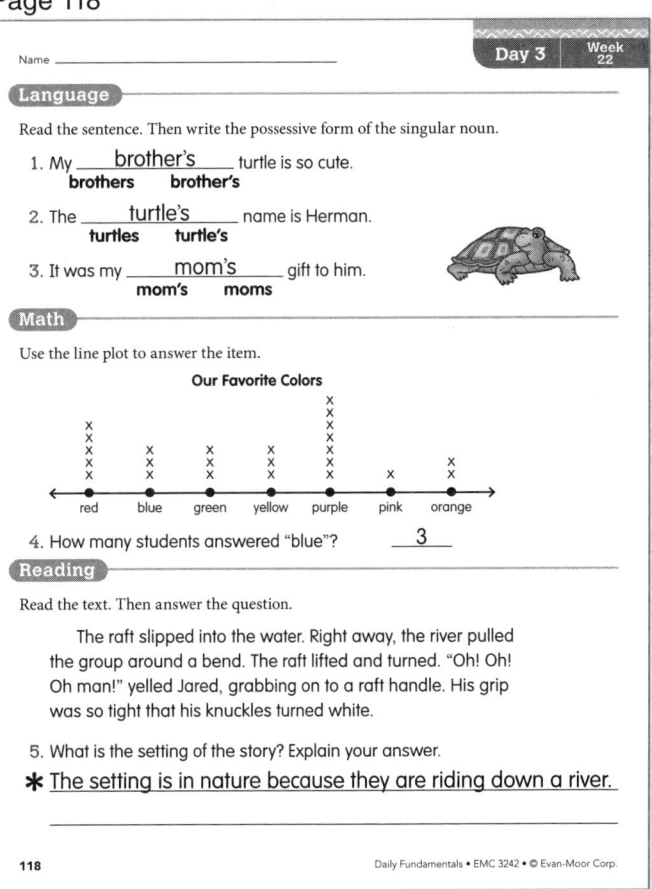

⁕ These answers will vary. Examples are given.

Page 119

Day 4 | Week 22

Language
Read the sentence pair. Then write the possessive to show who or what owns something. Use an apostrophe.
1. The red lunchbox belongs to Sam. It is __Sam's__ lunchbox.
2. The zipper on the backpack broke. The __backpack's__ zipper broke.
3. Give this sweater to Jeff. This is __Jeff's__ sweater.

Math
Use the line plot to answer the item.

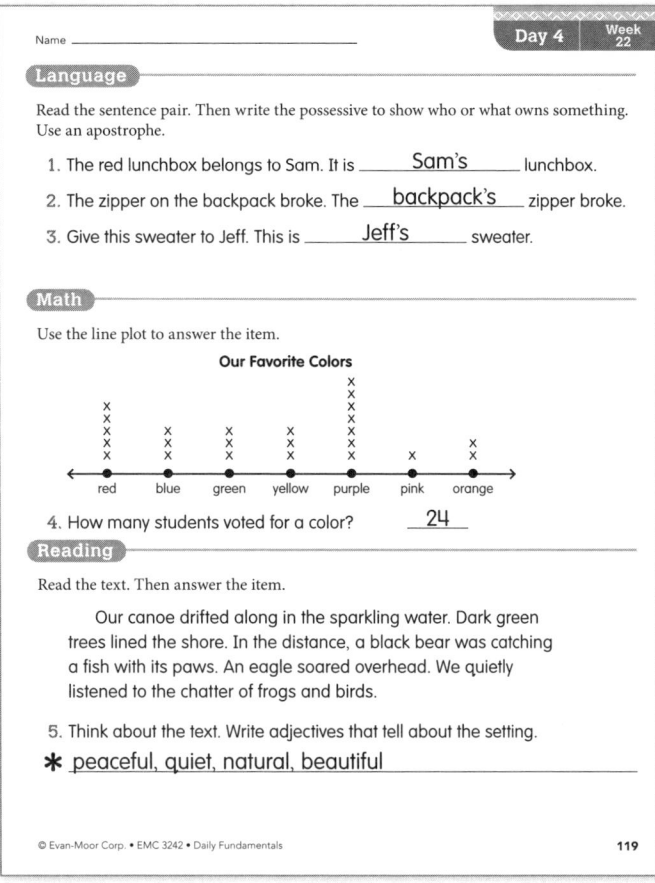

4. How many students voted for a color? __24__

Reading
Read the text. Then answer the item.

Our canoe drifted along in the sparkling water. Dark green trees lined the shore. In the distance, a black bear was catching a fish with its paws. An eagle soared overhead. We quietly listened to the chatter of frogs and birds.

5. Think about the text. Write adjectives that tell about the setting.
⁕ __peaceful, quiet, natural, beautiful__

Page 120

Day 5 | Week 22

Language
Read the sentence. Then write the possessive form of the plural noun.
1. My two __friends'__ birthdays fall on the same day.
   friend's   friends'
2. The __twins'__ names are Jordan and Austin.
   twins'   twin's
3. All the __guests'__ gifts are on that table.
   guest's   guests'

Math
Use the line plot to answer the item.

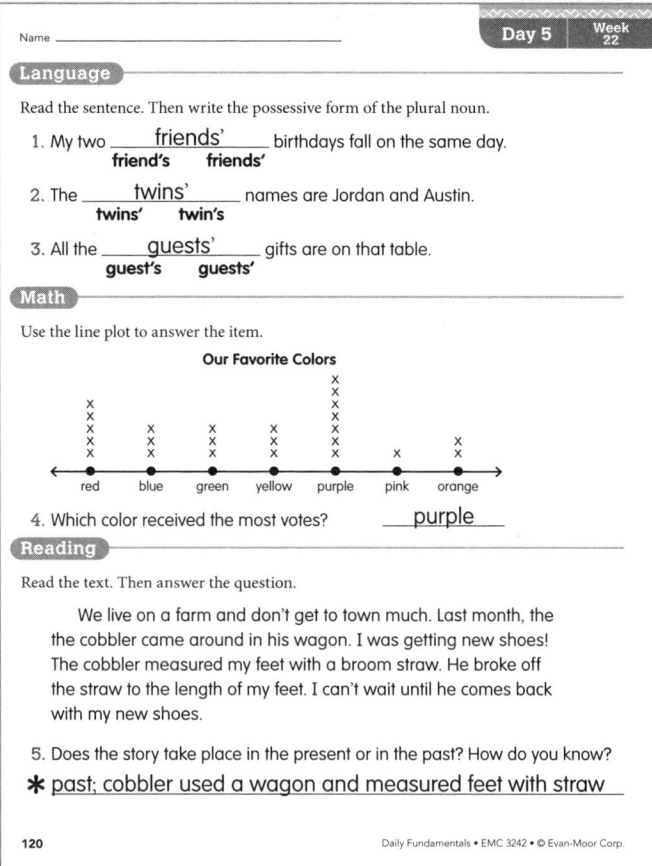

4. Which color received the most votes? __purple__

Reading
Read the text. Then answer the question.

We live on a farm and don't get to town much. Last month, the the cobbler came around in his wagon. I was getting new shoes! The cobbler measured my feet with a broom straw. He broke off the straw to the length of my feet. I can't wait until he comes back with my new shoes.

5. Does the story take place in the present or in the past? How do you know?
⁕ __past; cobbler used a wagon and measured feet with straw__

Page 121

Day 1 | Week 23

Language
Read the sentence. Then write the correct word to complete the sentence.
1. I am very __good__ at math.
   good   well
2. I did __well__ on my math test.
   good   well
3. I had a __good__ day at school today.
   good   well

Math
Use the data chart to complete the line plot.

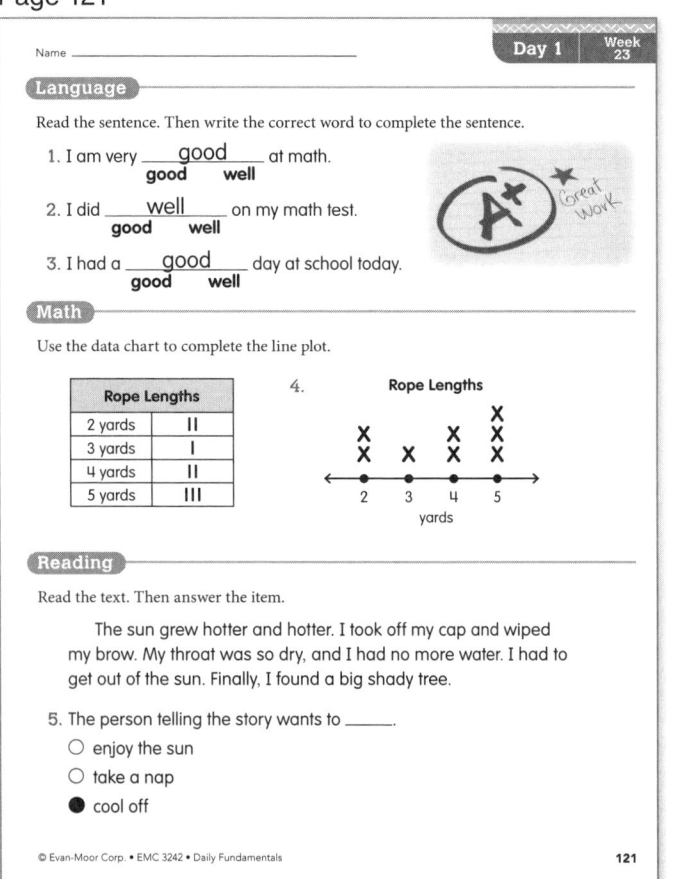

Reading
Read the text. Then answer the item.

The sun grew hotter and hotter. I took off my cap and wiped my brow. My throat was so dry, and I had no more water. I had to get out of the sun. Finally, I found a big shady tree.

5. The person telling the story wants to _____.
○ enjoy the sun
○ take a nap
● cool off

Page 122

Day 2 | Week 23

Language
Read the sentence. Then write the correct word to complete the sentence.
1. It is __good__ to be home.
   good   well
2. I don't feel __well__ today.
   good   well
3. The chicken soup tastes __good__.
   good   well

Math
Use the data chart to complete the line plot.

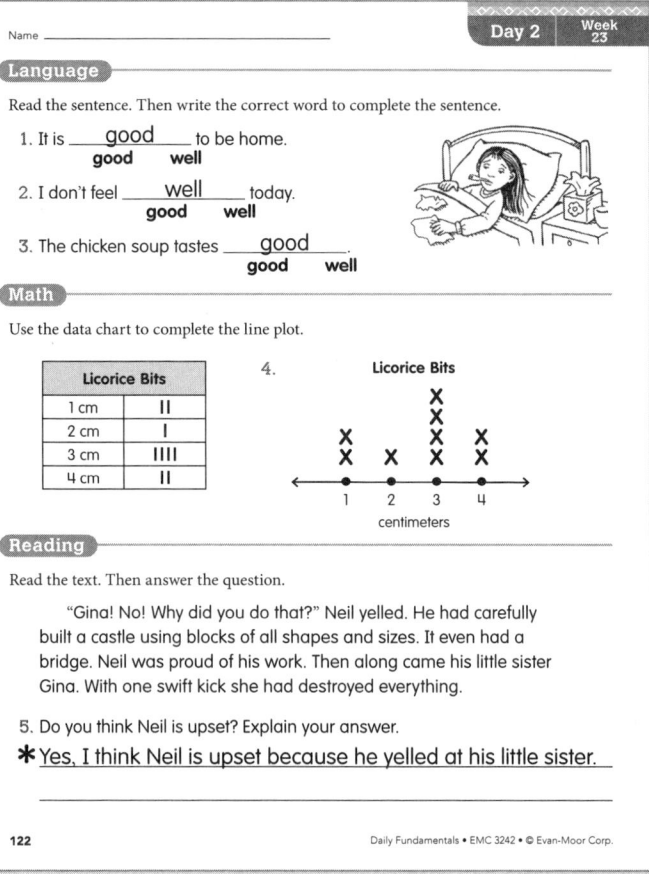

Reading
Read the text. Then answer the question.

"Gina! No! Why did you do that?" Neil yelled. He had carefully built a castle using blocks of all shapes and sizes. It even had a bridge. Neil was proud of his work. Then along came his little sister Gina. With one swift kick she had destroyed everything.

5. Do you think Neil is upset? Explain your answer.
⁕ __Yes, I think Neil is upset because he yelled at his little sister.__

✱ These answers will vary. Examples are given.

Page 123

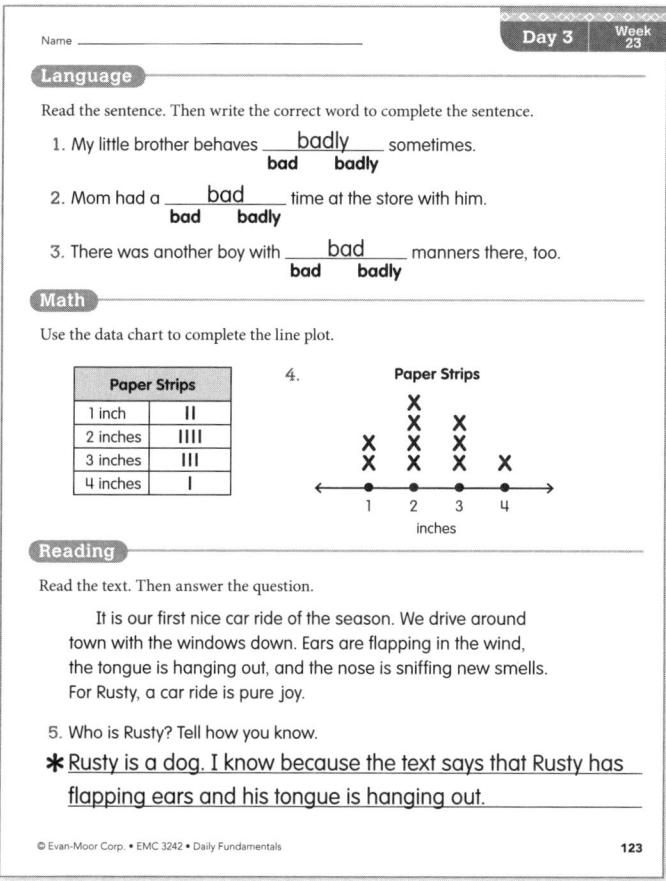

Page 124

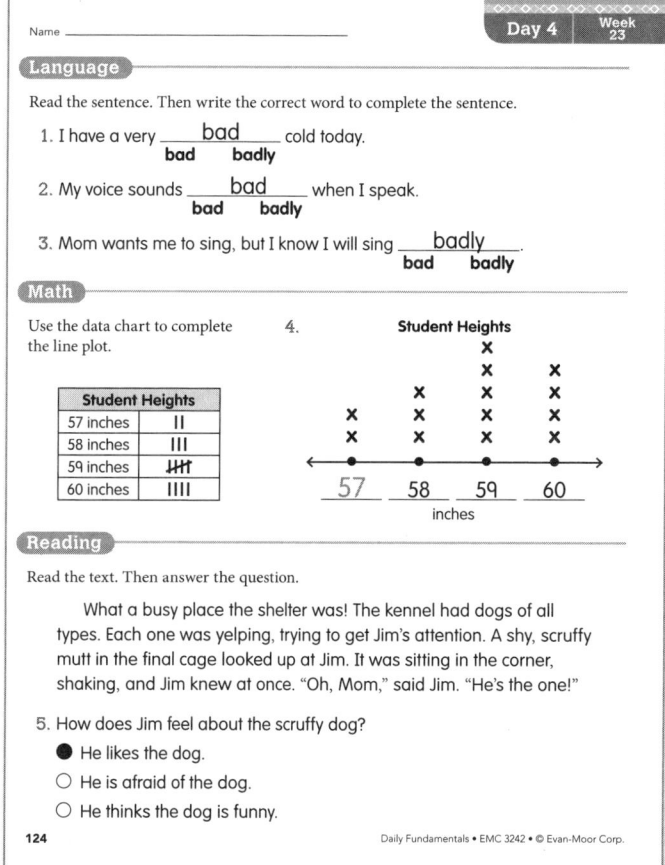

Page 125

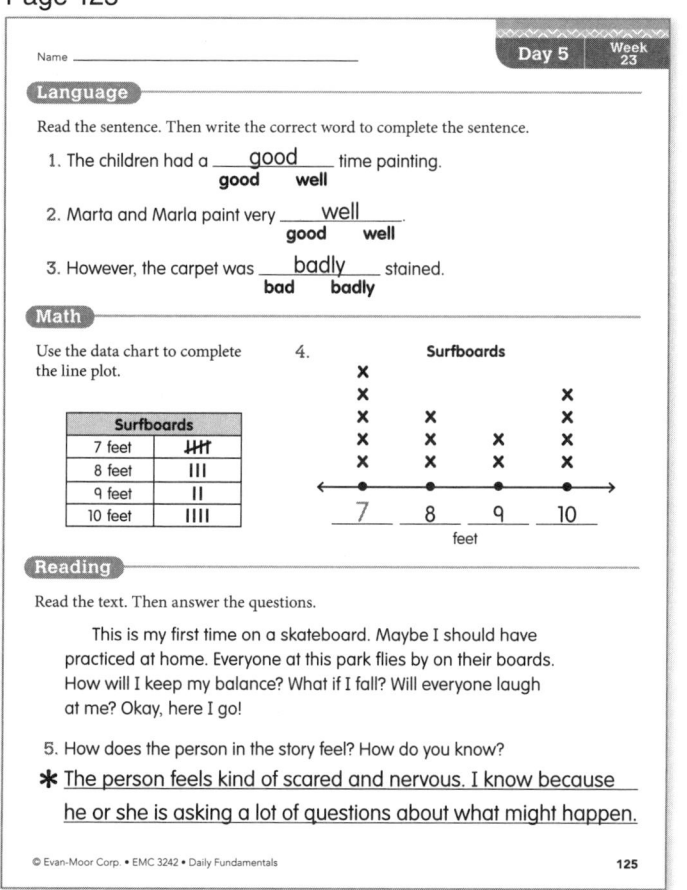

Page 126

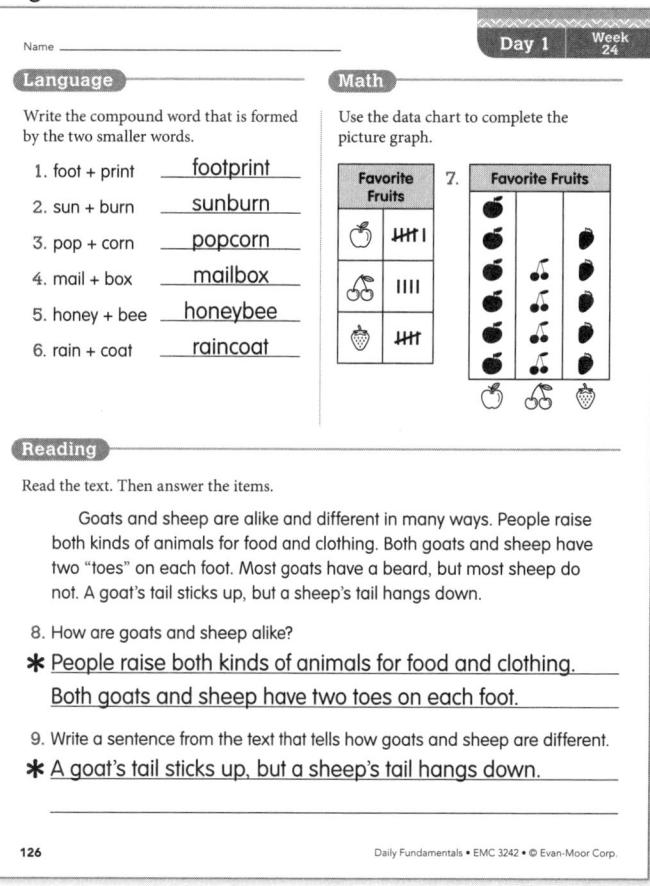

These answers will vary. Examples are given.

Page 127

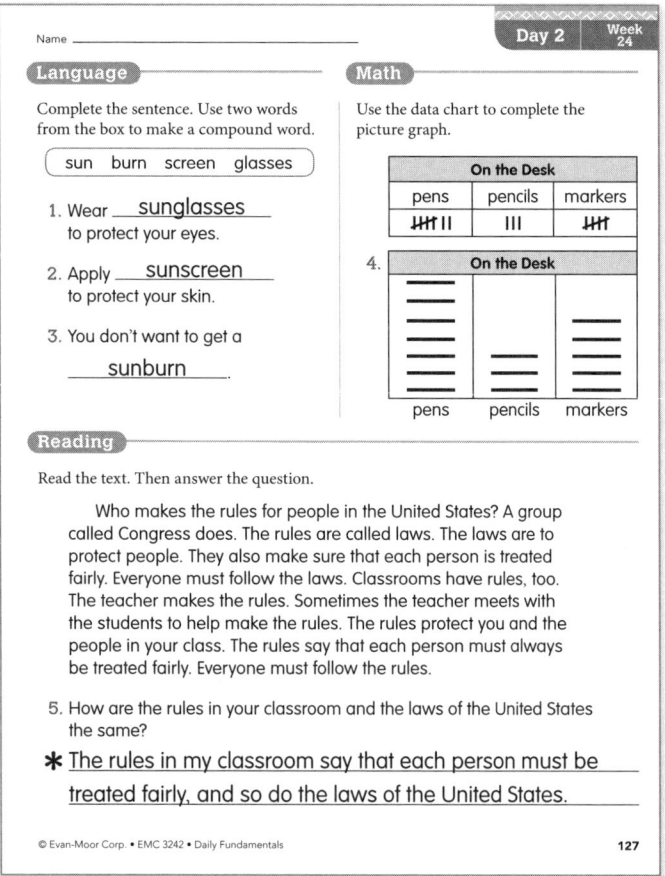

Page 128

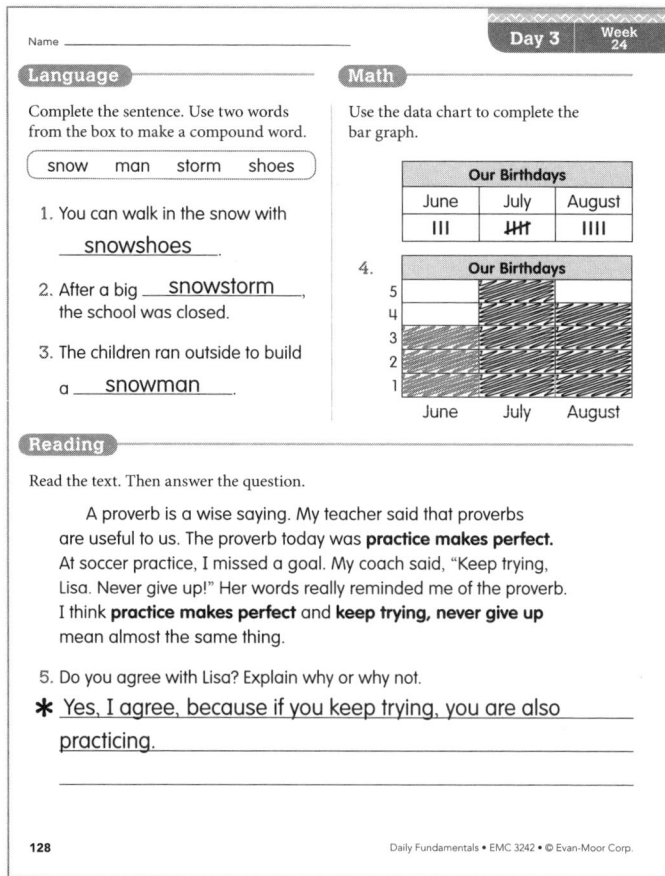

Page 129

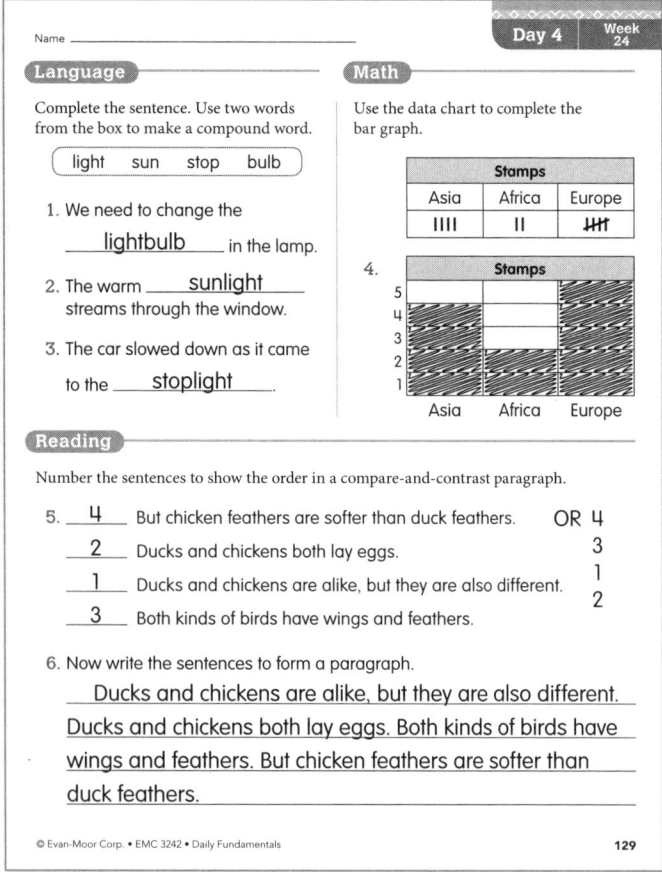

Page 130

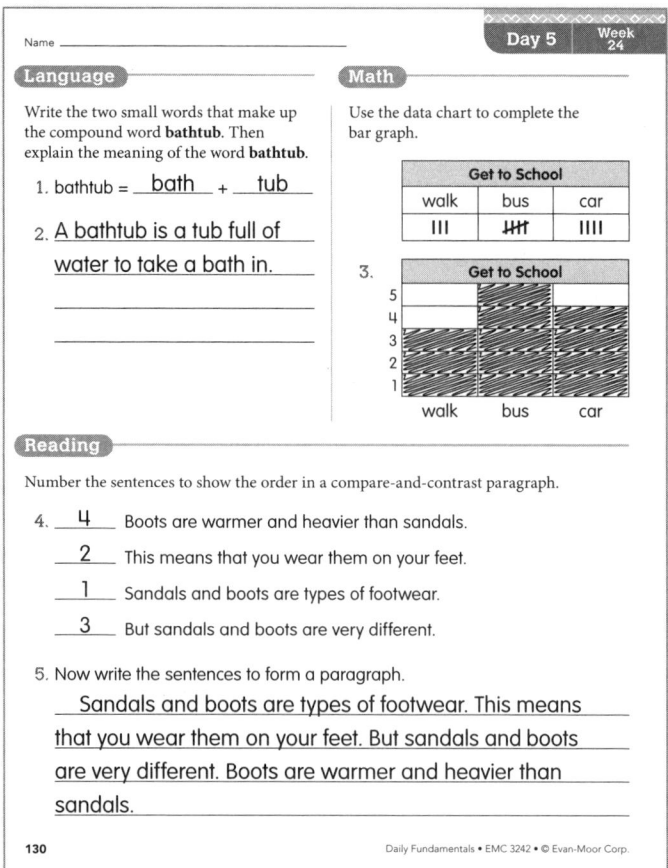

✱ These answers will vary. Examples are given.

Page 131

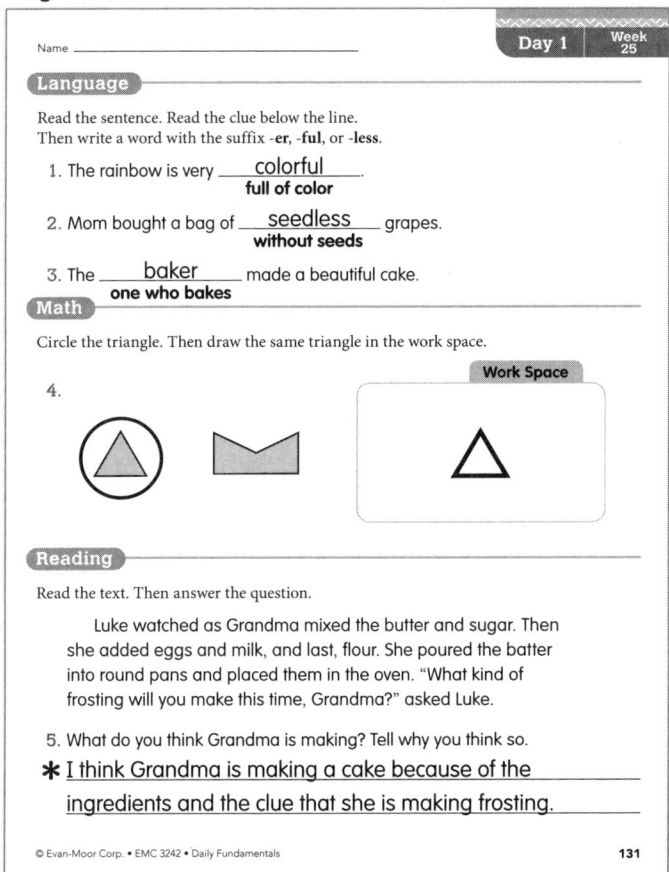

Language

Read the sentence. Read the clue below the line. Then write a word with the suffix -**er**, -**ful**, or -**less**.

1. The rainbow is very __colorful__.
   full of color
2. Mom bought a bag of __seedless__ grapes.
   without seeds
3. The __baker__ made a beautiful cake.
   one who bakes

Math

Circle the triangle. Then draw the same triangle in the work space.

4.

Reading

Read the text. Then answer the question.

Luke watched as Grandma mixed the butter and sugar. Then she added eggs and milk, and last, flour. She poured the batter into round pans and placed them in the oven. "What kind of frosting will you make this time, Grandma?" asked Luke.

5. What do you think Grandma is making? Tell why you think so.
✱ I think Grandma is making a cake because of the ingredients and the clue that she is making frosting.

Page 132

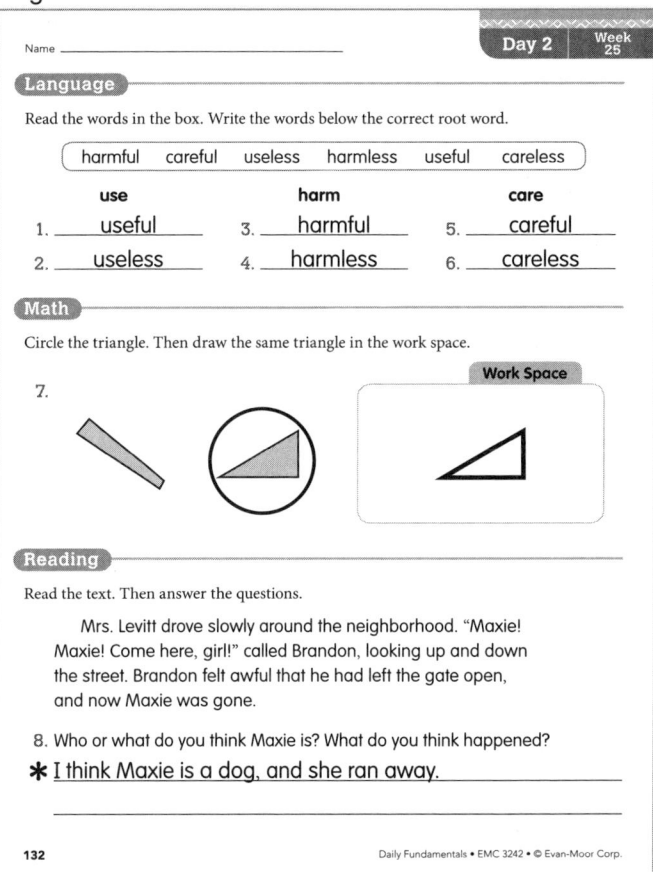

Language

Read the words in the box. Write the words below the correct root word.

| harmful | careful | useless | harmless | useful | careless |

use
1. useful
2. useless

harm
3. harmful
4. harmless

care
5. careful
6. careless

Math

Circle the triangle. Then draw the same triangle in the work space.

7.

Reading

Read the text. Then answer the questions.

Mrs. Levitt drove slowly around the neighborhood. "Maxie! Maxie! Come here, girl!" called Brandon, looking up and down the street. Brandon felt awful that he had left the gate open, and now Maxie was gone.

8. Who or what do you think Maxie is? What do you think happened?
✱ I think Maxie is a dog, and she ran away.

Page 133

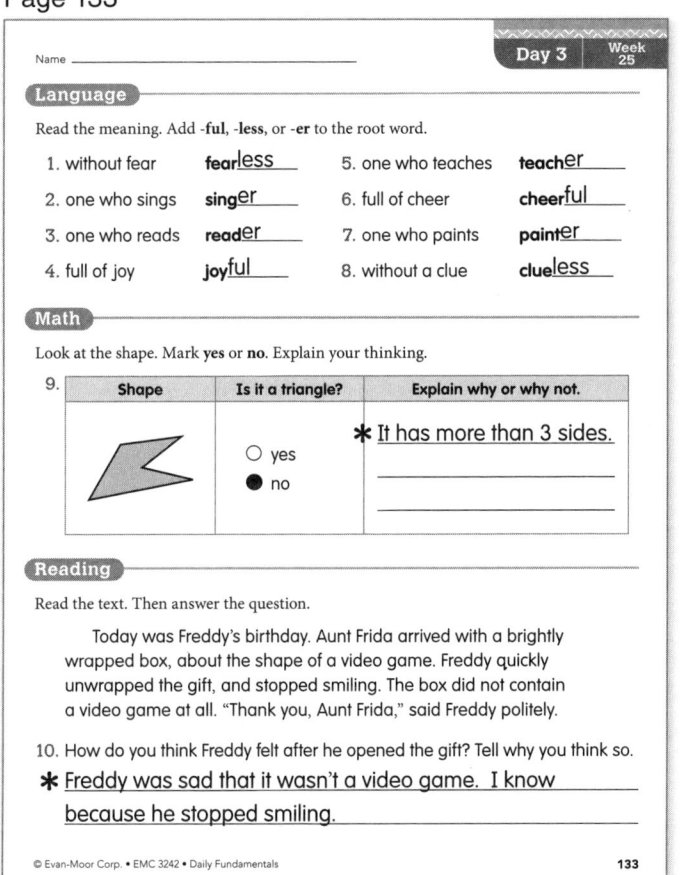

Language

Read the meaning. Add -**ful**, -**less**, or -**er** to the root word.

1. without fear — fear**less**
2. one who sings — sing**er**
3. one who reads — read**er**
4. full of joy — joy**ful**
5. one who teaches — teach**er**
6. full of cheer — cheer**ful**
7. one who paints — paint**er**
8. without a clue — clue**less**

Math

Look at the shape. Mark **yes** or **no**. Explain your thinking.

9.
Shape	Is it a triangle?	Explain why or why not.
	○ yes ● no	✱ It has more than 3 sides.

Reading

Read the text. Then answer the question.

Today was Freddy's birthday. Aunt Frida arrived with a brightly wrapped box, about the shape of a video game. Freddy quickly unwrapped the gift, and stopped smiling. The box did not contain a video game at all. "Thank you, Aunt Frida," said Freddy politely.

10. How do you think Freddy felt after he opened the gift? Tell why you think so.
✱ Freddy was sad that it wasn't a video game. I know because he stopped smiling.

Page 134

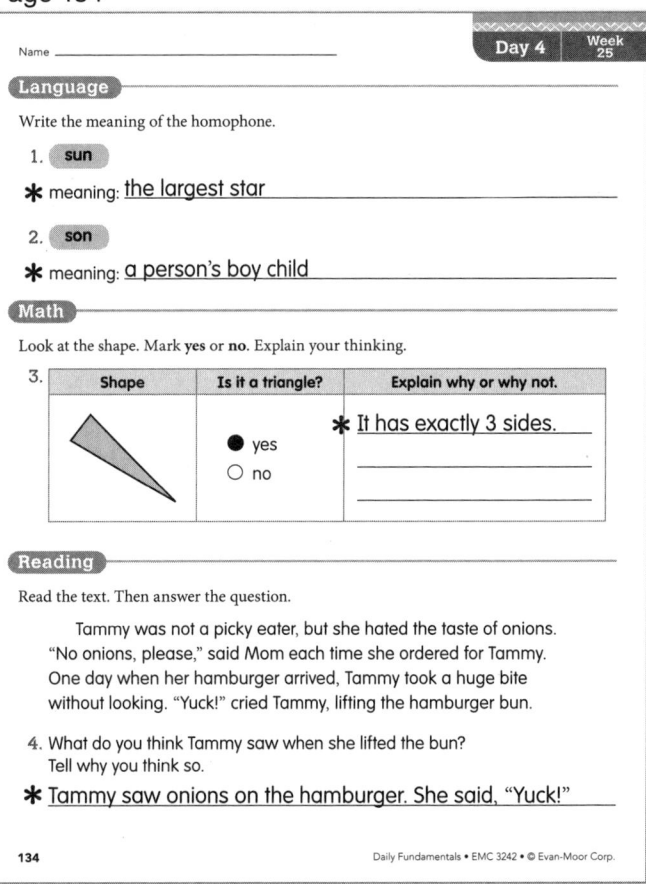

Language

Write the meaning of the homophone.

1. **sun**
✱ meaning: the largest star

2. **son**
✱ meaning: a person's boy child

Math

Look at the shape. Mark **yes** or **no**. Explain your thinking.

3.
Shape	Is it a triangle?	Explain why or why not.
	● yes ○ no	✱ It has exactly 3 sides.

Reading

Read the text. Then answer the question.

Tammy was not a picky eater, but she hated the taste of onions. "No onions, please," said Mom each time she ordered for Tammy. One day when her hamburger arrived, Tammy took a huge bite without looking. "Yuck!" cried Tammy, lifting the hamburger bun.

4. What do you think Tammy saw when she lifted the bun? Tell why you think so.
✱ Tammy saw onions on the hamburger. She said, "Yuck!"

★ These answers will vary. Examples are given.

Page 135

Day 5 · Week 25

Language
Read the sentence. Then complete the sentence with the correct homophone.
1. I saw a __deer__ in the forest.   **deer**   **dear**
2. The __sea__ is full of fish.   **see**   **sea**
3. Don't fall in the __hole__!   **whole**   **hole**
4. I need __flour__ to bake the cake.   **flour**   **flower**

Math
Draw a closed shape with three straight sides.
5.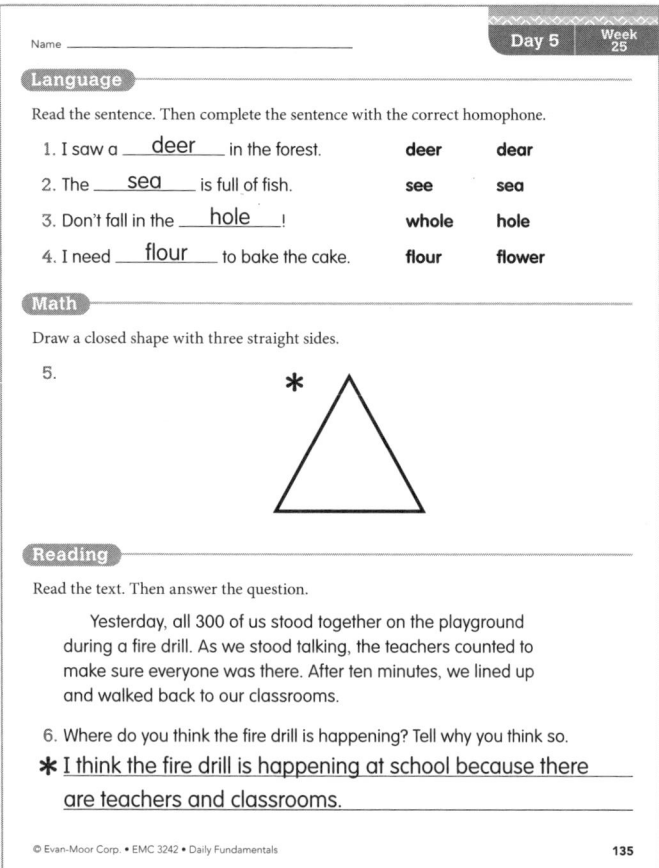
★

Reading
Read the text. Then answer the question.

Yesterday, all 300 of us stood together on the playground during a fire drill. As we stood talking, the teachers counted to make sure everyone was there. After ten minutes, we lined up and walked back to our classrooms.

6. Where do you think the fire drill is happening? Tell why you think so.
★ I think the fire drill is happening at school because there are teachers and classrooms.

Page 136

Day 1 · Week 26

Language
Read the sentence. Then write the correct verb to complete the sentence.
1. Anton __chose__ a sandwich from the menu.   **chose**   **choosed**
2. He __gave__ half the sandwich to Jesse.   **gave**   **gived**
3. He __felt__ the sandwich was too big for him.   **feeled**   **felt**

Math
Circle the quadrilateral. Then draw the same quadrilateral in the work space.
4.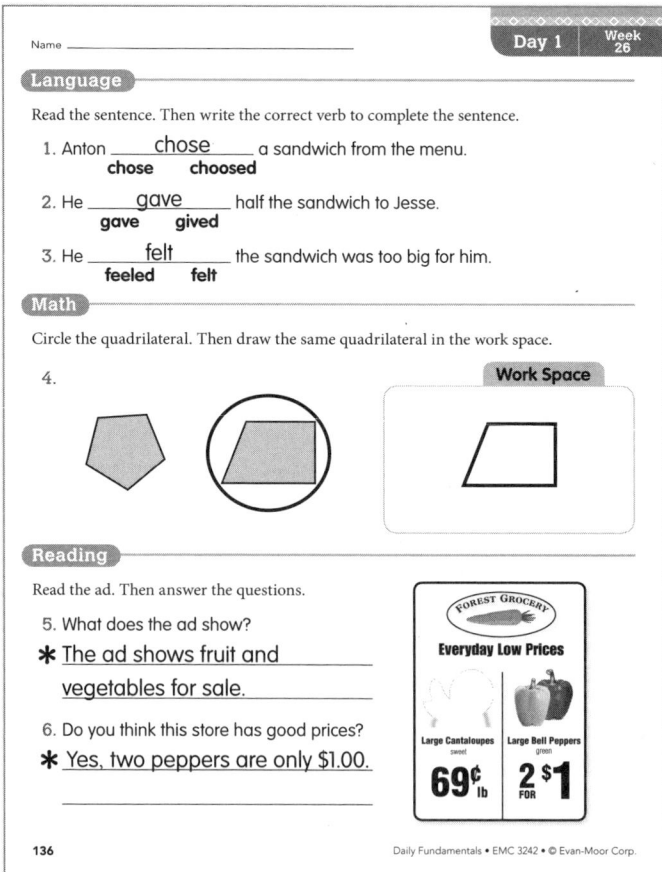

Reading
Read the ad. Then answer the questions.
5. What does the ad show?
★ The ad shows fruit and vegetables for sale.
6. Do you think this store has good prices?
★ Yes, two peppers are only $1.00.

Page 137

Day 2 · Week 26

Language
Read the sentence. Then write the correct verb to complete the sentence.
1. Nico __threw__ the ball to me.   **throwed**   **threw**
2. The ball __hit__ the table by the sofa.   **hitted**   **hit**
3. A vase __fell__ onto the floor.   **fell**   **falled**

Math
Circle the quadrilateral. Then draw the same quadrilateral in the work space.
4.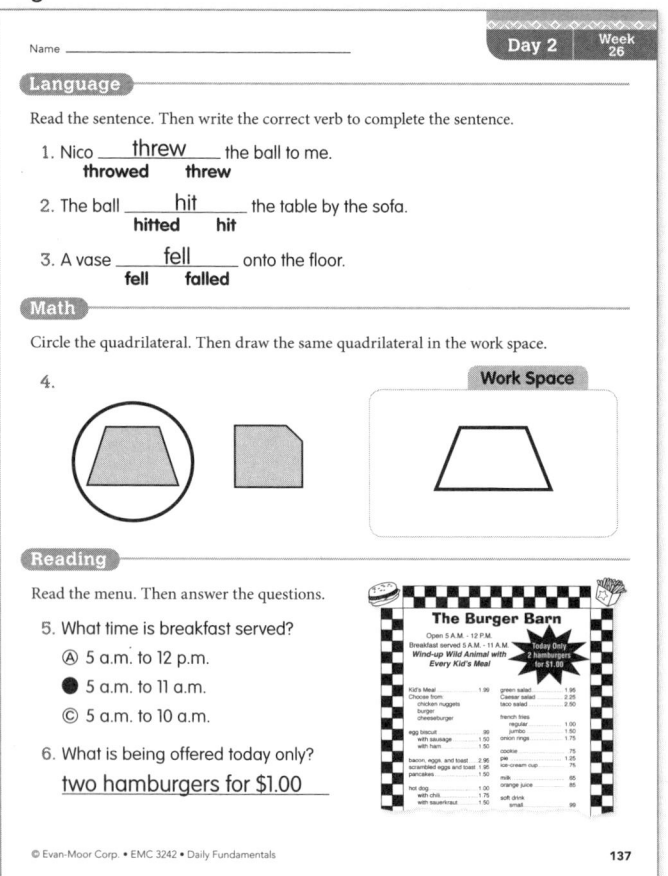

Reading
Read the menu. Then answer the questions.
5. What time is breakfast served?
   Ⓐ 5 a.m. to 12 p.m.
   ● 5 a.m. to 11 a.m.
   Ⓒ 5 a.m. to 10 a.m.
6. What is being offered today only?
   two hamburgers for $1.00

Page 138

Day 3 · Week 26

Language
Read the sentence. Then write the correct verb to complete the sentence.
1. We __rode__ our bikes around the block.   **rided**   **rode**
2. Sela __came__ with me on her blue bike.   **came**   **camed**
3. Sela __lost__ her sweater that day.   **losed**   **lost**

Math
Look at the shape. Mark **yes** or **no**. Explain your thinking.

4.
Shape	Is it a quadrilateral?	Explain why or why not.
(triangle)	○ yes ● no	★ It does not have 4 straight sides.

Reading
Read the recipe. Then answer the question.
5. What do the numbers in this recipe tell you?
   Ⓐ the amount of each soup ingredient
   ● the steps to make the soup
   Ⓒ how long you should cook the soup

Tom Kha Gai
1. Mix and cook: chicken broth, lime juice, chopped ginger, sugar, coconut milk
2. Add diced, cooked chicken.
3. Spoon over rice.
4. Add cilantro and crushed red pepper.

✱ These answers will vary. Examples are given.

Page 139

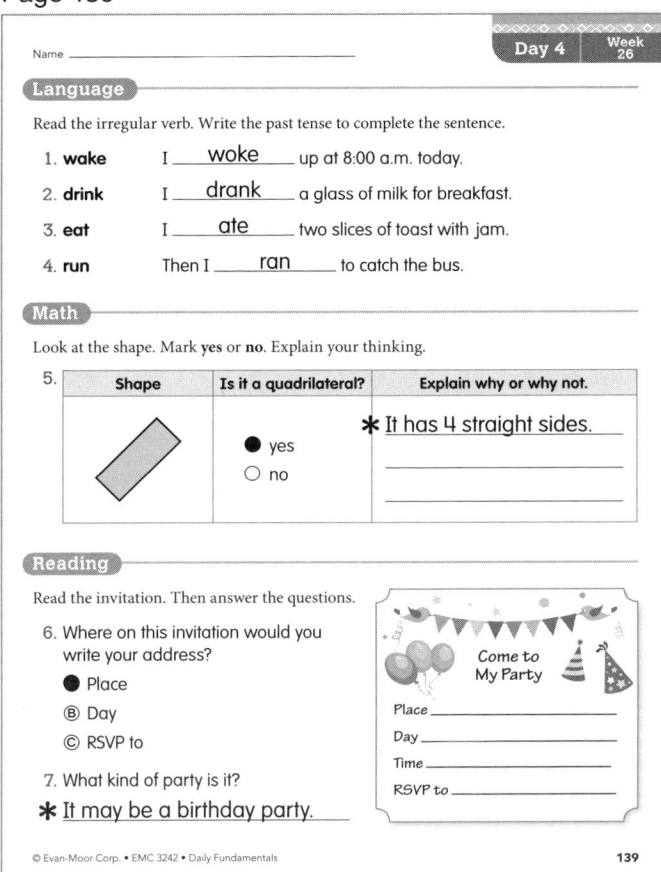

Day 4 — Week 26

Language
Read the irregular verb. Write the past tense to complete the sentence.
1. wake — I __woke__ up at 8:00 a.m. today.
2. drink — I __drank__ a glass of milk for breakfast.
3. eat — I __ate__ two slices of toast with jam.
4. run — Then I __ran__ to catch the bus.

Math
Look at the shape. Mark **yes** or **no**. Explain your thinking.
5. Shape — Is it a quadrilateral? ● yes ○ no — ✱ It has 4 straight sides.

Reading
Read the invitation. Then answer the questions.
6. Where on this invitation would you write your address?
● Place
Ⓑ Day
Ⓒ RSVP to
7. What kind of party is it?
✱ It may be a birthday party.

Page 140

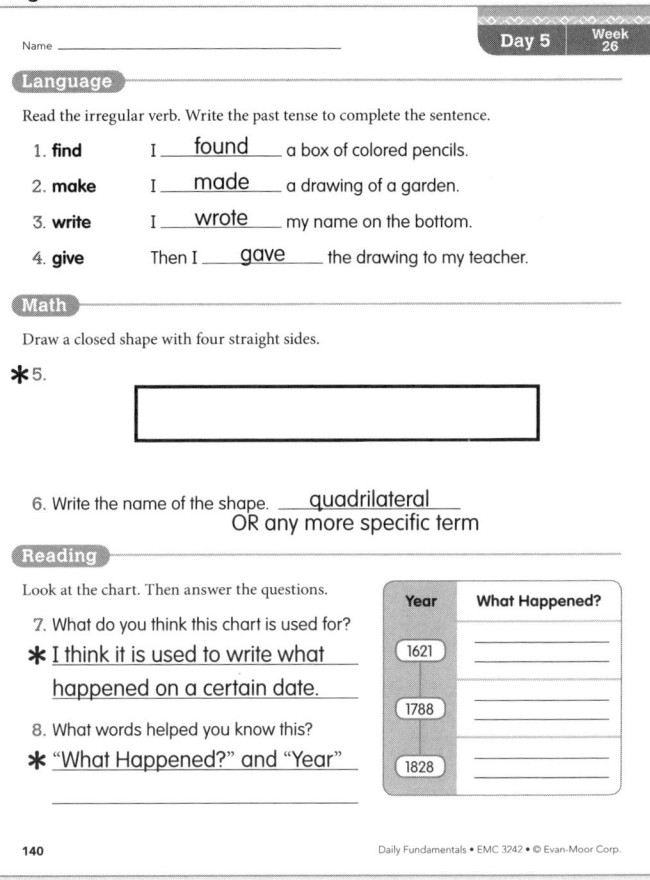

Day 5 — Week 26

Language
Read the irregular verb. Write the past tense to complete the sentence.
1. find — I __found__ a box of colored pencils.
2. make — I __made__ a drawing of a garden.
3. write — I __wrote__ my name on the bottom.
4. give — Then I __gave__ the drawing to my teacher.

Math
Draw a closed shape with four straight sides.
✱ 5. [rectangle drawn]
6. Write the name of the shape. __quadrilateral__ OR any more specific term

Reading
Look at the chart. Then answer the questions.
7. What do you think this chart is used for?
✱ I think it is used to write what happened on a certain date.
8. What words helped you know this?
✱ "What Happened?" and "Year"

Page 141

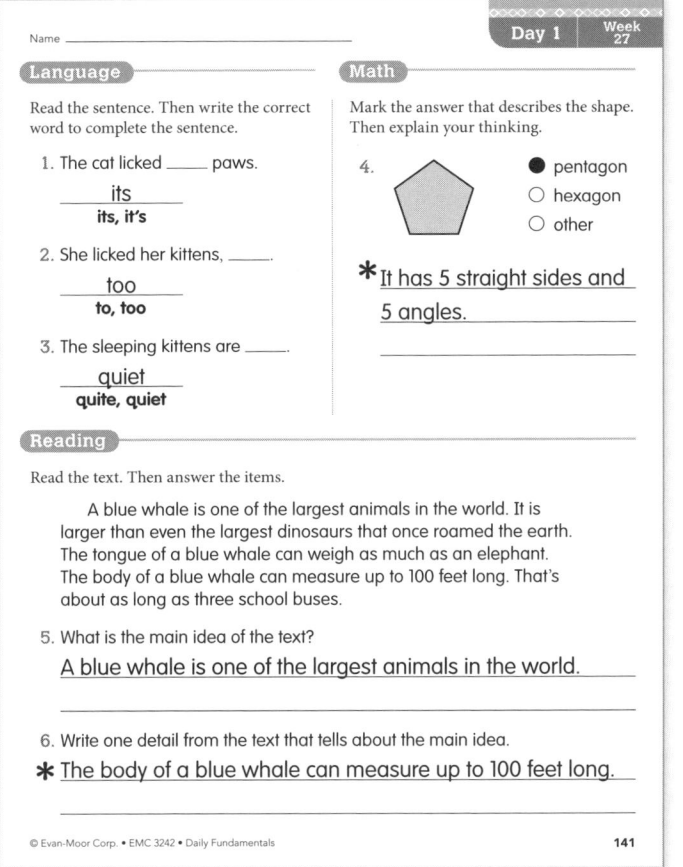

Day 1 — Week 27

Language
Read the sentence. Then write the correct word to complete the sentence.
1. The cat licked ___ paws. __its__ (its, it's)
2. She licked her kittens, ___. __too__ (to, too)
3. The sleeping kittens are ___. __quiet__ (quite, quiet)

Math
Mark the answer that describes the shape. Then explain your thinking.
4. [pentagon]
● pentagon
○ hexagon
○ other
✱ It has 5 straight sides and 5 angles.

Reading
Read the text. Then answer the items.

A blue whale is one of the largest animals in the world. It is larger than even the largest dinosaurs that once roamed the earth. The tongue of a blue whale can weigh as much as an elephant. The body of a blue whale can measure up to 100 feet long. That's about as long as three school buses.

5. What is the main idea of the text?
A blue whale is one of the largest animals in the world.
6. Write one detail from the text that tells about the main idea.
✱ The body of a blue whale can measure up to 100 feet long.

Page 142

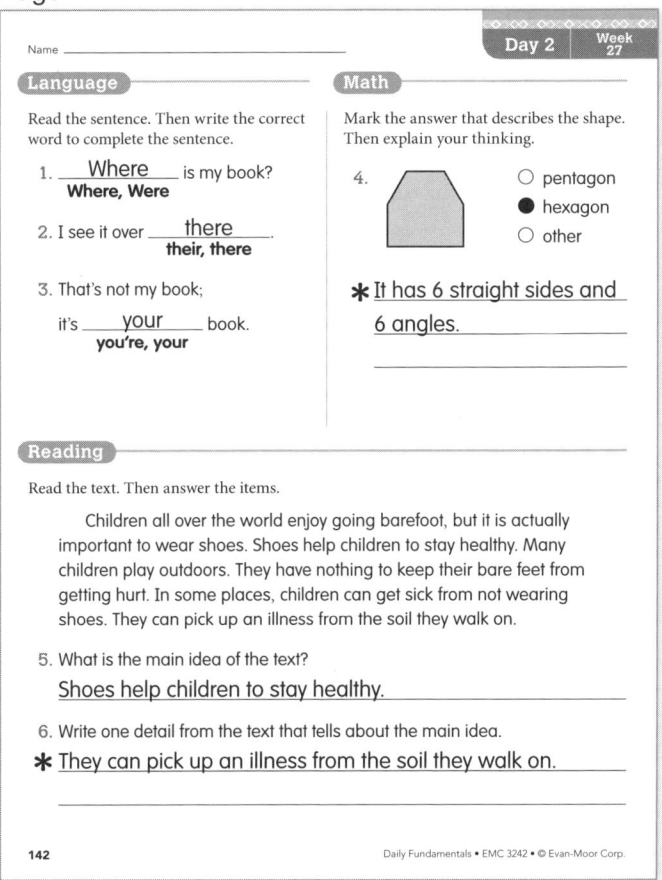

Day 2 — Week 27

Language
Read the sentence. Then write the correct word to complete the sentence.
1. __Where__ is my book? (Where, Were)
2. I see it over __there__. (their, there)
3. That's not my book; it's __your__ book. (you're, your)

Math
Mark the answer that describes the shape. Then explain your thinking.
4. [hexagon]
○ pentagon
● hexagon
○ other
✱ It has 6 straight sides and 6 angles.

Reading
Read the text. Then answer the items.

Children all over the world enjoy going barefoot, but it is actually important to wear shoes. Shoes help children to stay healthy. Many children play outdoors. They have nothing to keep their bare feet from getting hurt. In some places, children can get sick from not wearing shoes. They can pick up an illness from the soil they walk on.

5. What is the main idea of the text?
Shoes help children to stay healthy.
6. Write one detail from the text that tells about the main idea.
✱ They can pick up an illness from the soil they walk on.

* These answers will vary. Examples are given.

Page 143

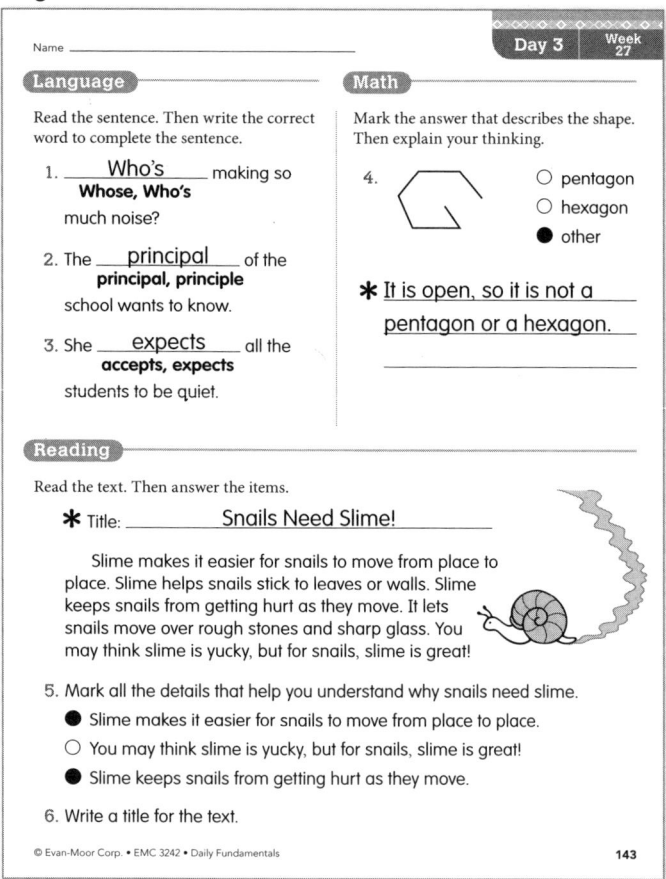

Day 3 • Week 27

Language

Read the sentence. Then write the correct word to complete the sentence.

1. **Who's** making so much noise? (Whose, Who's)
2. The **principal** of the school wants to know. (principal, principle)
3. She **expects** all the students to be quiet. (accepts, expects)

Math

Mark the answer that describes the shape. Then explain your thinking.

4. ○ pentagon ○ hexagon ● other

* It is open, so it is not a pentagon or a hexagon.

Reading

Read the text. Then answer the items.

* Title: **Snails Need Slime!**

Slime makes it easier for snails to move from place to place. Slime helps snails stick to leaves or walls. Slime keeps snails from getting hurt as they move over rough stones and sharp glass. You may think slime is yucky, but for snails, slime is great!

5. Mark all the details that help you understand why snails need slime.
● Slime makes it easier for snails to move from place to place.
○ You may think slime is yucky, but for snails, slime is great!
● Slime keeps snails from getting hurt as they move.

6. Write a title for the text.

Page 144

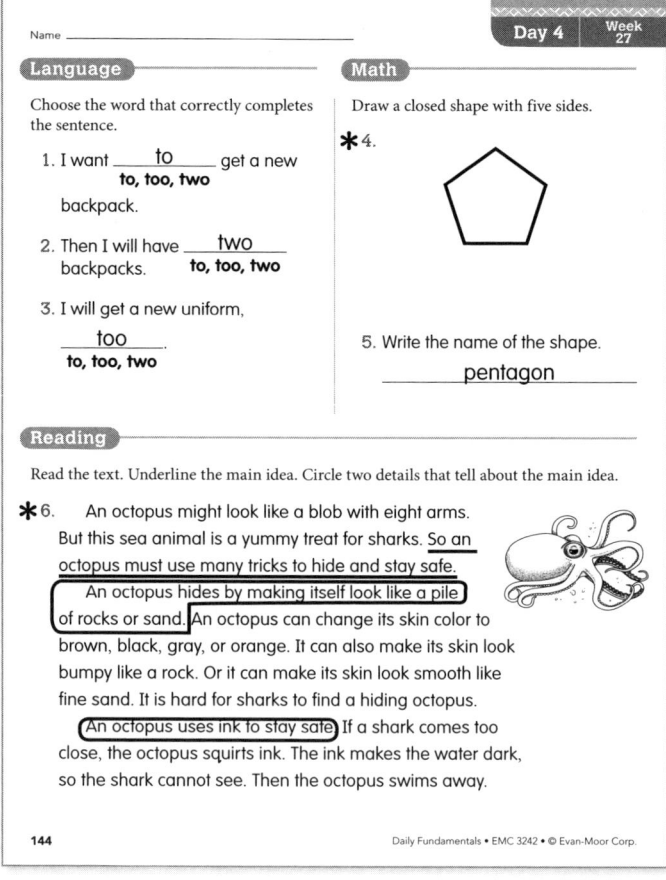

Day 4 • Week 27

Language

Choose the word that correctly completes the sentence.

1. I want **to** get a new backpack. (to, too, two)
2. Then I will have **two** backpacks. (to, too, two)
3. I will get a new uniform, **too**. (to, too, two)

Math

Draw a closed shape with five sides.

* 4.

5. Write the name of the shape. **pentagon**

Reading

Read the text. Underline the main idea. Circle two details that tell about the main idea.

* 6. An octopus might look like a blob with eight arms. But this sea animal is a yummy treat for sharks. <u>So an octopus must use many tricks to hide and stay safe.</u> (An octopus hides by making itself look like a pile of rocks or sand.) An octopus can change its skin color to brown, black, gray, or orange. It can also make its skin look bumpy like a rock. Or it can make its skin look smooth like fine sand. It is hard for sharks to find a hiding octopus. (An octopus uses ink to stay safe.) If a shark comes too close, the octopus squirts ink. The ink makes the water dark, so the shark cannot see. Then the octopus swims away.

Page 145

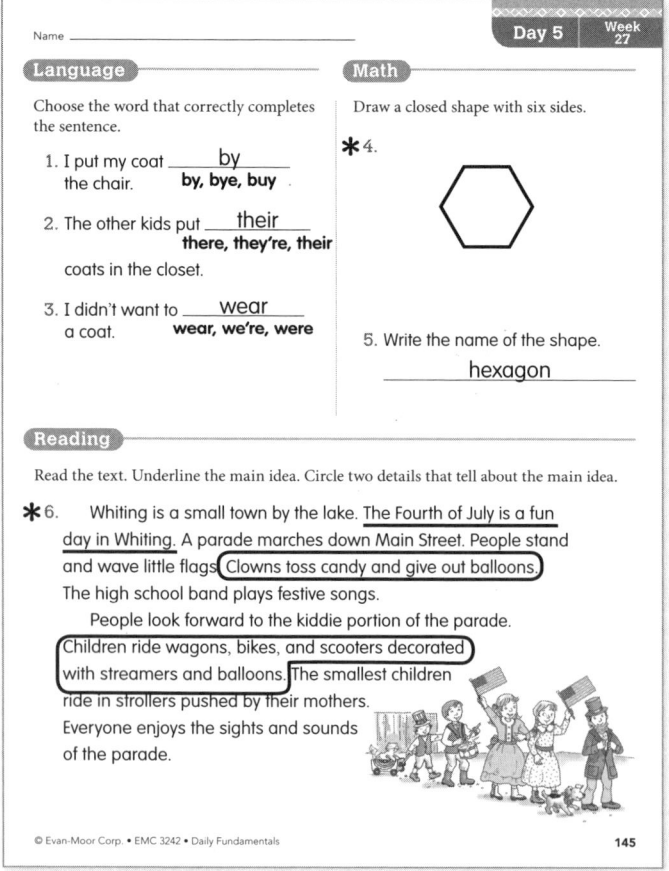

Day 5 • Week 27

Language

Choose the word that correctly completes the sentence.

1. I put my coat **by** the chair. (by, bye, buy)
2. The other kids put **their** coats in the closet. (there, they're, their)
3. I didn't want to **wear** a coat. (wear, we're, were)

Math

Draw a closed shape with six sides.

* 4.

5. Write the name of the shape. **hexagon**

Reading

Read the text. Underline the main idea. Circle two details that tell about the main idea.

* 6. Whiting is a small town by the lake. <u>The Fourth of July is a fun day in Whiting.</u> A parade marches down Main Street. People stand and wave little flags. (Clowns toss candy and give out balloons.) The high school band plays festive songs.
People look forward to the kiddie portion of the parade. (Children ride wagons, bikes, and scooters decorated with streamers and balloons.) The smallest children ride in strollers pushed by their mothers. Everyone enjoys the sights and sounds of the parade.

Page 146

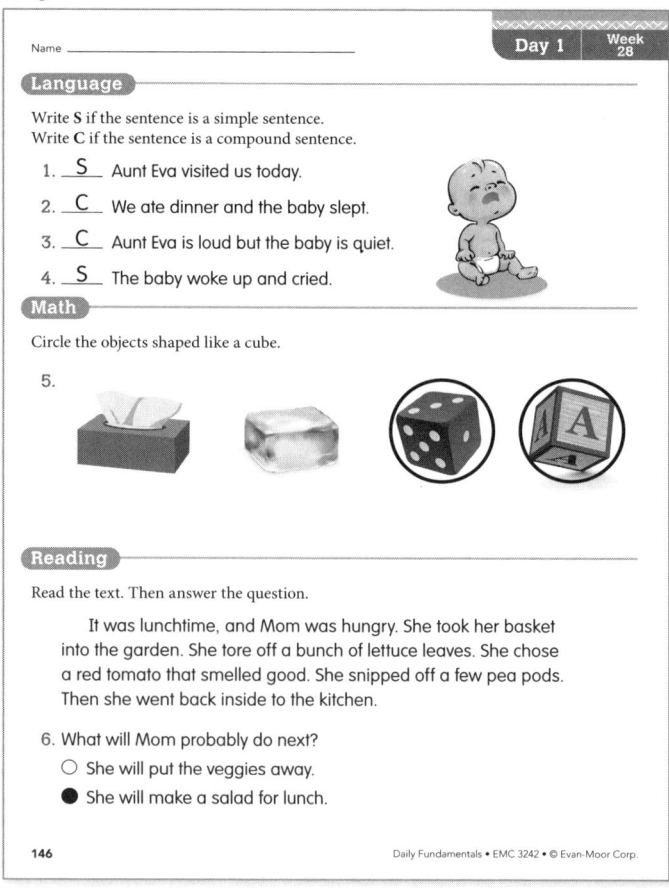

Day 1 • Week 28

Language

Write **S** if the sentence is a simple sentence.
Write **C** if the sentence is a compound sentence.

1. **S** Aunt Eva visited us today.
2. **C** We ate dinner and the baby slept.
3. **C** Aunt Eva is loud but the baby is quiet.
4. **S** The baby woke up and cried.

Math

Circle the objects shaped like a cube.

5. [tissue box] [ice cube - circled] [die - circled] [alphabet block - circled]

Reading

Read the text. Then answer the question.

It was lunchtime, and Mom was hungry. She took her basket into the garden. She tore off a bunch of lettuce leaves. She chose a red tomato that smelled good. She snipped off a few pea pods. Then she went back inside to the kitchen.

6. What will Mom probably do next?
○ She will put the veggies away.
● She will make a salad for lunch.

* These answers will vary. Examples are given.

Page 147

Day 2 — Week 28

Language
Write **S** if the sentence is a simple sentence.
Write **C** if the sentence is a compound sentence.

1. __S__ We picked three baskets of apples from our tree.
2. __C__ Sharon washed the apples and Kate peeled them.
3. __S__ Dad baked three apple pies for the bake sale.
4. __C__ You can buy a whole pie or you can buy just a slice.

Math
Answer the item.

5. How many edges does a cube have?
   ○ 8
   ○ 10
   ● 12

Reading
Read the text. Then answer the question.

Joel likes to save things that he finds in nature. On a shelf in his room, he has bumpy rocks and flat stones. He also has a long white feather. Next to that, there is a tiny nest that he found in the park. Joel made some room on the shelf. Today he is going to the beach!

6. What will Joel probably do at the beach? Tell why you think so.
* He will probably collect things from nature like shells and put them on his shelf.

Page 148

Day 3 — Week 28

Language
Combine the two simple sentences to make a compound sentence.

1. Mom came home. We sat down to eat dinner.
   Mom came home and we sat down to eat dinner.
2. Teri made a big salad. Julia baked some bread.
   Teri made a big salad and Julia baked some bread.

Math
Answer the item.

3. How many vertices does a cube have?
   ○ 6
   ● 8
   ○ 10

Reading
Read the text. Then answer the question.

Izzy hummed as she brushed her teeth. Suddenly, she stopped and gently touched her front tooth. Sure enough, the tooth wiggled. That morning at breakfast, Izzy ate only soft pancakes. She asked her mom to pack only soft foods in her lunch—no apples or chips!

4. How will Izzy probably feel if her mom packs hard foods in her lunch?
* She will feel scared that her tooth will fall out and it might hurt.

Page 149

Day 4 — Week 28

Language
Combine the two simple sentences to make a compound sentence.

1. I studied for the test. I got a low score.
   I studied for the test but I got a low score.
2. I can take the test again. I can accept the low score.
   I can take the test again or I can accept the low score.

Math
Answer the item.

3. How many faces does a cube have?
   ● 6
   ○ 8
   ○ 10

Reading
Read the text. Then answer the question.

The house next to Gabe's had been empty for a long time. There weren't any kids in his neighborhood. As he lay on his bed, feeling bored, he heard noises coming from outside. Gabe peeked out the window. A truck was parked in front of the house. Men were unloading furniture and boxes. Gabe wished he knew who was moving in.

4. If kids move into the house next door, what do you predict Gabe will do?
* I think he will go next door and meet them and ask if they want to play.

Page 150

Day 5 — Week 28

Language
Read the sentences. Then combine them to make a compound sentence.

1. Our dog can catch a ball. She can roll over.
   Our dog can catch a ball and she can roll over.
2. Dogs can wait outside. They aren't allowed in the restaurant.
   Dogs can wait outside but they aren't allowed in the restaurant.

Math
Follow the steps to draw a cube.

3. **First** — Draw a square. Draw a dot in the center.
   Then — Start at the dot. Draw another square the same size.
   Next — Draw straight lines to connect the corners.
   Workspace

Reading
Read the text. Then answer the questions.

Dad pulls out Sparky's leash and whistles. Sparky hurries over to Dad, wagging her tail. Dad hooks the leash to Sparky's collar, and Sparky runs toward the door. Dad carefully guides Sparky upstairs to give him a bath.

Answers will vary.

4. Did the story end like you thought it would?   ○ yes   ○ no
5. If you answered **no**, how did you think the story was going to end?
* I thought Dad was going to take Sparky for a walk.

✱ These answers will vary. Examples are given.

Page 151

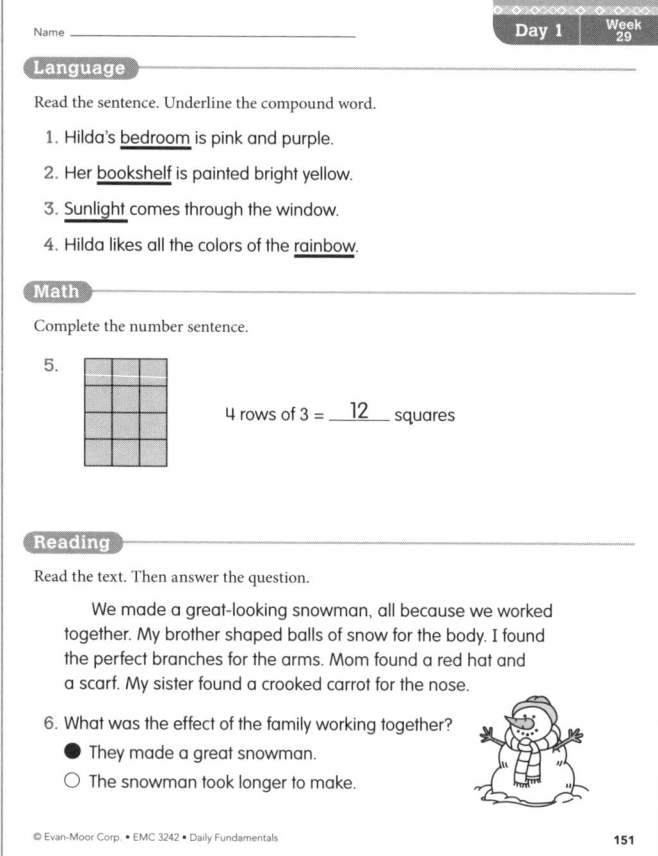

Page 152

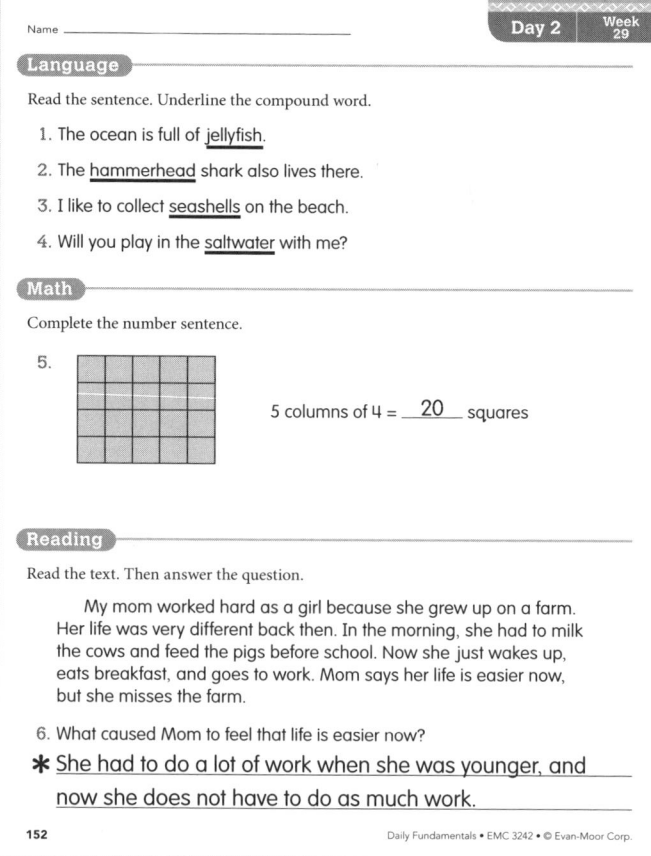

6. What caused Mom to feel that life is easier now?
✱ She had to do a lot of work when she was younger, and now she does not have to do as much work.

Page 153

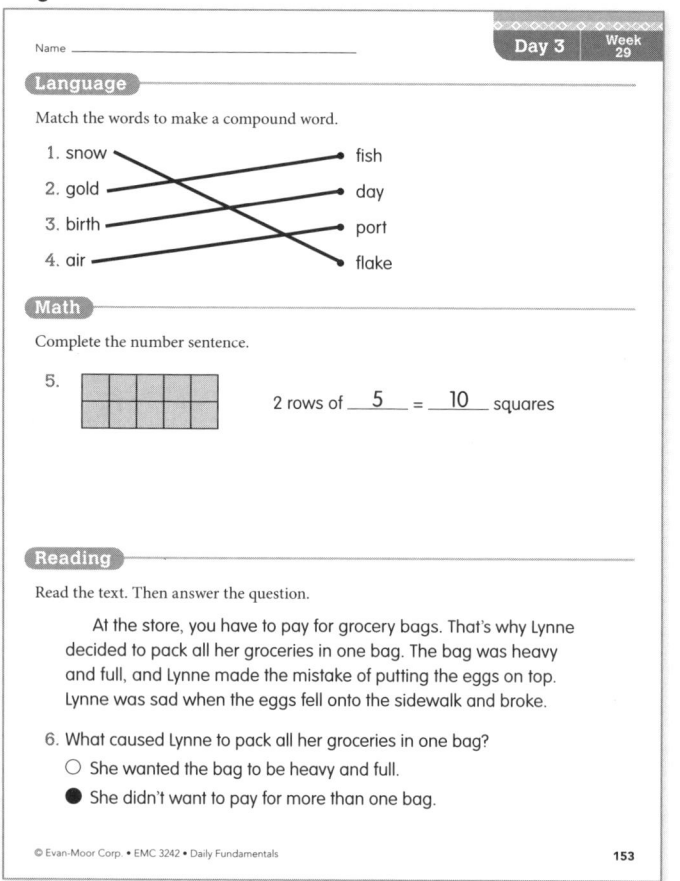

Page 154

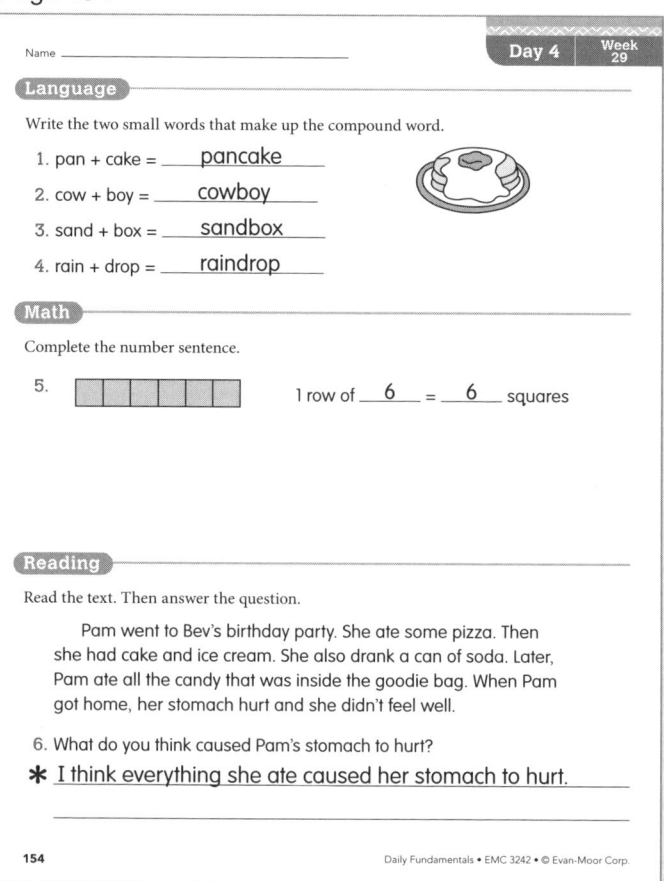

6. What do you think caused Pam's stomach to hurt?
✱ I think everything she ate caused her stomach to hurt.

✱ These answers will vary. Examples are given.

Page 155

Day 5 · Week 29

Language
Write the two small words that make up the compound word.
1. fish + bowl = fishbowl
2. sea + horse = seahorse
3. wind + mill = windmill
4. sun + shine = sunshine

Math
Divide the rectangle into 6 columns of 3 squares.

5.

Reading
Read the text. Then answer the question.

Thousands of wildfires occur each year in the United States. Some people are very careless. They leave campfires burning instead of putting them out. People should be very careful in hot, dry weather. That is when wildfires spread the fastest.

6. What is the effect of hot, dry weather?
● Wildfires spread fast in this weather.
○ People leave campfires burning.

Page 156

Day 1 · Week 30

Language
Circle the linking verb in the sentence.
1. This valentine (seems) pretty.
2. It (is) pink and red.
3. The cookie (feels) soft.
4. The cookie (smells) good.
5. This valentine cookie (tastes) sweet.
6. You (are) my best friend!

Math
Look at the shape. Mark the answer that names how much is shaded.

7.
○ two thirds
● one fourth
○ three fourths

Reading
Read the text. Then answer the questions.

I am helping Grandpa prepare dinner. I wash the carrots and peel the potatoes. Grandpa puts salt on the meat. I check to see if there is any rice made. There's not, so I put three cups of rice and some water into the rice cooker. Grandpa puts the meat, the carrots, and the potatoes in a pan and puts it into the oven to cook.

8. What does **prepare** mean?
○ to put away
● to get ready

9. What context clues helped you?
✱ washing the carrots and peeling the potatoes

Page 157

Day 2 · Week 30

Language
Circle the linking verb in the sentence.
1. Dinner (was) delicious.
2. That sofa (seems) cozy.
3. This pillow (is) very soft.
4. The cats (are) warm.
5. You all (look) happy together.
6. Everyone (is) sleepy and quiet.

Math
Look at the shape. Mark the answer that names how much is shaded.

7.
● two thirds
○ one third
○ one half

Reading
Read the text. Then answer the items.

Mars is one of the planets in our solar system. It is about half the size of Earth. Mars is as dry as a desert except for its ice caps at the north and south poles. Mars has very tall mountains and deep canyons. The soil is full of rust-colored iron dust. This makes Mars look red. Strong winds blow up big storms of red dust.

8. What does **except** mean? ● other than   ○ because of
9. Write a sentence using the word **except**.
✱ I like all fruits except for bananas.

Page 158

Day 3 · Week 30

Language
Circle the linking verb in the sentence.
1. I (am) a good speller.
2. Mr. Dunn (is) my spelling teacher.
3. We (are) a little nervous.
4. Mr. Dunn (is) very proud of us.
5. I (am) happy about the test.
6. We (are) all good spellers.

Math
Look at the shape. Color one third.

7.

Reading
Read the text. Then answer the items.

Ginny had been making mud pies in the backyard all afternoon. "You're a mess, kiddo!" said her dad. "It's into the bathtub with you."
"Dad!" screamed Ginny. "Come quickly. There's a spider in the bathtub!"
Dad came and took a look. "<u>You don't have to be afraid.</u> It won't harm you."
"I'm not afraid," explained Ginny. "<u>I know it won't hurt me.</u> I don't want it to drown when I turn on the water."

8. What does **harm** mean?
✱ to hurt or injure
✱ 9. Underline the context clues that helped you.

✱ These answers will vary. Examples are given.

Page 159

Day 4 | Week 30

Language
Write **is** or **are** to complete the sentence.

1. The county fair __is__ a fun place to visit.
2. There __are__ many animals.
3. The chicks __are__ the cutest.
4. They __are__ soft and fluffy.
5. The fair __is__ also fun because of the rides.
6. There __is__ a big Ferris wheel.

Math
Look at the shape. Color one fourth.

7.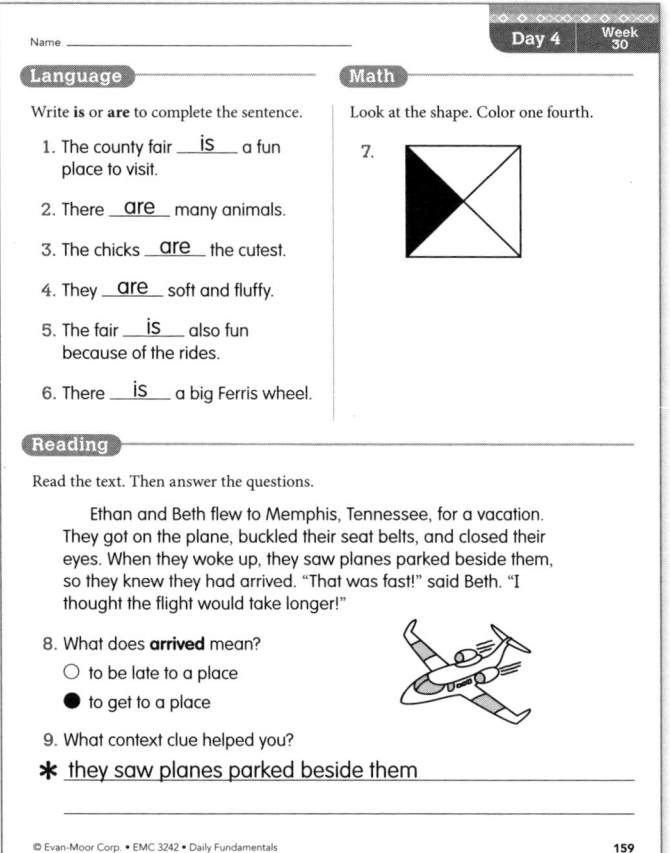

Reading
Read the text. Then answer the questions.

Ethan and Beth flew to Memphis, Tennessee, for a vacation. They got on the plane, buckled their seat belts, and closed their eyes. When they woke up, they saw planes parked beside them, so they knew they had arrived. "That was fast!" said Beth. "I thought the flight would take longer!"

8. What does **arrived** mean?
   ○ to be late to a place
   ● to get to a place

9. What context clue helped you?
   ✱ they saw planes parked beside them

Page 160

Day 5 | Week 30

Language
Write **am, are,** or **is** to complete the sentence.

1. I __am__ 8 years old.
2. Randy __is__ 12 years old.
3. The twins __are__ 10 years old.
4. I __am__ the youngest child.
5. My dad __is__ older than my mom.
6. My parents __are__ both very busy with us!

Math
Read the problem. Then answer the item.

Jelena ate one third of a round pizza. How much was left over? Draw the pizza. Color the part that was left over.

7.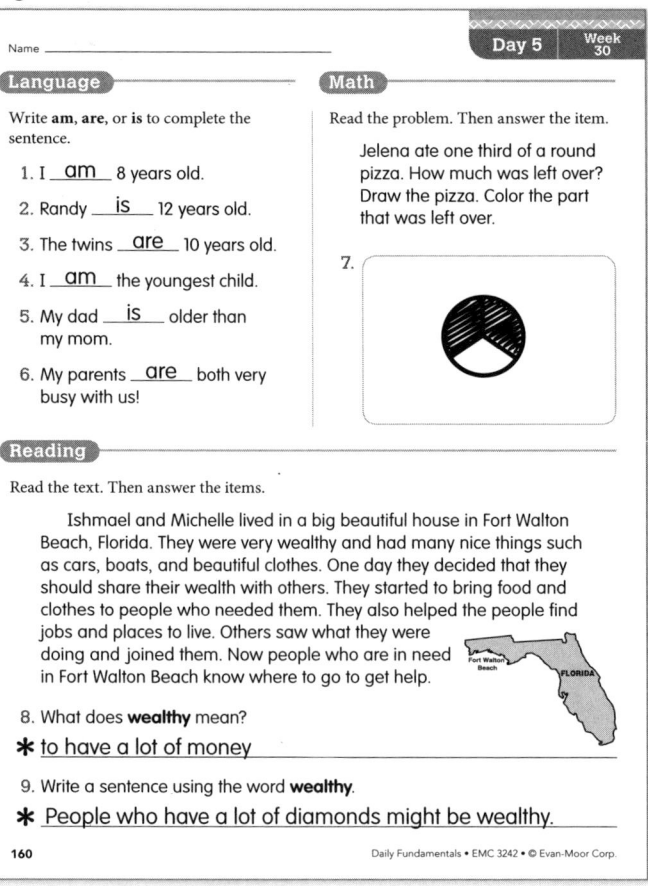

Reading
Read the text. Then answer the items.

Ishmael and Michelle lived in a big beautiful house in Fort Walton Beach, Florida. They were very wealthy and had many nice things such as cars, boats, and beautiful clothes. One day they decided that they should share their wealth with others. They started to bring food and clothes to people who needed them. They also helped the people find jobs and places to live. Others saw what they were doing and joined them. Now people who are in need in Fort Walton Beach know where to go to get help.

8. What does **wealthy** mean?
   ✱ to have a lot of money

9. Write a sentence using the word **wealthy**.
   ✱ People who have a lot of diamonds might be wealthy.

Take It to Your Seat Centers: Math

Grades K–6

Independent practice, perfect for students at all levels.

Take It to Your Seat Centers: Math

Hands-on practice of core math skills! Each of the 12 centers focuses on key math concepts and presents skill practice in engaging visual and tactile activities. The easy-to-assemble centers include full-color cards and mats, directions, answer keys, and student record forms. Ideal for any classroom and to support RTI or ELLs. 160 full-color pages. Correlated to state standards and Common Core State Standards.

www.evan-moor.com/tmcent

Teacher's Edition Print		Teacher's Edition E-book	
GRADE	EMC	GRADE	EMC
K	3070	K	3070i
1	3071	1	3071i
2	3072	2	3072i
3	3073	3	3073i
4	3074	4	3074i
5	3075	5	3075i
6	3076	6	3076i

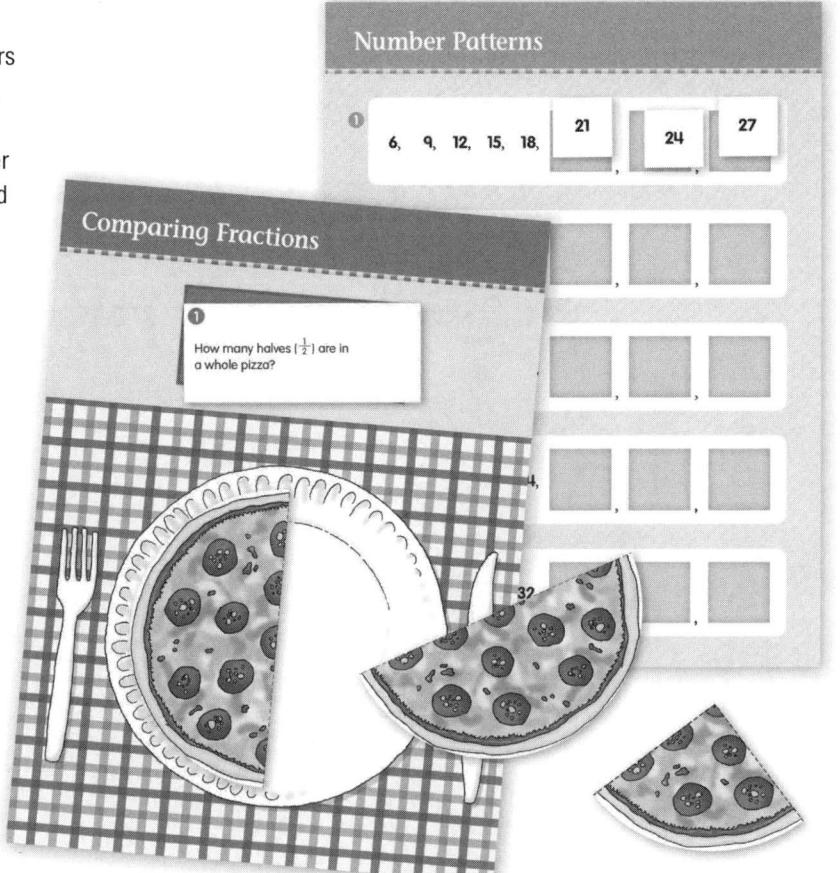

Daily Word Problems

Students' problem-solving skills improve day by day as they take part in meaningful, real-life math practice!

Grades 1–6

- Students learn to persevere in solving 180 word problems through engaging practice of meaningful, theme-based problems.
- The 36 weeks of practice activities address grade-level math concepts such as addition, fractions, logic, algebra, and more.
- Monday through Thursday activities present students with a one- or two-step word problem, while Friday's format is more extensive and requires multiple steps.

Correlated to state standards and Common Core State Standards.

www.evan-moor.com/dwp

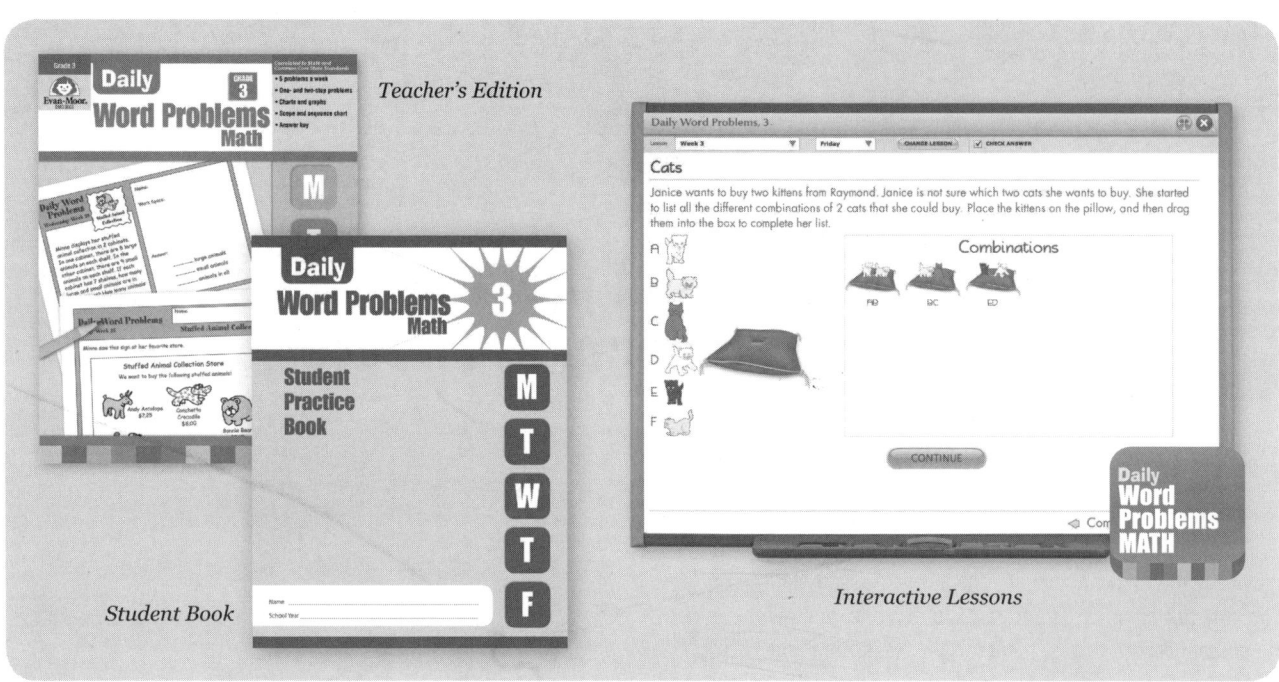

Student Book   *Teacher's Edition*   *Interactive Lessons*

Order the format right for you

Teacher's Edition Print		Teacher's Edition E-book		Student Book 5-Pack		Student Book		Interactive Lessons (No Student Licenses)		Interactive Lessons (With Student Licenses) — Best Value!
GRADE	**EMC**	**GRADE**	**EMC**	**GRADE**	**EMC**	**GRADE**	**EMC**	**GRADE**	**EMC**	**Includes All Grades (1–6)**
1	3001	1	3001i	1	6539	1	6691	1	5661r	**EMC** 5660
2	3002	2	3002i	2	6540	2	6692	2	5662r	
3	3003	3	3003i	3	6541	3	6693	3	5663r	
4	3004	4	3004i	4	6542	4	6694	4	5664r	
5	3005	5	3005i	5	6543	5	6695	5	5665r	
6	3006	6	3006i	6	6544	6	6696	6	5666r	